Effective Classroom Management

CARL J. WALLEN
Arizona State University

LaDONNA L. WALLEN

Effective Classroom Management

ALLYN AND BACON, INC.

Boston • London • Sydney

Library of Congress Cataloging in Publication Data

Wallen, Carl J
    Effective classroom management.

    Includes bibliographical references and index.
    1. Classroom management. I. Wallen, LaDonna L.,
joint author. II. Title.
LB3013.W35   371.1'02   77-10785
ISBN 0-205-05893-0
Second printing . . . September, 1978

Contents

Preface

We have long been concerned, both as teachers and parents, with the tunnel vision evidenced in so much of the literature dealing with classroom management. Simple, unidimensional solutions are offered to what are in actuality complex, multidimensional problems. The concerned teacher is offered a choice between such widely divergent and contradictory panaceas as *open education* and *behavior modification*. When the opportunity to write this book came along, we vowed that the view presented of classroom management would be suitably multidimensional. We have tried to accomplish this by focusing on three major roles of the teacher; instructional manager, group leader, and counselor. While these are obviously not all the roles a teacher is usually expected to carry out well, they appear to be the most important.

We have also attempted to avoid another weakness of the literature in educational method. A book is either so mundanely *practical* that it contains nothing more generalizable than a series of specific recipes, or it is so esoterically *theoretical* that practical application is unclear. We have tried to bridge the gap between theory and practice by the organization of the chapters within each of the three sections devoted to teacher roles. Theory is explored in the first chapter of a section, and its implications for practice identified. The second chapter in a section is devoted to explaining practical teaching strategies that follow from the theory. Instruments and procedures for assessing the effectiveness with which the teacher's practice is achieving the intended theoretical goals are presented in the third chapter. A fourth chapter describes situational examples.

We wish to express our gratitude to the two wonderful friends who read and commented on an early version of the manuscript, Dr. Jeanette Veatch and Mrs. Carmen O'Brien. We hope they feel that the final version of the book justifies their generous efforts.

We also appreciate the teachers in Chandler, Arizona, who participated in an inservice course in classroom management where an earlier version of the book's manuscript served as the course content. Their knowledgable and experienced responses provided an important basis for revision.

We also wish to thank Nancy Anderes for the dedicated attention she gave to typing the final manuscript.

C. J. W.
L. L. W.

1

Introduction

> *We must shift the emphasis from the three R's to the fourth R, human relations, and place it first, foremost, and always in the order of importance as a principle reason for the existence of the school . . . . We must train for humanity, and training in reading, writing and arithmetic must be given in a manner calculated to serve the ends of that humanity. For all the knowledge in the world is worse than useless if it is not humanely understood and humanely used. An intelligence that is not humane is the worst thing in the world.*
>
> **Ashley Montagu, On Being Human**

To be humanistic means to be responsive to human needs or desires. A humanistic teacher does not "force people to learn against their will, since that is impossible. Nor is it the task to trick them into learning. The responsibility of the teacher is to help each student discover and use means of satisfying his needs which are personally effective and socially desirable."[1]

It is our hope that this book will help you to turn perplexing problems of classroom management into interesting challenges. When you've read it and carried out the suggested activities in your

1. Donald Snugg and Arthur W. Combs, *Individual Behavior* (New York: Harper, 1949).

1

own classroom, you will likely discover that with reference to classroom management, you no longer say you have a problem, but rather an intriguing challenge. In chapter 1 we discuss the rationale and the organization and optimum use of the book.

RATIONALE

Stop a moment and think about what you really hope to gain from reading this book. Identify your concerns about classroom management. Distinguish between *instructing* and *managing*. Instructing is teaching people something, such as reading, writing, arithmetic, music, or art. *Managing, on the other hand, is organizing people and things so that instruction in group situations will be effective.* A teacher instructing one child at a time in a clinic is not concerned with classroom management. Teachers who instruct classroom groups of twenty to forty find that their competency as instructors is directly dependent on their effectiveness in managing classrooms.

Compare your list of concerns with those identified by a group of teachers enrolled in a course in classroom management. Their concerns are listed below in the order of the priority they assigned to them. Over half the teachers listed individualization as the most critical.

1. *Individualization.* Dealing with the wide range of abilities found in the average classroom. The slower students are still working long after the more able ones are finished. The less able need extra help and the more able additional challenge. Using time effectively so that more individual help can be provided for all students.

2. *Developing Self-Direction.* Helping students become responsible for their own behavior and completion of assignments. Students should be able to work independently.

3. *Motivation.* Stimulating students' interest and curiosity in learning, so that they will all work close to their capacity.

4. *Reaching Disruptive Students.* Helping children who don't seem to care to learn or to cooperate. Changing their negative behavior to positive behavior.

5. *Disciplining Students.* Controlling students in a way that is consistent and positive.

The major emphases of the approximately 4,500 locally organized Teacher Centers reflected the same humanistic concerns.[2] The four major emphases of these centers are *individualized instruction, classroom management, humanizing education,* and *open education.*

A Distinct Contrast

Teachers' humanistic concerns for making school more responsive to students' needs and desires is a distinct contrast with concerns of teachers a century ago. They are, however, quite consistent with the public's present concerns, though the consistency is not always obvious.

Teachers, a century ago, were concerned mostly with controlling students, making them responsive to the school's desires rather than the other way around. A teacher in 1848 wrote these rules of discipline for his classroom:

RULES	LASHES
1. Boys and girls fighting together	4
2. Quarreling	4
3. Fighting	5
4. Gameleing or beting	4
5. Tellying lyes	7
6. Nich naming each other	4
7. Swaring	8[3]

Obviously, not only spelling has changed in schools.

Horace Mann, the leading educational reformer of the period, reported that in a school of about 250 students there was an average of 65 floggings each day.[4] Physical abuse had some effect in controlling students in those dreary days only because it was accompanied by a very high pupil dropout rate. The rate is illustrated by this approximate registration in selected grades of the public schools of San Francisco in 1907:

2. Sam J. Yarger and Albert Leonard, *A Descriptive Study of the Teacher Center Movement in American Education* (Syracuse University: Syracuse Teacher Center Project, 1974).

3. E. W. Knight, *Education in the United States* (New York: Ginn and Co., 1951).

4. Pickens H. Harris, *Changing Conceptualizations of School Discipline* (New York: The Macmillan Company, 1928).

First Grade	10,000
Second Grade	5,000
Eighth Grade	2,000
Ninth Grade	1,240
High School Graduates	260[5]

This level of dropouts cannot be tolerated in a technologically advanced and democratic society which depends on universal education for its survival. As Thomas Jefferson once observed:

> It is safer to have a whole people respectively enlightened than a few in a high state of science and the many in ignorance. This last is the most dangerous state in which a nation can be.

The public is also concerned with humanism, though it is usually not obvious at first. The Seventh Annual Gallup Poll of Public Attitudes Toward Education[6] illustrates the difference between the public's apparent concern with controlling students, and their actual concern with having schools be more responsive to students' needs and desires. In six of the seven years that the poll has been conducted, discipline has lead the list of items identified by the public as the major problem confronting the public schools.

If one examines the poll no further, it could be concluded that the public wants to return to the school of Horace Mann's day, but they really don't, as other items in the poll indicate. Sixty-four percent are favorable toward nongraded schools, a form of individualization few had actually experienced personally. The nongraded school was described to them as a system in which a student is able to progress through school at his own speed and without regard to the usual grade levels. Further, the public views low student interest and motivation as even a more critical cause for the lack of student learning than poor discipline.

When asked to suggest reasons for the decline in students' performance on national tests, 29 percent of the public attributed it to a lack of student motivation while 28 percent attributed it to a lack of discipline in the home and school. The third most frequently mentioned cause of low student performance (22 percent) was a weak curriculum that was too easy and lacked sufficient emphasis

---

5. Don Robinson, "Fifty Years Ago," *California Teachers Association Journal* (May 1959).
6. George H. Gallup, "Seventh Annual Gallup Poll of Public Attitudes Toward Education," *Phi Delta Kappan* 57 (December 1975): 227–240.

on the basics. The public's concern with poor curriculum seems consistent with the teachers' concern with individualization, providing the less able students with extra help and the more able ones an additional challenge.

If you are interested in developing a more humanized classroom management, you can be reassured that most other teachers have the same interest, and so does the public. Disagreements about humanization are more a matter of semantics than substance. The semantic nature of the disagreement makes communication among teachers, and between teachers and the public, very important.

Students' Needs

The fundamental reason teachers have problems with classroom management is that they ignore the psychological dynamics of the learning process. Ignoring these dynamics often causes conflicts in the classroom and the failure of students and teachers. Education involves our whole being, not just our intellectual forebrain processes. Merely teaching the three *R*'s cannot be done without taking into account the *whole person*. The intellectual function is influenced by the student's personal traits and emotional responses. The importance of dealing with the whole student is not just a philosophical point of view with which the teacher has the option of agreeing or disagreeing, but rather, it is a critical factor in the entire educational process.

Teachers will be most effective when they utilize procedures that enable students to learn while at the same time allowing them to satisfy their psychological needs in constructive ways. The three basic psychological needs can be identified as: (1) the need to be an active learner; (2) the need to socialize; and, (3) the need to feel confident and secure.

Human beings are by nature active learners, moving about physically as well as intellectually in a constant search for information. They actively solicit and provoke stimuli, and find great enjoyment in discovery, manipulation, contemplation, speculation, creativity, and experimentation. People do not want to keep still. Teachers are most effective when they utilize the natural curiosity and exploratory urges of students in the learning process. In forcing students

The Need To Be an Active Learner

to be inactive, the teacher may well waste the energy students would normally use in learning. The teacher will get control at the expense of instructional effectiveness.

The Need To Socialize
People are by nature social beings. An infant who has been alone and quiet is excited by the appearance of mother, or even by hearing her voice. Children who dislike school, nevertheless enjoy those times when socialization is encouraged, such as recess and physical education. Unfortunately, many teachers have been reluctant to fit the satisfaction of social needs into their instructional planning because they believe social activities are a waste of time and interfere with serious "school work." Nothing could be farther from the truth.

The Need To Feel Confident and Secure
The need to feel confident and secure is so obviously basic that some psychologists view it as the explanation for all human behavior. A sense of security seems to function like a governor on a motor. It limits the degree to which the person will actively explore and socialize. People will venture out into the world—physically and intellectually—only if they have somewhere to come back to in case of emergency, or just plain fright. Many adults are permanently crippled intellectually because their parents and teachers did not provide them with an emotionally secure learning environment.

ORGANIZATION

The major problem teachers have in achieving effective classroom management is due to their possessing an inadequate repertoire of procedures for classroom management. The repertoire is inadequate either because the procedures are inappropriate for the psychological dynamics involved, or because the repertoire is too limited. Not only must different procedures be used for different psychological dynamics, procedures must also be varied because students are individuals and behave in different ways—what works today, even with one person, may not work tomorrow.

   In writing this book, we wish to help you generate classroom management procedures that are appropriate for the psychological dynamics involved, and to generate them in sufficient quantity that variation is possible. The identification of psychological dynamics that are both broad in scope and have practical application in classrooms is assured by organizing them around what Clark Trow et al. have identified as the three chief roles of the teacher: instructor, controller or democratic strategist, and therapist.[7] The three major sections of this book are entitled Instructional Manager, Group Leader, and Counselor.

You are helped to generate your own procedures by an emphasis on a *"practical theory" for use in decision making.* The practicality of the theory is assured by the organization of the chapters within each section. In the first chapter, the conditions (dynamics) relevant to a role are explained. In the second, strategies (general procedures) for managing classrooms consistent with the conditions are described. In the third, instruments that can be used in assessing your own effectiveness in altering a certain condition are identified.

For example, motivation is one condition identified for the Instructional Manager Role. Factors influencing student motivation are discussed in the first chapter in that section. Strategies that can be used in increasing student's motivation are described in the second chapter. Instruments for assessing actual student gains in motivation are shown in the third chapter.

OPTIMUM USE

In order for this book to be of much *practical help* to you, it should be used in a way that recognizes that your needs are the same as your students. You need to be an active learner, active physically and intellectually. You need to socialize. You need to feel confident and secure.

Active learning can be accomplished by viewing the book as a starting point, as containing some ideas to *try out.* As Sophocles said in 400 B.C.:

> One must learn
> By doing the thing; for though you
> Think you know it
> You have no certainty, until you try.

---

7. W. Clark Trow, Alvin Zander, William Morse, and David Jenkins, "Psychology of Group Behavior: The Class as a Group," *Journal of Educational Psychology* 41 (October 1950): 322-337. The three roles are also discussed in W. C. Trow, "Group Processes," in *Encyclopedia of Educational Research*, 3rd ed., Chester Harris, ed. (New York: The Macmillan Company, 1960), p. 610f.

Rather than read the entire book in one or two long sessions, and assume that by some mysterious process the ideas will be reflected in your practice, take the book one section at a time. Work on improving your effectiveness by carrying out one of the three roles. Be active intellectually by interpreting, modifying, and even rejecting ideas presented. Be active physically by trying out a strategy in your classroom. Administer one of the suggested assessment instruments to determine how effective it was. Modify the strategy and try again; assess again, and so forth.

Satisfy your need to socialize by discussing what you are doing with other teachers. A number of you might wish to work together. You are, after all, fellow professionals trying to improve your practice.

Satisfy your need to feel confident and secure by setting realistic goals that can be measured. For example, after assessing the current level of student motivation in your classroom, identify a slightly higher figure as your goal. Student motivation might have been 3.5 when one of the assessment instruments suggested in this book was given to your class. Set as your goal in motivation a figure slightly higher than 3.5. After you try out a strategy designed to increase student motivation, use the assessment instrument again and see if a higher figure hasn't been attained. Oftentimes you will find that even though motivation has increased, say from 3.5 to 3.8, you won't be satisfied simply because you are a dedicated teacher and your dreams always seem to exceed your grasp. After all, what else are dreams for? While you may not have achieved what you dreamed, you at least know that you have taken a definite step in the right direction. In the real world, dreams are usually achieved one step at a time.

Instructional Manager Role

2

Conditions

Few would disagree that a *true teacher* is one who elicits and reinforces each student's individual intellectual curiosity and strivings to learn, discover, manipulate, contemplate, speculate, create, and experiment. The true teacher is not a mere transmitter of knowledge who tries to fill students' memories. Yet, being a *true* teacher in Mark Hopkins' one-bench log hut is much easier than being one in a classroom crammed with twenty-five to thirty-five benches. In the log hut one can concentrate fully on being a teacher, but in a crowded classroom it is necessary to be a *manager* as well as a *teacher*, and, if one does not manage well, there will be little opportunity to teach.

In this section, we deal with four of the five major concerns teachers have about classroom management, *individualization, developing self-direction, motivation,* and *reaching disruptive students*. We do not deal with teaching, but instead with the management in classrooms of those instructional conditions that determine what and how well students can be taught in group settings. Three instructional conditions must be managed in group settings: individual differences, time and space, and motivation. While these conditions are present in a one-student, Mark Hopkins-type classroom, they seldom present the difficulty there that they do in normal-sized classrooms.

INDIVIDUAL DIFFERENCES

Individualization, that is, providing for individual differences, was cited as the major classroom management concern by the teachers identified in the introduction. Perhaps you also listed it as your major concern. Those teachers noted an obvious manifestation of the problem: *slower students are still working long after the more able have finished.* Solving this critical management problem requires an understanding of both the nature of the phenomena of individual differences and the attempts to devise suitable educational arrangements.

To Differ Is Natural

Individuals vary on every characteristic, whether physical or psychological. The naturalness of individual differences is obvious in physical attributes. The small intestines of adult humans have measured out anywhere from eleven feet to twenty-five feet, nine inches. Eleven different patterns have been plotted for the muscle that controls the index finger. Cell chemistries and the matching electrical impulses vary from individual to individual. None of us smells exactly alike— that is how the bloodhound earns his kennel rations.

Just as natural are differences in psychological attributes: subject-matter knowledge, intellectual development, motivation, intellectual curiosity, study habits, ability to think independently, creativity, and so on. The universalness of these differences causes one to speculate whether variety rather than uniformity is not nature's law.

The typical distribution of individual differences in psychological characteristics is shown in Figure 2.1. The characteristic is intellectual development, which is referred to here as mental age. A mental age of 144 indicates that the person's intellectual development is equivalent to an average person whose chronological age is 144 months or 12 years of age (12 months times 12 years of age equals 144 months). A mental-age score of 156 indicates an intellectual development equivalent to a person whose chronological age is 156 months or thirteen years (12 × 13 = 156). (Mental age should not be confused with I.Q. scores.) Students were drawn randomly. All are in the sixth grade and have chronological ages ranging from 138 months (11 years and 6 months) to 154 months (12 years and 10 months). Notice that the greatest number of students cluster around the average, which is a mental age of 144 months. Decreasingly fewer students have progressively higher and lower scores.

In a survey of intellectual development in classes that had been assigned on the basis of chronological age, Cook found the range of mental-age equivalent was five years at the primary level, six years at the intermediate, and eight years at the high school level.[1] This means that within a typical fifth-grade classroom, one can expect to find the dullest student having an intellectual level equivalent to the average second grader, while the brightest has a level equivalent to the average eighth grader. Moreover, a similar range of individual differences can be expected with almost any psychological characteristic tested.

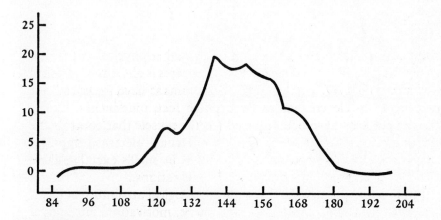

Figure 2.1

1. W. W. Cook, "Individual-Train Differences in Public Schools with Implications for School Organization and Curriculum Development," *Teachers College Journal* 19 (1947): 56–57, 67–70.

The differences shown in Figure 2.1 are *inter-individual*, meaning differences between students on one characteristic. Students also differ *intra-individually*, meaning differences within one student on different characteristics. The achievement profile of one student is shown in Figure 2.2. The student has a mental-age equivalency of 138. The profile indicates nine characteristics. Scores are reported as *grade equivalents*. A score of 6.8 is equivalent to the average performance of students who were tested during the eighth month of the sixth grade. (The six indicates the grade and the eight indicates the month in that grade.) The horizontal line beside 6.0 indicates that this student was tested before the end of the first month in the sixth grade. A score of 6.0 therefore, indicates average performance on that characteristic.

Notice that the overall achievement score (Battery Median) is 5.8, which is only slightly below what one would expect from the *average* student who is tested at the beginning of the sixth grade. The student's overall achievement score of 5.8 seems to

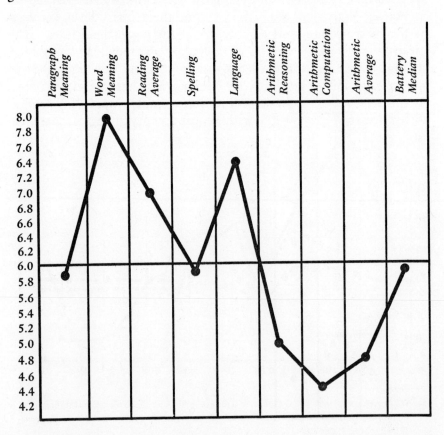

Figure 2.2

correlate fairly well with his level of mental development, which at 138 months is average for a student beginning the sixth grade. But notice the intra-individual variability that is obscured if average achievement is the only thing considered. The student's paragraph-meaning ability is equivalent to the average fifth grader in the eighth month of school (5.8), while his word-meaning ability is equivalent to an average seventh grader in the eighth month of school (7.8). This constitutes a full two grade-level variation in just reading ability. There is over a three and one-half grade-level variation between the student's word-meaning ability (7.8) and his arithmetic-computation ability (4.2).

Intra-individual variability does not occur in the same way with every student, as an examination of Figure 2.3 shows. A composite achievement profile for four students is given. All are in the sixth grade. All have a mental age of 138 months, and all were tested during the first month of sixth grade, as the horizontal line beside 6.0 indicates.

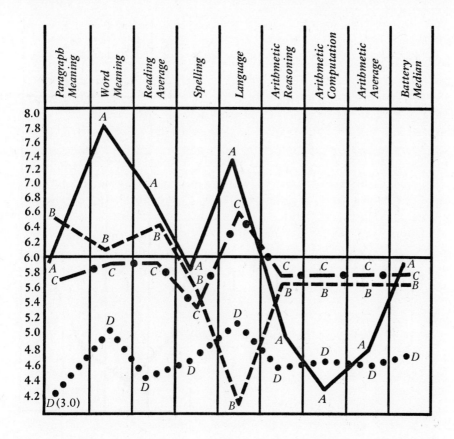

Figure 2.

Notice that if only the average achievement score is considered, then three of the four students have scores fairly close to the expected average. (The average is 6.0 and they have scores of 5.8, 5.7, and 5.6.)

While the variability of achievement scores shown in Figure 2.3 is almost mind boggling, remember that the four students shown there all have the *same* level of intellectual development. Imagine what a composite achievement profile for the entire class looks like when it includes students with a full average range of mental development.

Anastasi concluded that intra-individual variability averages from 75 to 80 percent as large as the inter-individual variability found with a single characteristic.[2] Stated another way, *each student in the class can be expected to have about four-fifths as much variation in the different abilities possessed as all the students vary from each other in the single characteristic of intellectual development.* This ratio of inter- to intra-individual variability has been found with groups of students in elementary school, high school, and vocational school, as well as adults.

Differences Not Recognized

Many teachers are unaware of the immense variability, both inter and intra, among students in their classes. There are three reasons for this lack of recognition. *First,* they lack the data base because frequent and comprehensive achievement and mental tests are not given. The variability shown in Figures 2.1, 2.2, and 2.3 can be recognized only if reliable standardized tests are administered. Schools committed to providing for individual differences must have comprehensive testing programs.

The *second* reason for the failure to recognize the actual variability of individual differences is misunderstanding the interpretation of standardized tests. Two misunderstandings are discussed here.

Differences Are Quantitative Not Qualitative Many teachers mistakenly interpret students' performance on achievement tests and other test-like situations as indicating that the students either possess a characteristic or they do not. They can read or they cannot. They are artistic or they are not. In reality, the opposite

2. A. Anastasi, *Differential Psychology* (New York: The Macmillan Company, 1960).

is true. Everyone possesses basically the same characteristics; they vary in the *degree* to which they possess them. Every human has a height, usually somewhere between eighteen and eighty inches. Every student possesses some degree of language ability. It is not that one student can read and another cannot; rather, it is the relative degree of language ability each possesses. All students possess some degree of such psychological characteristics as subject-matter knowledge, intellectual development, creativity, and self-direction.

Confusion about the quantitative nature of individual differences is often the result of failing to distinguish between the testing instruments that are intended to assess a characteristic and the reality of the characteristic itself. If the measure used in determining height starts at a yardstick high, then we will find that many children are less than a yardstick in height. It is not that they have no height, only that the instrument is not suitable for measuring their height. Likewise, if the only measure of language ability is one requiring the pronunciation of written words, we will find some students who cannot do it. It is not that they have no language ability, only that our measure is not suitable for them.

Teachers who misunderstand the quantitative nature of individual differences are quite naturally inclined to operate in their classrooms on the assumption that because a student did not show up on the test situation that he simply does not possess the assessed characteristic in any degree. The student who cannot pronounce written words when she enters first grade is erroneously labeled a "nonreader." The student who does not make the varsity basketball team is labeled a "nonathlete." Students and teachers come to accept these mislabels as fact, and act on the assumption that little can be done to alter such basic conditions.

Many teachers mistakenly assume that average or better performance in a test situation indicates that a student is normal, and below average performance indicates abnormality. What these teachers are failing to realize is that *average is only a mathematical point in a range of scores*. While these teachers would not assume that all fifth-grade students are abnormal if they are not fifty-five inches tall, that being the mathematical average height for fifth graders, they often mistakenly assume that all fifth-grade students should be able to read on the *average* level of 5.0, as indicated by their performance on a standardized achievement test.

The consequences of teachers misunderstanding the mathematical

Average Is Not the Same as Normal

concept of *average* were spotlighted by an extensive study of reading instruction in the United States in the early 1960s. Austin and Morrison found that most elementary teachers they surveyed were unable to ignore the idea that they were "third" or "fourth" grade teachers.[3] They felt compelled to teach the reading skills considered suitable for their grade, regardless of the real differences existing among children. They were unable to shake this idea even though most had organized a number of reading groups in their classroom, had assigned students to the groups on the basis of their performance on standardized test scores, and had provided different groups with reading materials of differing levels of difficulty. A student in the fourth grade was still considered *below grade level* if he was reading in a second-level text, even though he was progressing satisfactorily. Students were seldom assigned to reading materials above grade level because they were considered above average and therefore satisfactory. The misunderstanding about averageness resulted in the establishment of remedial reading programs for those achieving below grade level, developmental programs for those at grade level, and nothing for those achieving above grade level, except perhaps some additional developmental work.

When averageness is equated with normality the result is school programs that are intended to erase individual differences. As Lee J. Cronbach noted:

> Most tactics the school uses are intended to minimize the nuisance of individual differences so that it can go on teaching the same unaltered course. This is true of remedial instruction, which adds onto the common program rather than redesigning it. Remedial work takes it for granted that the classroom work is largely a fixed program. Many a pupil needs help that the standard program does not give him, and supplementary instruction is thereby provided, with the intention of repairing the gaps in skill and putting him back on the pace. That is, to say, remedial instruction attempts to erase individual differences.[4]

A *third* reason for not recognizing individual differences is that many teachers mistakenly assume that variability indicates poor teaching. In fact, just the opposite is true. Good nutrition, for example, does not cause everyone to be the same height. Rather, it

3. M. Austin and C. Morrison, *The First R: The Harvard Report on Reading in Elementary Schools* (New York: The Macmillan Company, 1963).
4. L. J. Cronbach, "How Can Instruction Be Adapted to Individual Differences?" in *Learning and Individual Differences*, R. Gagne, ed. (Columbus, Ohio: Charles E. Merrill Publishing Co., 1966), chapter 2.

increases the range of differences and raises the average. During the Middle Ages most men could fit into the armor suits worn by knights. Today, partly because of improved nutrition, only a few men can. Good teaching likewise does not eradicate differences in mathematical ability, causing everyone in the first grade to perform at the level of 5.0. The effect is just the opposite; it increases the range of mathematical ability and raises the average.

Individual differences in psychological characteristics among students are a natural occurrence with which teachers must contend, just as they must with differences in physical characteristics. The differences arise from students' different inherited capacities, different learning rates, and different past learning experiences. The best teaching occurs when individual differences are recognized and the most appropriate instruction provided. The *true teacher* identifies where each student is on each psychological characteristic and takes the student from there.

Easier said than done, you say? You are correct. But *the idea is right,* and has been a major thrust of American education for the last half century.

Historical Perspective

Prior to 1920, little adjustment was made for individual differences. Students were initially assigned to classrooms on the basis of age, and everyone in the same classroom received identical instruction. Students having difficulty were retained or encouraged to drop out, either overtly or covertly. In the schools of that day it was not unusual to see fourteen year olds in the fifth grade, waiting none too patiently until they were no longer compelled by law to attend school.

After 1920, two things occurred: the development of standardized achievement tests and growth in the size of public schools. Thus, more groups had to be created within a school, and test scores provided a means of accomplishing that. In 1925, Carleton Washburne stated:

> The widespread use of intelligence tests and achievement tests during the past few years has made every educator realize forcefully that children vary greatly as individuals and that any one school grade contains children of an astonishingly wide variety of capacity and achievement. It has become palpably absurd to expect to achieve uniform results from uniform assignments made to a class of widely differing individuals. Throughout

the educational world there has therefore awakened a desire to find some way of adapting schools to the differing individuals who attend them.[5]

During the next few decades, the only area where much provision was made for individual differences was in reading. Children were often assigned to classrooms on the basis of chronological age, and then to one of three groups within the classroom on the basis of reading test scores. Each group received different instruction, suitable for its level of achievement.

Contemporary Perspective

In the last decade or so, two significant educational changes occurred that profoundly affected the movement toward individualization. *First,* the publishing industry expanded greatly and produced a wealth of *self-instructional materials*—devices that a student could operate by himself with little or no teacher guidance. Workbooks, for example, were designed so students could correct their own answers. If oral instructions from the teacher were necessary, they were delivered by means of a tape recording and earphones.

The *second* significant change was the recognized development of a method called open education or open classrooms which featured student *self-selection of instructional activities.* The method, developed initially by British teachers for primary schools, was described this way by Joseph Featherstone:

> Children are trained to work for the most part independently, in an environment thoughtfully laid out to permit choices from an array of materials—water, clay, practical math apparatus, science stuff, all kinds of books for individual reading, private dictionaries and word books, free-writing notebooks, powder paint and easels, puppet theatres, and play houses. Teachers and children in some schools are given choices to such an extent that there is no longer a fixed curriculum or set timetable. (This is called, variously, the free or integrated day.) Children move freely around the classroom at their tasks and within limits are encouraged to talk to each other.[6]

5. Carleton N. Washburne, in the Introduction to *Adapting Schools to Individual Differences,* Twenty-fourth Yearbook of the National Society for the Study of Education, Part II (Chicago: The University of Chicago Press, 1925), p. 24.

6. J. Featherstone, "Report Analysis: Children and Their Primary Schools," *Harvard Educational Review* 38 (Spring 1968): 317–328.

At the present time, teachers have available two different but complimentary, ways of individualizing.

Individual differences are accounted for by varying the rate, or speed, with which students move through a fixed curriculum. For example, if the content is the list of words in the sixth-grade spelling text, rate is varied by allowing students to move through lessons as quickly as they are able to spell correctly all the words in each lesson. Some students are able to master two lessons a week, others require three weeks to master one lesson. The fastest learners are able to complete the entire sixth-grade text by the end of the second month while the slowest have completed only the first four or five lessons by the end of the school year.

Vary the Rate, Keep the Content Constant

Individual differences are accounted for by having different students working on different curriculums. For example, in contrast to the spelling illustration discussed previously, students might be given *weekly* spelling tests, but the number, composition, and difficulty of the words included in each lesson would be varied according to each student's ability and interests. One student in the sixth grade might be working on the words in a second-grade text, another might decide to take only half of the words in the sixth-grade text, a third might supplement the words from the sixth-grade text with words the student selects from a special area of study, such as science. With programs that vary content, students are given the freedom to make real decisions about the *goals* they wish to attain, the *procedures* they will use in attaining them, and the *evaluation* of their attainment of the goals.

Vary the Content, Keep the Rate Constant

These two presently available ways of individualizing differ markedly from the single option previously available to the teacher and obviously still available: *rate and content are held constant and level of mastery is considered variable.* For example, to expand on the spelling illustration, all students in the sixth grade are given one week to learn all the words in one lesson in the sixth-grade spelling text. All have the same time to learn the same words. On Friday they are tested and their variations in level of mastery noted and graded. Some students are able to spell correctly one hundred percent of the words, others seventy-five percent, and still others fifty percent or less. Next week they begin a new lesson with new words. The unlearned words remain unlearned.

The two, newer available instructional options require different classroom-management strategies than the earlier single option where everyone did the same thing at the same time. Variation of rate and content involve a more decentralized classroom situation because each student is doing something different. The more decentralized classroom situation requires a higher level of student self-direction and a wider variety of available instructional activities. The teacher who attempts to use the same management strategies with the more decentralized classroom that were used effectively with the earlier, more teacher-centered program is doomed to have serious difficulties with classroom management.

Strategies for managing more decentralized classrooms are described in the next two chapters. A *continuous-progress curriculum* is used in varying the rate at which students are guided through a given content, such as reading, writing, and mathematics. *Independent activities* and *student contracts* can be used in varying the content provided students. *Grouping* can be used as an aid to varying either the content or the rate. The other strategies facilitate successful management in a more decentralized classroom.

TIME AND SPACE

The effective use of time was given as an obvious manifestation of the problem of individualization by the teachers identified in the introduction who cited individualization as their overwhelming concern in classroom management. They stated the problem as: *using time effectively so that more individual help can be provided all students.* The use of space was also frequently mentioned as a problem by those teachers.

The major difficulty teachers have with time and space is recognizing and accepting alternative ways of arranging them. Not only do people tend to confuse the way things are with the way they could or should be, they fail to view the arrangements from a perspective of wholeness. In this section, we intended to provide a perspective about time and space arrangements with the hope that you will be encouraged to try alternatives that might better serve educational purposes.

Unconsciously Learned Concepts

Concepts of time and space are learned unconsciously. One way of making our unconscious concepts conscious is to compare them with those held by people in other cultures. Their concepts of time and space are different from ours because their culturally determined learning experiences are different.

Time is not thought of in the same way by people from different cultures. The European-American views time as a ribbon stretching into the future, along which one progresses through sequential and discrete compartments. The reading period begins promptly at 9:10 and ends at 10:10. It is not resumed until tomorrow at the same time. To the Indian-American, on the other hand, time is more relative because it is determined by the situation one is in.

The differences between the two conceptualizations of time become most obvious when the two cultures meet. A European-American visitor to an Indian ceremonial dance drives a long distance over a primitive desert road in order to view a dance that began at 10:00 p.m. last year, and will presumably begin at the same time this year. The visitor risks permanent damage to his car so that he will be there on time, but once there, he has to wait impatiently in the cold until well after one o'clock in the morning before the dancers appear. It is not that the dance is late, it is just that the time to begin the dance is when the participants "feel ready." Indian-Americans do not follow an external machine-determined schedule like European-Americans. They follow an internally-determined, "readiness time" schedule.

Space is also not thought of in the same way by persons from different cultures. A particularly curious space arrangement is the unconscious distance speakers maintain between each other. When a North American converses with another person she normally maintains a distance of about twenty inches, but a Latin American normally maintains a distance under twenty inches. Very subtle conflicts occur when people with the two different conceptualizations of space meet, as when a North American is talking with a Latin American. To the North American, the Latin American keeps moving so close that it evokes sexual or aggressive feelings. To the Latin American, the North American's tendency to keep moving away evokes feelings of unfriendliness or rejection.

One of the authors recalls that soon after reading about space arrangements between speakers he had the opportunity of testing them out at a party. He found that he could literally move people about a room without saying anything about moving. They remained totally unaware of the movement. If the author decided to move a person backwards, he simply moved ever so slowly closer to the person while continuing the conversation. When he had moved closer than twenty inches, the person unconsciously took a step backwards.

If he wanted to move the person forward, he simply slipped slowly backward. When the distance had become somewhat over twenty inches, the person unconsciously took a step forward. Without realizing the reason for their actions, or even being aware of them, they attempted to maintain the twenty-inch conversational distance with which they felt comfortable. Try it.

Present Practice

Attempts to alter time and space arrangements for educational purposes should be based on a recognition of two characteristics of culturally determined concepts. *First,* change is uncomfortable. If a North American wants to avoid offending Latin Americans, she can consciously maintain conversational distances of less than twenty inches, but she has to expect, and be prepared to deal with, her own initial feelings of discomfort. *Second,* learning is the major solution to dealing with unconsciously acquired concepts. The North American who had decided to maintain closer conversation distances when speaking to Latin Americans had evidenced the first stage of learning, a conscious recognition of space arrangements.

If we can accept that time and space arrangements are not absolute and immutable, our challenge is to become conscious about the arrangements we use so that we might rationally devise alternatives that will result in better education for our students. As a way of helping teachers become more conscious of the culturally determined arrangements they live by in school, Sarason suggests the fantasy of a visiting being from outer space who finds himself and his invisible space platform hovering directly above an elementary school.[7] The space being is able to see everying going on, but is not able to understand what is said. Being a good scientist, the space being records and categorizes events, and uses the data to identify regular patterns of behavior among the earth people. He notices that the school follows a 5–2 plan; school is open for five days and closed for two. This puzzles him. Why this plan instead of another, such as two on, one off, three on, and one off? The value of the fantasy is that it provides a frame of reference for identifying regular arrangements of time and space, of questioning the rationale for the arrangements, and, hopefully, of suggesting better alternatives.

If you were to hover in a space ship over elementary school

---

7. S. B. Sarason, *The Culture of the School and the Problem of Change* (Boston: Allyn and Bacon, Inc., 1971).

classrooms, what you would likely observe is suggested by a study of Adams and Biddle.[8] They found these things. Students are usually divided into groups of around thirty, with each group having a wall around it. A teacher lives with each group. Seventy-five percent of the time in the classroom is spent with students in aggregations consisting of the teacher and fifty percent of the students, the remainder of the students being either unorganized or in much smaller groups. Fifty percent of the time the teacher is engaged with the large group is spent in disseminating information, with the teacher doing most of the talking. Slightly less than seven percent of the time is spent with questions students initiate.

About two-thirds of the students' time is devoted to responding to questions asked by the teacher. The arrangement of time and space that emerges is the *recitation*: teachers ask questions to large groups of students, and individual students or groups of students answer. The arrangement is presumably based on two assumptions, that students are so crowded only one person at a time can be heard, and students lack motivation and self-control. Recitation thus appears to be the only way to carry out clearly audible instruction, maintain order, and keep all students under observation and working.

Alternative Arrangements

The unsuitability of the recitation was suggested in 1925 by Carleton Washburne, among others. Earlier in this chapter Washburne was quoted as saying, "It has become palpably absurd to expect to achieve uniform results from uniform assignments made to a class of widely differing individuals. Throughout the educational world there has therefore awakened a desire to find some way of adapting schools to the differing individuals who attend them."

Alternative arrangements to recitation are possible, but the comparative advantages and disadvantages should be recognized. Here are three examples. First, divide students into several groups of roughly equal size and teach each group separately. The groups might be formed on the basis of interest, ability, or attention span. Grouping has the advantage of reducing the range of individual differences within one instructional group. It has the disadvantage of requiring different sets of instructional materials for each group.

Second, bring in additional teachers to share the load of teaching

---

8. R. S. Adams and B. J. Biddle, *Realities of Teaching* (New York: Holt, Rinehart, and Winston, 1970).

and management. If regular teachers are used, this may be accomplished by combining classes so that two or three teachers are housed in a large room with sixty to ninety students. The additional teachers could be in the form of volunteer or paid aides and older students. Teaming, whether by regular teachers or combinations of teachers and aides, provides more possibilities for individualizing teaching and management. It also presents its own unique problems of the division of labor and authority. Who, for example, initiates the reading lesson? Who cleans the sink? How will the conflict be resolved that arises when a student asks one teacher for permission to go to the library, is refused, and then is given permission to go by the other teacher?

Third, open up the boundaries of classroom space by using areas not previously considered part of the classroom such as hallways, patios, and offices. Spreading out reduces the problems of noise and crowding but brings different management problems, especially for teachers who are accustomed to exercising control in face-to-face situations.

Teachers interested in seeking new time and space arrangements should answer four questions.

1. *Given the existing physical structure of the school and classroom, what different time and space arrangements are possible?* Don't confine yourself to one or two just yet. Now is the time to be wildly creative. Later you can be mundanely realistic.

2. *How well do each of these arrangements facilitate the attainment of educational goals?* For example, in terms of the alternative arrangements mentioned earlier, the recitation makes virtually no provision for individual differences, but is easily manageable. The open classroom, where children are not confined to the classroom, results in more activity, interest, and individualization, but not necessarily more learning because many students may not use unsupervised time productively.

3. *What unique problems must be solved with each arrangement?* For example, with the open classroom some ways must be found for supervising student learning when the teacher is not present.

4. *What are the solutions of these problems?* For example, with the open classroom, teaching materials could be used that are self-instructional, self-checking, and self-recording. The materials might also provide for periodic tests given by the teacher.

A helpful perspective for answering the four questions was suggested by a school principal with considerable experience directing professional reading conferences. She noted that devising alternative time and space arrangements is much like having the responsibility for arranging a weekend reading conference. A certain number of people are expected to arrive at a specified time—assuming European-American time concepts. People must be divided into groups, and the size and schedule for each group made dependent on the purpose for each group. For example, a lecture by a noted authority who plans to give a speech might be scheduled for an hour in a room holding one hundred. A seminar by a teacher who plans to demonstrate a lesson with students and then discuss it with the audience might be scheduled for two hours in a room holding twenty-five. Finally, a printed schedule describing the arrangements must be prepared and distributed so that everyone knows where to go and when.

If all that has been said in this section is taken literally, you will spend awhile hovering in a space ship over the school collecting data that suggests physical constraints, present arrangements, and, perhaps, a rationale for the arrangements. Once the space ship returns to earth, you will approach the school and classroom as if it were a year-long professional conference. The literal implications are not far from the actual task.

The instructional management strategies explained in the next chapter involve arrangements of time and space that are different from those found in many schools. In contemplating the use of these strategies you must be realistic about the problems that arise whenever different time and space arrangements are attempted. Hopefully, you are so firmly committed to improving instruction in your class that you are willing to give any of the new arrangements a try.

MOTIVATION

Motivation is listed as the third most pressing problem by the teachers identified in the introduction. They expressed their concern as: *stimulating student's interest and curiosity in learning, so that they will all work close to their capacity.* Motivation is obviously also related to their fourth most pressing problem, reaching disruptive students. They expressed that concern this way: *helping students who don't seem to care to learn or to cooperate.* Whether students care to learn is a problem when trying to motivate learning.

Motivation is an immense topic. Entire books are written on the subject. Most texts in educational psychology contain one or more chapters on the subject. In this section we will be concerned only with those varieties of human motivation that are highly relevant to the process of learning and the procedures of instruction.

What Is It?

Motivation is likened to our common sense—we are, on the surface, *motivated* to do what we do—but upon investigation nothing proves to be more controversial. Harlow, a prominent student of motivation, wrote:

> Motivationally, man is a strange, if not bizarre, creature: he is the only known organism to arise in the morning before he is awake, work all day without resting, continue his activities after diurnal and even crepuscular organisms have retired to rest, and then take narcotics to induce an inadequate period of troubled sleep. But lest we decry man's motivational mechanisms, we should point out that without them we would not have the steam engine, the electric light, the automobile, Beethoven's Fifth Symphony, Leonardo de Vinci's undigested "Last Supper," gastric ulcers, coronary thrombosis, and clinical psychologists. Indeed, we might well regard this aggregate as the human motivation syndrome.[9]

Ausubel, an eminent educational psychologist, stated:

> After fifty years or more of research on motivation, perhaps the most striking conclusion that emerges from consideration of the staggering mass of research data and theory in this area is how little we really know about it, and how much is still a matter of conjecture and speculative preference.[10]

Because the topic of motivation is immense, a set of clear definitions will give us a grasp on it. Motivation is usually defined as the combination of forces that initiate, direct, and sustain behavior toward a goal (Lindsey 1957). Goals are achieved by satisfying needs. *Needs* are the relatively permanent tendencies people have to be motivated in certain ways (McDonald 1959). The needs may be physical, such as for food, water, and safety, or they may be psychological. The three basic psychological needs identified and discussed

---

9. H. F. Harlow, "Motivation as a Factor in the Acquisition of New Responses," in *Current Theory and Research in Motivation: A Symposium* (Lincoln, Nebr.: University of Nebraska Press, 1953), p. 24.

10. D. P. Ausubel, *Educational Psychology: A Cognitive View* (New York: Holt, Rinehart and Winston, Inc., 1968), p. 363.

in the introduction are: (1) the need to be an active learner; (2) the need to socialize; and, (3) the need to feel confident and secure.

For example, if food and water are placed across the room from a person who is hungry and thirsty—one who has unfilled physical needs for food and water—he will be motivated to fulfill those needs. Upon seeing the food and water, he will move in a way obviously intended to obtain them. Likewise, a person desiring social contact—someone with a psychological need for socialization—will try to start a conversation, and otherwise interact with another person.

School environments typically provide many kinds of rewards and punishments that are intended to motivate students such as grades, prizes, teacher and student approval. The devices the school uses to motivate are called *incentives*. In order to be effective in motivating students the incentives must provide some degree of need satisfaction. When teachers talk about motivating students to do school work, they are generally referring to the use of incentives. Yet, teachers should realize that motivation for learning is not something magically produced by the use of incentives, but a process involving complex conditions within the individual and the total school environment (Hilgard and Russell 1950).

One of the major reasons motivation is such a vast topic is due to the fact that motivational patterns are learned. People growing up in different cultures, therefore, learn different ways of satisfying the same basic needs. The statement, "One man's food is another man's poison," is another way of saying this. As a consequence of culturally determined learning experiences that occurred prior to their entering school, some students will find the incentive of teacher approval to be motivating and, in turn, fulfilling the need for confidence; others will not. In order to effectively motivate all students, teachers must be aware of each student's "foods and poisons" and then devise ways of providing "food."

Why Is Motivation Important?

Teachers ought to be vitally concerned with student motivation for two reasons. First, research indicates that motivation is a highly significant factor in and greatly facilitates learning, though it is not an indispensable condition for learning (Ausubel 1968). Highly motivated students are likely to be learning at or near their intellectual capacities. Poorly motivated students are likely to be learning well below their capacities. This close relationship between motivation and learning allows teachers to improve the effectiveness of their teaching by utilizing procedures that increase students' level of motivation.

Second, more highly motivated students are better behaved. Kounin provides evidence of the close relationship between student motivation and behavior.[11] Highly motivated students and poorly motivated students respond to incidents in the classroom differently. Highly motivated students more often feel discipline is fair and, so, tend to take the teacher's side in conflicts with misbehaving students. Poorly motivated students see discipline as punishment and tend to side with the misbehaving students. Highly motivated students see the teacher in task-related ways. They are interested in the teacher's competence in explaining materials and organizing assignments. Poorly motivated students see the teacher in feeling-related ways. They tend to discuss the teacher's fairness, or unfairness, and other personal qualities. The close relationship between student motivation and behavior allows teachers to reduce discipline problems by increasing the level of students' motivation.

Increasing Level of Motivation

A practical and widely applicable set of principles for increasing motivation is suggested by Herbert Klausmeier and William Goodwin. Our discussion is organized around their seven principles:

1. Focus student attention on desired objectives.
2. Encourage the development of positive motives.
3. Use learning sets and advance organizers.
4. Help students set and attain realistic goals.
5. Provide incentives and punish, if necessary.
6. Create a warm, orderly atmosphere.
7. Avoid high stress and disorganization.[12]

Focus Student Attention on Desired Objectives

Motivation to learn is affected by the basic purpose for attending school in the first place. Students must want to be in the school setting before it is likely to have much effect on them. Young children frequently have rather weak motivation to attend school,

---

11. J. S. Kounin, *Discipline and Classroom Management* (New York: Holt, Rinehart and Winston, Inc., 1970).

12. H. J. Klausmeier and W. Goodwin, *Learning and Human Abilities* (New York: Harper & Row, Publishers, 1966), pp. 446–465.

preferring the familiar environment of the home (Gagne 1970). Studies of older, lower-class students indicate that they consider going to school a "sissy" thing, dominated by females who extol the virtues of neatness, cleanliness, and orderliness (Riessman 1962). They have a sort of Huckleberry Finn attitude toward school.

Positive motivation toward school can be ensured by providing very attractive classroom activities. It can also be a result of developing a healthy classroom atmosphere, one that makes group membership highly rewarding for students. Providing attractive activities is discussed in the next two chapters of this section. The development of healthy classroom atmospheres is the major theme of section 2 of this book. Once students have been motivated to attend school, the next concern is motivating them to eagerly engage in learning activities.

A considerable amount of research on motivating students to learn suggests the importance of making the objectives in a given learning task as explicit as possible, and of attempting to help students know the reasons why the objectives are important *for them.* In the case of nonpractical and remote objectives, the relationship between the learning task and other kinds of goals should be clarified. If students know why they are reading a selection, they will learn more. One of the reasons for involving students in genuine decision making about goals and procedures is to increase their understanding and acceptance of school objectives.

Many experiments show that students learn more effectively when responding to explicit instructions. Numerous studies show that when students intend to remember something, the longevity and amount of retention increases. The inability to recognize a need for a subject is the reason students mention most frequently for losing interest in high school studies (Young 1932). A lack of interest in what one is doing results in relatively little permanent learning (Cantor 1953). A large number of studies indicate that students will learn more effectively if they have a positive attitude toward the materials used.

Many of the management strategies described in the next two chapters are designed to focus students' attention on desired objectives. The central feature of a *continuous-progress curriculum* is an explicitly stated set of objectives. When *independent activities* are organized properly, the objectives of specific learning tasks are explicit and accepted. With *student contracts,* students play a critical role in making decisions about objectives and the procedures for attaining them. An important step in using *incentive techniques* is clarifying objectives.

Anatole France once said, "The whole art of teaching is only the art of awakening the natural curiosity of young minds for the purpose of satisfying it afterward." He didn't, unfortunately, suggest how to accomplish this. Teachers, probably since time immemorial, have frequently been unsuccessful in "awakening students' natural curiosity" and, so, have resorted to compulsive means of motivating them. Plato recognized this tendency, and advised teachers in *The Republic* to "avoid compulsion and let your children's lessons take the form of play." A hundred years ago in this country, motivation commonly was instilled through whippings, as you may recall from the discussion in the introduction.

Corporal punishment should never be used to motivate students. It not only is morally questionable, but, of critical importance to the school's mission, it just doesn't work. In fact, it is usually counterproductive. Students obviously do not wish to attend schools where corporal punishment is common, and so, any later attempts to motivate them to learn are uphill battles. Further, as Skinner has noted, punishment, even of the mild variety, is ineffective in causing learning because:

> We want to *generate* behavior, and it is not enough to "suppress not-behaving." Thus we do not strengthen good pronunciation by punishing bad, or skillful movements by punishing awkward. We do not make a student industrious by punishing idleness, or brave by punishing cowardice, or interested in his work by punishing him when he learns slowly, or to recall what he had learned by punishing him when he forgets, or to think logically by punishing him when he is illogical.[13]

Even to the degree that punishment succeeds temporarily, it does not supply the inner stimulation necessary for continued motivation and achievement. Glasser points out quite dramatically that guns, force, threats, shame, and punishment have been proven by history to be poor motivators.[14] They work only as long as the force or threat is being used and the person is afraid. If fear disappears, or the agent causing it leaves, motivation immediately ceases. The procedures for motivating students should have both a short-term and long-term value. Hilgard and Russell remind us that fear usually does not have a long-lasting effect:

---

13. B. F. Skinner, *The Technology of Teaching* (New York: Appleton-Century-Crofts, 1968), p. 149.

14. W. Glasser, *Schools Without Failure* (New York: Harper & Row, 1969).

Motivation is important not only as an energizer and director of learning but as a habit-system in itself. Children learn to respond to the set of motives used in the school. This is one reason why a teacher who appeals to fear fails to get results in a situation where the fear element is removed. It is one reason high grades or stars in spelling sometimes produce perfect spelling lessons but also produce incorrect writing.[15]

A classical and often cited experiment by Hurlock shows that incentives that provide reward are more powerful motivators of learning than incentives that provide mild punishment.[16] Also, rewarding and punishing the student are more powerful than ignoring the student. Hurlock studied the relative effectiveness of praise, reproof, and ignoring of students' learning of arithmetic. The praise and reproof were administered to students as a group so there was no informative value of specific errors or correct responses. She found that students made the most progress in arithmetic under conditions of praise, next under reproof, and least when students were ignored.

While rewards are much more effective for motivating students to learn than are mild punishments, rewards have many disadvantages. First, as Lewin points out, the teacher who uses rewards must provide a barrier against students attaining them by any short cut not requiring the completion of the desired instructional task.[17] Examinations require proctors because there is a tendency to try to reach the goal by shorter routes.

Second, because rewards are regulated by authority, too much emphasis on them encourages docility and deference to authority. Students soon learn that *one does things solely to obtain rewards from the person in authority.* Students who have learned to do things solely to get rewards from the person in authority are impeded from obtaining satisfaction from other sources such as experiencing a pleasing feeling of self-actualization from simply completing an activity they set out to do. Students, for example, can become so accustomed to reading books and then being rewarded for preparing book reports on them that they never learn to enjoy the activity of

15. E. R. Hilgard and D. H. Russell, "Motivation and Learning," in *Learning and Instruction,* N. B. Henry, ed. (Chicago: University of Chicago Press, 1950).

16. E. B. Hurlock, "An Evaluation of Certain Incentives Used in School Work," *Journal of Educational Psychology* 15 (1925): 145–159.

17. K. Lewin, "Field Theory and Learning," in *The Psychology of Learning,* Forty-First Yearbook of the National Society for the Study of Education, Part II, National Society for the Study of Education. (Chicago: University of Chicago Press, 1950), pp. 215–242.

reading itself. Or, alas, as Lewin pointed out earlier, they sometimes learn not to read the book at all and only skim it sufficiently enough to prepare a book report.

Recognizing the deficiencies in using reward and mild punishment to motivate students to learn has resulted in a trend in recent research to examine other factors. This research indicates the powerful motivating effects of such factors as curiosity (Berlyne 1960), and the opportunities the task offers for exploration (Montgomery 1954), activity (Hill 1956), manipulation (Harlow 1950; Terrell 1959), and gaining a sense of mastery or competence (White 1959). These factors have been shown to be so sufficiently powerful as motivators that Ausubel elevates them to the status of needs.[18] For example, the research indicates that people with high needs for achievement are more persistent (Feather 1961), learn more effectively (Kight and Sassenrath 1966), and tend to reach solutions in problem-solving tasks more often than do those with low achievement needs (French and Thomas 1958).

In summary, the research on motivation indicates that students will be motivated to learn when their instructional activities are organized in such a way that they can satisfy the three basic needs identified earlier, *activity* (particularly intellectual activity), *security*, and *socialization.* For example, the research would give one some confidence in predicting that Lesson *A*, described below, will likely result in a higher level of student motivation, and thus, probably also learning, than Lesson *B*, even though both lessons were designed for the same objective in arithmetic. The objective for both lessons is: *knowing the addition facts.* They are review lessons and intended to provide additional practice.

Lesson A. The teacher has students pretend that they are to spend $20.00 for family Christmas presents. They are given old mail-order catalogues and instructed to shop until they find gifts that total only a few pennies more or less than $20.00. On their papers they are to list each recipient's name, the gift selected, the cost of each gift, and subsequently the cost of all gifts. The gifts should be appropriate for the recipients. Students are encouraged to share ideas and catalogues with each other.

Lesson B. Students are given a printed worksheet containing fifty problems, such as: 24 + 18 = _____. They are to work alone.

Lesson *A* involves more activity and socialization, and, depending on how the teacher treated the worksheet completed in Lesson *B*,

---

18. Ausubel, *Educational Psychology: A Cognitive View*, p. 365.

probably also more security. Lesson *A* thus provides for more positive motives.

Even with a traditional school incentive like grades, the more chance students have of meeting one or more of the three basic needs, the greater the motivational power of the incentive will be. For example, Page studied the motivational effect of two grading procedures.[19] After taking an objective examination, students were randomly divided into two groups. For one group, the teacher wrote only a letter grade on the exam paper. With the second group, the teacher wrote both a letter grade and a short personal note on each exam. Students were later given a second exam covering different material. Student performance on the second exam was intended to be an indicator of the relative motivational power of each grading procedure. The better the students performed on the second exam, the more highly motivated they were due to the grading procedure used on the first exam. Page found that the students in the group that received a grade plus a personal note on the first exam performed significantly better on the second exam than those that had received only a grade on the first exam.

Students seem to be more motivated to learn when grading involves a personal, written note from the teacher than when it involves only a letter grade. One might presume that a personal note shows more concern and interest on the teacher's part, and thus, contributes more to the students' satisfaction of the need for confidence and esteem—My teacher cares enough about me to write a note. The more information the note provides about the students' performance may also give them a greater sense of mastery, thus satisfying the need for activity. The same dynamics may account for the results Hurlock found in her study of praise, reproof, and ignoring as incentives.

Incentives should not be used when students are engaged in tasks that already interest them, such as Lesson *A* shown earlier. A sizable body of research indicates that adding incentives to an already interesting task does not—as common sense would suggest—increase motivation. Rather, under these conditions they tend to decrease it, to "turn off" students. For example, grading students on their performance of an intrinsically interesting task like Lesson *A* will usually result in a lower level of motivation than if no grades are given and the teacher simply acknowledges completion of the task.

19. E. B. Page, "Teacher Comments and Student Motivation: A Seventy-Four Classroom Experiment in School Motivation," *Journal of Educational Psychology* 49 (1958): 173–181.

Somehow, the teacher's external application of incentives reduces students' satisfaction of basic needs when they are involved in tasks that already have the potential of being very satisfying.

Many of the management strategies described in the next two chapters are designed to allow students to satisfy the three basic needs. Also, the effective use of school incentives is dealt with under the title of *incentive techniques.*

Use Learning Sets and Advance Organizers

An abundance of research supports the value of using learning sets and advance organizers to facilitate the learning of meaningful material. Since meaningfully understanding is a personal experience, it can be done only if the learner is *willing* to take the time to integrate new conceptualizations into his unique organization of existing ideas (Carter 1935). Learning sets and advance organizers maximize student understanding of new ideas by building on previously learned ideas, and, more related to this discussion, they encourage the learner to actively participate in the instructional task. It follows that learning, at anything higher than the lowest rote levels, simply does not occur when it is forcibly imposed on passive students.

Many of the suggestions given in the next two chapters on management strategies are ways of using learning sets and advance organizers. For example, an essential part of a *continuous-progress curriculum* is a student record form that lists all the desired objectives in a particular subject and shows the student's present attainment of them. The record form is highly motivating partly because it provides the student with a sense of continuity about learning experiences. A critical characteristic of well organized *independent activities* is that they are meaningfully related to other things going on in the classroom and school. In a learning center, students experiment with different electrical circuits. This activity is directly related to the unit on electricity being studied in science. A group project devoted to producing and putting on plays in other classrooms is related to a school program emphasizing the arts. One of the major purposes of *parent communication* is to provide continuity between home activities related to learning and school activities.

Help Students Set and Attain Realistic Goals

The topic of helping students set and attain realistic goals is closely related to the prior discussion of focusing student attention on desired objectives. The failure of teachers to focus students' attention on goals or objectives is demonstrated in a study by Johns concerning how elementary school students view the goal of reading.[20] He found that students view reading largely as "saying a bunch of words" and "doing workbook pages." If the objectives for reading cannot be made more explicit and personally relevant *for students* than that, it is unlikely that there will be any motivational benefits from teacher efforts at helping students attain them.

A major cause for low student motivation is the failure of teachers to provide students with a clear understanding of exactly what they are doing, why they are doing it, and how they are progressing. Often, students just perform a hazy sequence of activities, "saying words and doing workbook pages," without any idea of a purpose, a beginning, or a conclusion. The haziness of it all reduces, and even eliminates, the possibility for students to successfully experience their goals. As Klausmeier and Goodwin point out, "Nothing encourages continued effort and realistic goal setting more effectively than a backlog of successfully attained goals."[21] Stated another way, the successful attainment of goals is motivating.

Helping students understand and accept the *what* and *why* of objectives was discussed earlier. The discussion here will focus on two other aspects, identifying *realistic* goals and *knowing* when one attains them.

How realistic students are in setting goals that they will be able to attain successfully is directly related to their expectations for completing tasks that they think they are able to complete. Many studies have been done in this area under the topic *level of aspiration.* A study by Sears demonstrates the general conclusion from this line of research. [22]

Sears chose three groups of students from the fourth, fifth, and sixth grades. Students who had experienced success in school, as indicated by their grades and expressed feelings of success, were placed in a "Success" group. Students who had experienced failure in school were placed in a "Failure" group. The groups were comparable in age, intelligence, and sex. Each group was given a series of tasks, which consisted of reading and arithmetic assignments, and were frequently tested on them. After completing each assignment in the series, they were asked to estimate the time they would likely

---

20. J. J. Johns, "Reading: A View from the Child," *The Reading Teacher* 23 (April 1970): 647–648.

21. Klausmeier and Goodwin, *Learning and Human Abilities*, p. 451.

22. P. S. Sears, "Levels of Aspiration in Academically Successful and Unsuccessful Children," *Journal of Abnormal and Social Psychology* 35 (1940): 498–536.

need to complete the next assignment in the series. The more realistic a student's level of aspiration, the closer his or her estimated time matched the actual time required. Sears found that students in the "Success" group were more realistic. Students in the "Failure" group usually set their goals either too high or too low.

The inability of the "Failure" students to set realistic goals indicates that they are likely to continue being and feeling unsuccessful until the teacher is effective in helping them set more realistic goals. And, as long as they experience failure, their level of motivation will be low. Two of the strategies described in the next two chapters are effective in helping students learn to set realistic goals, *continuous-progress curriculum* and *student contracts.*

Of critical importance to learning is students *knowing,* at all times, whether they are performing satisfactorily (Glaser and Cooley 1973). Knowledge of results helps a student better understand what is being studied, and in less time. It also has a motivational benefit. Gagne points out that a continual knowledge of results allows students to reinforce themselves.[23] Their needs for activity and mastery will be met without the teacher having to use any incentive such as praise. In this vein, Ausubel stated, "Meaningful learning provides its own rewards."[24] However, meaningful learning will provide its own reward *only* if a continual knowledge of results is provided to students. A knowledge of the successful completion of tasks also allows students to become confident. When knowledge of results is provided as a matter of course, it is reasonable to assume that it will have an important effect on the students' motivation to continue learning.

Three of the management strategies described in the next two chapters are effective in communicating a knowledge of results to students. The diagnostic-teaching procedure followed with a *continuous-progress curriculum* keeps both the student and teacher well aware of the student's progress through a series of instructional tasks. The negotiation and evaluation steps of *student contracts* are effective in communicating a knowledge of results to students. The clarity with which tasks are defined when *incentive techniques* are used provides what is probably the most powerful and long-term payoff of their use, a clear and continual knowledge of results.

23. R. M. Gagne, *The Conditions of Learning,* 2nd ed. (New York: Holt, Rinehart and Winston, Inc., 1970), p. 317.
24. Ausubel, *Educational Psychology: A Cognitive View,* p. 367

The general use of incentives was discussed earlier in this section on motivation. Two essential conclusions that might be drawn from those earlier discussions are:

Provide Incentives and Punish, If Necessary

1. An incentive that rewards is more effective than one that mildly punishes. An incentive that mildly punishes is more effective than nothing.
2. Incentives are not likely to have as much long-term motivational effect as such other factors as opportunities to satisfy curiosity, to explore, to be active, to manipulate, and to gain a sense of mastery or competence. In fact, when these other factors are present, incentives may even be counterproductive.

However, as the noted behavior psychologist B. F. Skinner has pointed out most forcefully over the years, the major problem we have with incentives (he calls them "contrived reinforcers"), is the sloppy way they are used. All too often the teacher fails to organize the instructional situation in such a way that the incentive used is effective in altering the student's behavior in the way the teacher desires. Or, stated another way, the incentive and desired student behavior are not organized into an effective contingency relationship. It is not a matter of finding other reinforcers that count more (finding something more powerful than teacher praise, or substituting candy for gum); it is not a matter of the absolute magnitude of reinforcement (giving more profuse praise or more pieces of candy); it is, instead, a matter of designing better contingencies than those already available.

Compounding the organizational problem of using incentives in school settings is the fact that, in comparison with many other agencies outside the school, the teacher usually works with very weak variables. The economic system offers money; the judicial system offers a choice between freedom and incarceration; the teacher can offer nothing more powerful than praise or reproof. As it is unlikely that the incentives available to teachers will be increased in power—like being able to offer a $1,000.00 bonus for a perfect spelling paper—improvements in the use of incentives must come through the organization of more effective contingency relationships.

Skinner's work suggests two steps teachers can take:

1. *Make reinforcement contingent on the student exhibiting the desired behavior.*
2. *Minimize errors, and thus increase the student's opportunities to receive reinforcement.*

Each step will be discussed.

Reinforcement Contingent on Desired Behavior. The contingency relationship between the student exhibiting the desired behavior and the student receiving an incentive can be thought of as an application of *Grandmother's Rule:* "When you eat the vegetable, you get the dessert." Getting to do the preferred activity, eating dessert, is made contingent on the person doing the nonpreferred activity, eating the vegetable. The theoretical assumption behind this contingency coupling of activities is that the person feels reinforced when doing the preferred activity and so is willing to do the nonpreferred activity, which is not reinforcing. The contingency coupling has the possibility of changing the person's feelings about the nonpreferred activity because after the person has done the nonpreferred activity for awhile, it begins to be enjoyed for its own sake, and thus, becomes reinforcing.

Once the person feels reinforced when doing the activity which originally was not reinforcing, the contingency coupling of a nonpreferred activity with a preferred activity is no longer necessary. Grandmother feels justified in using dessert as bribery because she believes vegetables are good for you thus, any reasonable means of getting you to eat them is acceptable. She also believes that after you have eaten vegetables for awhile you will get to like them so much that you no longer have to be bribed with dessert.

Attempting to establish a contingency relationship between a reinforcer and all the many things the teacher hopes to have students doing is logistically impossible. The teacher must *concentrate on certain target behaviors* of the student. Work on the student's penmanship first, then his use of I for me, then on his capitalizing the first letter of each sentence, and so on. Don't try to tackle all of these language behaviors at once.

Initial attempts to motivate a student to exhibit a certain kind of behavior, such as spell more words correctly, should be *accomplished in small steps,* so that reinforcement is made more frequent and is easier to obtain. For example, instead of providing the incentive for correct spelling only on the basis of the student's performance on the final test given on Friday, base it on spelling five words correctly each day, or even provide reinforcement *immediately* after each word is spelled correctly.

Once the teacher has successfully established a certain ratio of desired behaviors and reinforcements—*each* time the student spells a word correctly she is immediately reinforced, and now she is spelling all the words correctly—the teacher should then endeavor to stretch that ratio *as rapidly as possible.* Move to providing reinforcement after every two words are spelled correctly, then after every four words, then after every ten words, and so forth. The only factor that limits the rapidity of this stretching is continued success. If the student continues to spell words correctly when reinforced after every five words, but starts spelling words incorrectly when the ratio is increased to every ten words, drop back to five. You might want to try other intermediate ratios, such as after every six or seven words. Then, as soon as a ratio of seven words to one reinforcer is successful, move immediately to a higher ratio. The teacher's goal is to be able to move out of the business of having to provide reinforcement in order to have students spell words correctly.

Minimize Errors. Success is the goal of contingency coupling. Students will continue to exhibit the desired behavior only as long as they are successful in obtaining reinforcement. The ratio relationship between behavior and reinforcement may stretch, yet only in the final stages should the possibility of being reinforced be eliminated, but the teacher should not confuse assuring success with providing only *easy* tasks. As Whitehead pointed out, "An easy book ought to be burned for it cannot be educational."[25] Successful performance and educational progress are accomplished by *setting standards of work consistent with a student's present level of ability*. Hilgard and Russell state it this way: "The job of the teacher is apparently that of keeping a nice balance between the ease of tasks that conveys no challenge and the difficulty of tasks that frustrates . . . ."[26]

The suggestions given later in this book for using incentive techniques are intended to help the teacher effectively accomplish the two steps of making reinforcement contingent and minimizing errors.

The creation of a warm and orderly atmosphere in the classroom is the major purpose of the teacher's role as a Group Leader. This topic is dealt with in depth in section 2 of this book.

Create a Warm, Orderly Atmosphere

---

25. A. N. Whitehead, "The Aims of Education 1929," quoted in C. J. Curtis and M. E. Boultwood, *A Short History of Educational Ideas* (London: University Tutorial Press, 1953).

26. E. R. Hilgard and D. H. Russell, "Motivation and Learning," in *Learning and Instruction*, Forty-Ninth Yearbook, Part 1, National Society for the Study of Education, N. B. Henry, Ed. (Chicago: University of Chicago Press, 1950).

Avoid High Stress   The reduction of the stress felt by students is one of the two major
and Disorganization   purposes of the teacher as a Counselor. The other goal is the development of a healthy self-concept. Both factors strongly affect stu-
dent motivation to learn. The topic is dealt with in depth in section
3 of this book.

CONCLUSION

Your goal as an instructional manager is to organize instructional
conditions in such a way that teaching can be carried out effectively
in group settings. The analogy of the one-bench, log hut and the
thirty-bench, typical classroom was used to illustrate the differences
between the task of *teaching*, which occurs whether you have one
student or thirty, and the task of *managing*, which becomes a problem when thirty students are taught in one setting.

Three instructional conditions that must be managed were
identified: individual differences, time and space, and motivation.
Your management of individual differences comes in one of two
ways: *varying the rate* with which all students move through the
same content, and *varying the content*. Your management of time and
space comes primarily by realistically assessing the present arrangements and physical constraints in the classroom and school and then
proposing alternatives that are likely to achieve the school's educational objectives. Your management of motivation comes in the ways
the combination of forces which initiate, direct, and sustain behavior toward a goal are handled.

Strategies for managing the three instructional conditions are
explained in the next two chapters. Instruments for assessing how
effectively the conditions are being managed are suggested in the
subsequent chapter.

REFERENCES

Ausubel, D. P. 1968. Educational psychology: a cognitive view. In *Motivational
      factors in learning.* New York: Holt, Rinehart and Winston, Inc.

Berlyne, D. C. 1960. *Conflict, arousal, and curiosity.* New York: McGraw-Hill.

Cantor, N. 1953. *The teaching-learning process.* New York: The Dryden Press.

Carter, H. D. 1935. Effects of emotional factors upon recall. *Journal of Psych-
      ology* 1:49–59.

Feather, N. T. 1961. The relationship of persistence at a task to expectation of success and achievement related motives. *Journal of Abnormal and Social Psychology* 63:552-561.

French, E. G., and Thomas, F. H. 1958. The relation of achievement motivation to problem solving. *Journal of Abnormal and Social Psychology* 56: 45-48.

Gagne, R. M. 1970. *The conditions of learning.* 2nd ed. New York: Holt, Rinehart and Winston, Inc.

Glaser, R., and Cooley, W. M. 1973. Instrumentation for teaching and instructional management. In R. M. Travers, ed., *Second handbook of research on teaching.* Chicago: Rand McNally and Company.

Harlow, H. F. 1950. Learning and satiation of response in instrinsically motivated complex puzzle performance by monkeys. *Journal of Comparative Physiological Psychology* 43:289-294.

Hilgard, E. R., and Russell, D. H. 1950. Motivation and learning. In *Learning and instruction,* N. B. Henry, ed. Chicago: University of Chicago Press.

Hill, W. F. 1956. Activity as an autonomous drive. *Journal of Comparative Physiological Psychology* 49:15-19.

Kight, H. R., and Sassenrath, J. M. 1966. Relation of achievement motivation and test anxiety to performance in programmed instruction. *Journal of Educational Psychology* 57:14-17.

Lindsley, D. P. 1957. Psychophysiology and motivation. In *Nebraska symposium on motivation,* M. R. Jones, ed. Lincoln, Nebr.: University of Nebraska Press.

McDonald, F. J. 1959. Motivation and learning. In *Educational psychology.* Belmont, Calif.: Wadsworth Publishing Company, Inc.

Montgomery, K. C. 1954. The role of exploratory drive in learning. *Journal of Comparative Physiological Psychology* 47:60-64.

Riessman, F. 1962. *The culturally deprived child.* New York: Harper & Row.

Terrell, G. 1959. Manipulatory motivation in children. *Journal of Comparative Physiological Psychology* 52:705-709.

White, R. W. 1959. Motivation reconsidered: the concept of competence. *Psychological Review* 66:297-333.

Young, R. M. 1932. Causes for lack of interest in high school subjects as reported by 631 college students. *Journal of Educational Research* 25:110-115

FOR FURTHER READING

For an extensive discussion of the nature of individual differences see:

Anastasi, A. *Differential Psychology.* New York: The Macmillan Company, 1960.

Gagne, R., ed. *Learning and Individual Differences.* Columbus, Ohio: Charles E. Merrill Publishing Co., 1966.

For additional information on educational attempts to individualize instruction see:

Howes, V. M. *Individualization of Instruction.* New York: The Macmillan Company, 1970. A book of readings.

_____. *Individualizing Instruction in Reading and Social Studies.* New York: The Macmillan Company, 1970. A book of readings.

Veatch, J. *Reading in the Elementary School.* New York: The Ronald Press Company, 1966. Describes individualized reading programs.

For an authoritative discussion of the new instrumentation available see:

Glaser, R., and Cooley, W. M. "Instrumentation for Teaching and Instructional Management." Chapter 26 in R. M. Travers, ed., *Second Handbook of Research on Teaching.* Chicago: Rand McNally and Company, 1973.

For discussions of open education see:

Central Advisory Council on Education. *Children and Their Primary Schools,* vol. 1, *The Report;* vol. 2, *Research and Surveys.* London: H.M.S.O., 1967. Known more popularly as the Plowden Report.

Hassett, J. D., and Weisberg, A. *Open Education: Alternatives Within Our Tradition.* Englewood Cliffs, N.J.: Prentice-Hall, Inc., 1972.

Walberg, H. J., and Thomas, S. C. "Open Education: An Operational Definition Validation in Great Britain and the United States." *American Educational Research Journal* (Spring 1972):1.

Time and space concepts are discussed in:

Hall, E. T. *The Silent Language.* New York: Doubleday and Company, 1959.

The reader interested in delving deeper into the topic of motivation will want to examine these books:

Cofer, C. N., and Appley, M. N. *Motivation: Theory and Research.* New York: John Wiley & Sons, Inc., 1967.

Farquhar, W. W. *Factors Related to Academic Achievement,* U.S. Dept. of Health Education and Welfare, Office of Education, Cooperative Research Project No. 846. East Lansing, Mich.: Michigan State University, January 1963.

Hall, J. F. *Psychology of Motivation.* Philadelphia: J. B. Lippincott Co., 1961.

Maslow, A. H. *Motivation and Personality.* New York: Harper & Row, 1945.

McClelland, D. C.; Atkinson, J. W.; Clark, R. A.; and Lowell, E. L. *The Achievement Motive.* New York: Appleton-Century-Crofts, 1953.

For additional reading on the motivational effectiveness of providing explicit instructions see:

Bromer, J. A. "A Comparison of Incidental and Purposeful Memory for Meaningful and Nonsense Material." *American Journal of Psychology* 55 (1942):106–108.

Huang, I., and Lee, W. E. "Experimental Studies on the Role of Repetition, Organization, and the Intention to Learn in Rote Memory." *Journal of General Psychology* 31 (1944):213–217.

Myers, G. C. "A Study in Incidental Memory." *Archives of Psychology* 5, no. 26 (1913).

Postman, L., and Senders, V. L. "Incidental Learning and Generality of Set." *Journal of Experimental Psychology* 36 (1946):153–165.

Reed, H. B. "Factors Influencing the Learning and Retention of Concepts." *Journal of Experimental Psychology* 36 (1946):71–87.

For further reading on the motivational effectiveness that student intention to remember has on the longevity and amount of retention see:

Ausubel, D. P., and Schpoont, S. H. "Prediction of Group Opinion as a Function of Extremeness of Predictor Variables." *Journal of Social Psychology* 46 (1957):19–29.

Beil, W. C., and Force, R. C. "Retention of Nonsense Syllables in Intentional and Incidental Learning." *Journal of Experimental Psychology* 32 (1943): 52–63.

Geyer, M. T. "Influence of Changing the Expected Time of Recall." *Journal of Experimental Psychology* 13 (1930):290–292.

Peterson, J. "The Effect of Attitude on Immediate and Delayed Recall: A Class Experiment." *Journal of Educational Psychology* 7 (1916):523–532.

Prentice, W. C. "Retroactive Inhibition and the Motivation of Learning." *American Journal of Psychology* 56 (1943): 283–292.

Thisted, M. N., and Remmers, H. H. "The Effect of Temporal Set on Learning." *Journal of Applied Psychology* 16 (1932): 257–268.

For further reading on the motivational effectiveness of a positive attitude toward what is being learned see:

Clark, K. B. "Some Factors Influencing the Remembering of Prose Material." *Archives of Psychology* 36, no. 253 (1940).

Edwards, A. L., and English, H. B. "Political Frames of References as a Factor Influencing Recognition." *Journal of Abnormal and Social Psychology* 36 (1941): 34–50.

Fitzgerald, D., and Ausubel, D. P. "Cognitive versus Affective Factors in the Learning and Retention of Controversial Material." *Journal of Educational Psychology* 54 (1963):73–74.

Gustafson, L. "Relationship Between Ethnic Group Membership and the Retention of Selected Facts Pertaining to American History and Culture." *Journal of Educational Sociology* 31 (1957):49–56.

Jones, E. E., and Kohler, R. "The Effects of Plausibility on the Learning of Controversial Statements." *Journal of Abnormal and Social Psychology* 57 (1958):315–320.

Levine, J., and Murphy, G. "The Learning and Forgetting of Controversial Material." *Journal of Abnormal and Social Psychology* (1943):507–517.

Taft, R. "Selective Recall and Memory Distortion of Favorable and Unfavorable Material." *Journal of Abnormal and Social Psychology* 49 (1954):23–28.

Watson, W. S., and Hartmann, G. W. "The Rigidity of a Basic Attitudinal Frame." *Journal of Abnormal and Social Psychology* 34 (1939): 314–335.

For further reading on the value of using learning sets and advance organizers in facilitating the learning of meaningful material see:

Ausubel, D. P. "The Use of Advance Organizers in the Learning and Retention of Meaningful Verbal Material." *Journal of Ed. Psych.* 51 (1960):267–272.

Carey, J. E., and Goss, A. E. "The Role of Mediating Verbal Responses in the Conceptual Sorting of Children." *Journal of Genetic Psychology* 90 (1957): 67–74.

Gagne, R. M.; Mayor, J. R.; Garstens, H. L.; and Paradise, N. E. "Factors in Acquiring Knowledge of a Mathematical Task." *Psychology Monographs* 76, no. 526 (1962).

_____, and Paradise, N. E. "Abilities and Learning Sets in Knowledge Acquisition." *Psychology Monographs* 75, no. 518 (1961).

Haselrud, G. M. "Transfer from Context to Sub-Threshold Summation." *Journal of Educational Psychology* 50 (1959): 254–258.

Kendler, H. H., and Karsik, A. D. "Concept Formation as a Function of Competition Between Response Produced Cues," *Journal of Experimental Psychology* 55 (1958): 278–283.

Keppel, G., and Postman, L. "Studies of Learning to Learn: III. Conditions of Improvement in Successive Transfer Tasks." *Journal of Verbal Learning and Verbal Behavior* 5 (1966): 260–267.

Liublinskaya, A. A. "The Development of Children's Speech and Thought." In *Psychology and the Soviet Union,* B. Simon, ed. Stanford, Calif.: Stanford University Press, 1957, pp. 197–204.

Merrill, M. D., and Stolurow, L. M. "Hierarchical Preview versus Problem Oriented Review in Learning an Imaginary Science." *American Educational Research Journal* 3 (1966): 251–262.

Morrisett, L., and Hovland, C. I. "A Comparison of Three Kinds of Training in Human Problem Solving." *Journal of Experimental Psychology* 58 (1959): 52–55.

Newton, J. M., and Hickey, A. E. "Sequence of Effects in Programmed Learning of a Verbal Concept." *Journal of Educational Psychology* 56 (1965): 140–147.

Norcross, K. J., and Spiker, C. C. "Effects of Mediated Associations on Transfer in Paried-Associate Learning." *Journal of Experimental Psychology* 55 (1958): 129–134.

Overing, R. L., and Travers, R. M. "Effect Upon Transfer of Variations in Training Conditions." *Journal of Educational Psychology* 57 (1966):179–188.

Postman, L. "Learned Principles of Organization in Memory." *Psychology Monographs* 68, no. 374 (1954).

Reynolds, J. R. "Cognitive Transfer in Verbal Learning." *Journal of Educational Psychology* 57 (1966): 382–388.

Sassenrath, J. M. "Learning Without Awareness and Transfer of Learning Sets." *Journal of Educational Psychology* 50 (1959): 205–211.

Scandura, J. M. "Algorithm Learning and Problem Solving." *Journal of Experimental Psychology* 34 (1966):1–6.

_____. "Problem Solving and Prior Learning." *Journal of Experimental Psychology* 34 (1966):7–11.

Stevenson, H. W., and Langford, T. "Time as a Variable in Transposition by Children." *Child Development* 28 (1947): 365–370.

Underwood, B. J., and Richardson, J. "The Influence of Meaningfulness, Intralist Similarity, and Serial Position in Retention." *Journal of Experimental Psychology* 52 (1956): 119–126.

Wittrock, M. D., and Keislar, E. R. "Verbal Cues in the Transfer of Concepts." *Journal of Educational Psychology* 56 (1956):16–21.

For reviews of the literature on level of aspiration see:

Lewin, K. et al. "Level of Aspiration." In *Personality and the Behavior Disorders,* J. McV. Hunt, ed. New York: Ronald Press Co., 1944, pp. 333–378.

Silvertsen, D. "Goal Setting, Level of Aspiration, and Social Norms." *Acta Psychologia* 13 (1957):54–60.

For additional reading about Skinner's work see:

Skinner, B. F. *The Behavior of Organisms.* New York: Appleton-Century-Crofts, 1938.

_____. *Science and Human Behavior.* New York: Macmillan, 1953.

_____. "The Experimental Analysis of Behavior." *American Scientist* 45 (1957): 343–371.

_____. "Reinforcement Today." *American Psychologist* 13, 3 (1958).

_____. *The Technology of Teaching.* New York: Appleton-Century-Crofts, 1968.

For further reading on the negative effects incentives can have on motivation see:

Calder, B. J., and Staw, B. M. "Interaction of Intrinsic and Extrinsic Motivation: Some Methodological Notes." *Journal of Personality and Social Psychology* 31 (1975):76–80.

_____. "Self-perception of Intrinsic and Extrinsic Motivation." *Journal of Personality and Social Psychology* 31 (1975):599–605.

Deci, E. L. "Effects of Externally Mediated Rewards on Intrinsic Motivation." *Journal of Personality and Social Psychology* 18 (1971)105–115.

_____. *Intrinsic Motivation.* New York: Plenum Press, 1975.

Leeper, M. R., and Greene, D. "Turning Play Into Work: Effects of Adult Surveillance and Extrinsic Rewards on Children's Intrinsic Motivation." *Journal of Personality and Social Psychology* 31 (1975):479–486.

Leeper, M. R.: Greene, D.; and Nisbett, R. "Undermining Children's Intrinsic Interest with Extrinsic Reward: A Test of the 'Overjustification' Hypothesis." *Journal of Personality and Social Psychology* 28 (1973):129–137.

Maehr, M. L., and Stallings, W. M. "Freedom from External Evaluation." *Child Development* 43 (1972):143–161.

Notz, W. W. "Work Motivation and the Negative Effects of Extrinsic Rewards." *American Psychologist* 30 (1975):884–891.

Salili, F.; Maehr, M. L.; Sorensen, R. L.; and Fyans, L. J., Jr. "A Further Consideration of the Effects of Evaluation on Motivation." *American Educational Research Journal* 13 (1976):85–120.

Staw, B. M. *Intrinsic and Extrinsic Motivation.* University Programs Modular Series. Morristown, N.J.: General Learning Press, 1976.

3

Strategies (1)

Teaching in group settings can be effective if teachers are competent in using the instructional-manager strategies that create the management conditions that facilitate teaching. Eight instructional-manager strategies are:

1. Continuous-progress curriculum
2. Grouping
3. Independent activities
4. Team teaching
5. Instructional aides
6. Student contracts
7. Incentive Techniques
8. Parent communication

These instructional strategies are interrelated. In order to individualize instruction by varying rate, the teacher would use a continuous-progress curriculum. Individualization is facilitated by the ways students are grouped into classrooms within the school, and then grouped again within each classroom. Because individualization requires that the teacher frequently instruct one student or a small group of students, a provision is made for the rest of the students to work productively at tasks where they are responsible for independently instructing themselves. These independent activities are highly motivating. They also allow the teacher to vary the content.

The dynamic time and space arrangements that accompany teachers instructing individual students while the rest are engaged in independent activities result in a need for different staffing patterns such as team teaching and the use of parents and students as instructional aides. Individual differences, time and space, and motivation are affected by having student contracts in which students identify their goals and commit themselves to achieving them. Incentive techniques might be used with students who are particularly unmotivated by most school activities, or with instructional tasks that simply cannot be made intrinsically motivating. Also, an effective program of parent communication should be in operation. Parents often think "teaching" means the teacher stands before the class and the students listen attentively or recite. The acceptance of new arrangements is more likely if parents understand why they are important.

The first four strategies are explained in this chapter; the last four are explained in the next chapter.

CONTINUOUS-PROGRESS CURRICULUM

A continuous progress curriculum will be explained in terms of two elements, the *materials* that are needed and the *procedures* for using the materials.

Materials

A continuous-progress curriculum consists of:

1. a defined sequence of progressively arranged objectives (from lowest to highest)
2. a separate test for each objective
3. a separate instructional task for each objective
4. a record form showing students' attainment of each objective

The objectives refer to small enough bits of information that can be learned in short periods of time, from a few minutes to a few days. The first three parts are shown in Figure 3.1.

No grade-level designation is assigned to objectives. That is, one group of objectives is not assigned to Grade Two, another

Objectives	Tests	Instructional Tasks
Objective #1	Test #1	Task #1
Objective #2	Test #2	Task #2
.	.	.
.	.	.
.	.	.
Objective #23	Test #23	Task #23
Objective #24	Test #24	Task #24
.	.	.
.	.	.
.	.	.

Figure 3.1

set to Grade Three, and so forth. Students simply move up the sequence of objectives regardless of what grade they may be in. There will be some students in the first grade working on Objective #23, as well as some students in the fourth grade working on the same objective. This is the nature of individual differences. Grade-level designations unnaturally constrain individual differences and are especially harmful to those at either end of the range. The more able students in the first grade may not be allowed to progress to Objective #23, though they are quite capable of mastering it, because it is considered a second grade objective. This is not really unlike withholding food from students who are about to grow taller than the height someone has arbitrarily decided they should grow. At the other end of the scale, students in the fourth grade who are ready for instruction for Objective #23, and quite capable of mastering it, receive little more than pitying remarks about their disability and assignment to a remedial teacher. This arbitrary grading of objectives leads to encouraging some students to think of themselves, falsely, as disabled.

The fourth part of a continuous-progress curriculum is a record form that shows the current status of each student's attainment of the objectives. There are two types of record forms, group and individual. A portion of a group record form used in teaching reading is shown in Figure 3.2. It contains the names of all the children and lists a limited number of reading objectives.

The major advantage of a group record form is that it shows a profile of the progress of the entire class on each objective, and so is particularly helpful in forming groups for instruction. A glance at the record form shown in Figure 3.2 indicates that the teacher could instruct four students at one time for the objective, *phonic word attack: initial consonant h* (Sam, Roger, Marion, Steve). Notice that only one student needed instruction for the objective, *phonic word attack: initial consonant d* (Steve). On the other hand, six

---

Group Record Form

Teacher_____ Dates_____to_____ Grade_____

Names	Objectives													
	Phonic Word Attack Initial Consonants													
	b	c(k)	c(s)	d	f	g	h	j	k	l	m	n	p	r
Tania A.	0	0	0	0	0	0	0							
Sam A.	0	X	X	0	X	X	/							
Roger B.	X	X	X	0	X	X	/							
Marion	0	X	X	0	0	X	/							
Steve	X	X	X	X	X	X	/							
Betty	0	X	X	0	X	0	0							

Key

0 means that the student *performed adequately* on the pretest for the objective, and so *no instruction for the objective is necessary.*

/ means that the student *performed inadequately* on the pretest for the objective, and so *instruction for the objective is necessary.*

X means that the student initially *performed inadequately* on the pretest, was instructed, and then *performed adequately* on the posttest. (The X is a crossed /.)

Figure 3.2

students needed instruction for the objective, *phonic word attack: initial consonant c (k)* (Sam, Roger, Marion, Steve, Betty).

The teacher using the group record form shown in Figure 3.2 had three instructional groups in reading, each working on different places in the sequence of objectives. One group was working on a portion of the sequence of objectives at a place *below* those shown in Figure 3.2, on auditory discrimination of sounds. Another group was working on the objectives shown in Figure 3.2. A third group was working on a portion of the sequence of objectives at a place *above* those shown in Figure 3.2, on phonic word attack of vowels.

A portion of an individual record form used in teaching reading is shown in Figure 3.3. An individual record form in reading is used with one student and lists all the reading-skill objectives that the student should achieve in school, grades kindergarten through six, or kindergarten through twelve, depending on the organization of the school district. The same form stays with the student during all these school years. The sequence of objectives for the portion of the record form shown in Figure 3.3 is visual discrimination for all letters, back again to the first letter to do auditory discrimination, and then back again to the first letter to do phonic word attack. Thus, Objective #1 is *visual discrimination: initial consonant b.* Objective #2 is *visual discrimination: initial consonant c.* Objective #74 is *auditory discrimination: initial consonant b.* (Remember, back again to the first letter.) Objective #148 is *phonic word attack: initial consonant b.* The portion of the individual record form shown here contains 222 objectives, which will require one year of study for some students and as many as five or six years for others.

An examination of the portion of Mary Wilson's record shown in Figure 3.3 indicates that she is in the first grade, has learned all the objectives dealing with visual discrimination (without needing instruction for any of them), and is now ready for instruction for the objective *auditory discrimination: final consonant d.* While the record seems to contain an unmanageable number of separate objectives, it is not as time consuming as it may first appear because Mary did not require teaching for *any* of the visual-discrimination objectives and only a *few* of the auditory-discrimination objectives for which tests have been given. In actuality, the kindergarten teacher dawdled along far too slowly. The teacher should have identified much more quickly where Mary would actually benefit from instruction: the first objective for which Mary actually needed instruction was Objective #75, *auditory discrimination: initial consonant c (hard).*

INDIVIDUAL RECORD FORM

Name   Mary Wilson

Teachers: K   Wallace   4 _____
           1   Bacchetti   5 _____
           2   _____   6 _____
           3   _____

Initial Consonants

	VD	AD	PWA
b-	0	0	
c- (hard)	0	X	
c- (soft)	0	X	
d-	0	0	
f-	0	0	
g- (hard)	0	X	
g- (soft)	0	X	
h-	0	0	
j-	0	0	
k-	0	0	
l-	0	0	
m-	0	0	
n-	0	0	
p-	0	0	
q-	0	0	
r-	0	0	
s-	0	0	
t-	0	0	
v-	0	0	
w-	0	0	
y-	0	0	
z-	0	0	

Initial Consonant Blends

	VD	AD	PWA
bl-	0	X	
br-	0	X	
cl-	0	X	
cr-	0	X	
dr-	0	0	
fl-	0	0	
fr-	0	0	
gl-	0	X	
gr-	0	0	
pl-	0	X	
pr-	0	0	
sc-	0	X	
sl-	0	0	
sk-	0	X	
sm-	0	0	
sn-	0	0	
sp-	0	0	
st-	0	0	
str-	0	X	
sw-	0	0	
tr-	0	0	

Initial Consonant Digraphs

	VD	AD	PWA
ch-	0	0	
ph-	0	0	
sh-	0	0	
th-	0	0	
wh-	0	0	

Final Consonants

	VD	AD	PWA
-b	0	X	
-d	0	/	
-f	0		
-g	0		
-k	0		
-l	0		
-m	0		
-n	0		
-p	0		
-r	0		
-s	0		
-t	0		

Final Consonant Blends

	VD	AD	PWA
-ld	0		
-lt	0		
-mp	0		
-nd	0		
-ng	0		
-nk	0		
-nt	0		
-st	0		

Final Consonant Digraphs

	VD	AD	PWA
-ch	0		
-ck	0		
-ll	0		
-sh	0		
-th	0		
Other			

Key

The designations 0, /, and X are used to indicate student attainment of objectives. The letters VD stand for *visual discrimination.* AD stands for *auditory discrimination.* PWA stands for *phonic word attack.*

Figure 3.3

Procedures

A diagnostic-teaching procedure is used in carrying out a continuous-progess curriculum.

1. *Diagnosis Before Teaching.* A student is tested for an objective in order to determine whether instruction for it should be given. If the student performs *adequately* on the test then instruction for it *should not* be given, and the student is then tested for the next objective in the sequence. On the other hand, if the student performs *inadequately* on the test for the objective, then instruction for it should be given.

2. *Teaching.* The student who performs inadequately on the test for the objective is given instruction for that objective. Instruction continues until the student performs satisfactorily with little teacher guidance.

3. *Diagnosis After Teaching.* Before going on to the next objective, the student is tested again to make certain that he can perform adequately on the test for the objective for which instruction is provided. If the student does not perform adequately on the test for the objective then additional instruction for it is provided.

For example, let's examine how diagnostic-teaching procedure might be used with two boys, Roger and Randy. Roger performs adequately on the Diagnosis Before Teaching. Randy performs inadequately on the Diagnosis Before Teaching.

Roger
1. Roger is given the test for Objective #23. He performs adequately on the test. His test performance indicates that he has already attained Objective #23, and so no instruction for it is necessary. Roger is then tested for Objective #24.

Randy
1. *Diagnosis Before Teaching.* Randy is given the test for Objective #23. He performs inadequately on the test. His test performance indicates that he has not already attained Objective #23 and so instruction for it is necessary.

2. *Teaching.* The instructional task designed for Objective #23 is used with Randy. Teaching continues until he seems to have mastered the task.

3. *Diagnosis After Teaching.* Randy is then given another test for Objective #23. If he is now able to perform it adequately

he will be tested for Objective #24. If he is still not able to perform it adequately, additional teaching for Objective #23 will be provided. Instruction for Objective #23 continues until Randy is able to perform adequately on the test for that objective.

Advantages

Higher Achievement   Research indicates that when the materials and procedures that characterize a continuous-progress curriculum are used, student achievement is as good or higher than it is with more traditional curriculums. Also, the most encouraging results have been obtained with disadvantaged, rural, special education, Indian, and Mexican-American students. When teachers organize their own continuous-progress curriculums, their teaching is what Berliner and Rosenshine call "direct teaching." In a review of studies dealing with the effect of teachers on students' learning, Berliner and Rosenshine concluded that "an emerging body of literature dealing particularly with children from low-income families at the primary grades indicates that teacher behavior focused on direct instruction results in increased acquisition of student knowledge and skills."[1]

Student Is the   The organization of a continuous-progress curriculum allows the
Working Unit of   *student to be the working unit of instruction.* The tests allow the
Instruction   teacher to determine what specific instruction is appropriate for each student. The teacher is not artificially confined to teaching for only those objectives considered *average* for students at a certain grade level. Also, the availability of tests and instructional tasks for all objectives makes it possible for any one student to work anywhere along the sequence of objectives, and for different students to be working at different places—Mary is on Objective #12, Tony on Objective #15, Jose on Objective #21.

In contrast, with a grade level curriculum, the highest degree of individualization can be accomplished by assigning students to grade levels on the basis of their performance on standardized tests. For example, all students whose mathematics achievement scores are between 4.0 and 4.9 are placed in the grade-four mathematics text and receive identical instruction. Whatever actual variation may

1. D. C. Berliner and B. Rosenshine, *The Acquisition of Knowledge in the Classroom*, Technical Report IV-1, Beginning Teacher Evaluation Study, Prepared for California Commission for Teacher Preparation and Licensing by the Far West Laboratory, San Francisco, California, February 1976, p. 26.

exist within that group is ignored. Further, because of intra-individual variation, students should be reassigned to different grade-level groups in different subjects because many students who score between 4.0 and 4.9 on the mathematics test will not score within that range on tests for reading and language.

A continuous-progress curriculum creates a higher level of student *motivation* because the separate bits of information are small enough that students can learn them in anywhere from a few minutes to a few days, and the tests provide students with concrete evidence of academic progress. When students can see a concrete demonstration of genuine progress after only a few minutes or few days of instruction, their personal sense of accomplishment is great. Progress is concretely demonstrated because students take the test, perform inadequately, are instructed for a short period of time, perform adequately when retested, and then get to make an indication of their accomplishment on the record form.

> *Motivation through Demonstrated Accomplishment*

In contrast, with the grade-level curriculum, students complete lessons but are provided no concrete bench marks by which to judge their academic progress. The lessons just seem to go on day by day, page by page. Because a grade-level curriculum provides no intrinsic motivation through demonstrated accomplishment, intrinsic motivation must be developed in other ways. For example, the traditional first step in teaching reading lessons with a grade-level curriculum is called *motivation.* Its purpose is to get students interested in doing the reading lesson. It consists of talking about interesting features of the story to be read, relating it to students' experiences, and so forth. The abundant use of pleasing stories and colorful pictures in reading texts are also attempts to develop intrinsic motivation. While these things are important, they usually do not match the motivational strength of demonstrated accomplishment.

Another important advantage of a continuous-progress curriculum is that it is *student centered.* The organization of it focuses the teacher's attention on students' performance. The test provides a frame of reference for selecting the most appropriate instructional tasks in situations where many different instructional tasks could possibly be used. An instructional task is appropriate if it looks like it will enable students to perform adequately on the test, and inappropriate if it does not. For example, in teaching for a specific objective in addition, teachers might consider using an almost infinite variety of ways to teach. When a continuous-progress curriculum is used, the *one* best way to teach for the objective in addition is the

> *Student-Centered Curriculum*

one that appears to provide the best preparation for the test for the objective. The purpose of the teacher's instructional activities is always in the direction of adequate student performance on the test.

A continuous-progress curriculum also *provides teachers tangible evidence of their worth as teachers.* This is the counterpart of students having tangible evidence of their academic progress. When students are progressing through the sequence of objectives, teachers *know* they are effective.

In contrast, a grade-level curriculum is *teacher and material centered.* The organization of it requires that the teacher's attention is on what the teacher is doing with students. It provides no frame of reference for selecting the most appropriate instructional task in situations where many could be possible. For example, when teaching for an objective in addition, teachers have no way of selecting what will probably be the *one* most effective instructional task from a book listing a virtually infinite variety of possible ways to teach addition. Consequently, teachers tend to try them all and then find that they do not have enough time.

A major reason for teachers not having sufficient time to teach is their inability to sort through the many possible instructional tasks and select the *one* most appropriate for a specified objective. Further, they share with their students a sense of not making progress. Many teachers feel hopelessness and failure because they see little relationship between their teaching efforts and their students' progress. Also, they are continually frustrated in their futile efforts to find the ultimate teaching plan. Their efforts are destined to be futile since the focus of a grade-level curriculum is on teacher and material, and so teachers aren't prepared to recognize the solution even if it should come.

Limitations

Objectives Behaviorally Defined
A continuous-progress curriculum can be developed only for those learnings in which desired student performances can be behaviorally defined. Examples of behaviorally definable *attainment objectives* are shown in Figure 3.4. The behavior a student is expected to exhibit with each of the objectives shown in Figure 3.4 is fairly clear. The teacher could determine whether a student was able to point to the city of Lima on a map or to the vena cava on a diagram of a heart. Also, notice that some of the objectives involve very high-level conceptualization and problem solving. Not all call for a simple, memorized response.

Attainment Objectives

1. *To be able to find the city of Lima on a map.*
2. *To be able to identify the vena cava on a diagram of a heart.*
3. *To be able to spell the words plow, sea, volley, and adapt.*
4. *To be able to name the ten characteristics of mammals.*
5. *To be able to identify the base line, scale, and label when shown the figure of a bar graph.*
6. *To be able to identify those shapes that are triangles when shown pictures of geometric shapes that have not been shown before.*
7. *To be able to describe three examples that illustrate the principle that "man's adaptations to his natural environment have resulted in changes in man's ways of living." The examples should not be identical or even highly similar to those the child might have been presented earlier during instruction.*
8. *To be able to propose a satisfactory solution to Geography Problem 18. (In this problem the student is given a map showing the topographical features of an area containing five towns. In the problem the student buys land in one or more of the towns, with the expectation that the land located in the town that later grows into a city will be most valuable, and thus he will realize the greatest gain on his investment. In solving the simulation problem the student has to apply what he knows about the relationship between topographical features and major cities.) He has not seen Problem 18 prior to the time he is asked to do it.*

Figure 3.4

Teachings not suitable for a continuous-progress curriculum are those in which the objectives refer to processes that are not easily observed. *Process objectives* identify the actions a student is expected to carry out, the results of which are presumed to be undefinable. Process objectives refer to activities such as painting, writing stories, participating in plays, and so forth. The teacher does not identify the specific behaviors students are expected to display in a play because "the play's the thing" rather than some expected level of performance. Almost anything dealing with creativity has process objectives for if the teacher stated exactly what the student was expected to create prior to the activity it would not be creative.

The subject areas that suitable continuous-progress curriculums can be designed for are those for which standardized achievement tests have been developed—reading, language, mathematics, and to a lesser degree, social science and science.

Assigning Grades

Another limitation of a continuous-progress curriculum is the assignment of grades. A grade of *A, B,* and so forth, cannot be assigned based on a student's performance on a test because the tests have been designed to be interpreted in only one of two ways. The student either *should be instructed* for a specified objective or, the student *should not be instructed* for the objective. If teachers must assign grades, they should not attempt to use any part of a continuous-progress curriculum to do it. If a conflict arises between the relative importance of grading and teaching, teaching should be considered the more important. The primary purpose of the school is, after all, to nurture and improve; it is not to grade and categorize. A grading system that prevents teachers from helping students improve should be carefully examined and then changed.

Developing a Continuous-Progress Curriculum

Programs having a continuous-progress curriculum are available from many publishers. Most publishers of major programs in reading, language arts, mathematics, science, and social science, at both the elementary and high school levels, have such programs for sale. The most consistent, obvious, and yet disturbing feature of these published programs is the near total dependence on technology for teaching. The materials are almost entirely self-instructional, meaning the materials handle the job of teaching. They are "teacher free."

Among the more highly developed and fully evaluated published programs are: (1) Individually Prescribed Instruction, (2) Individually Guided Education, and, (3) Program for Learning in Accordance with Needs (PLAN). A type of program still under development and so not yet widely published is computer-assisted instruction.

A continuous-progress curriculum can also be developed by a teacher or a group of teachers. There are a number of advantages to teachers producing their own continuous-progress curriculums. First, they can design the programs in such a way that the teacher plays a significant, personal role in carrying out testing and teaching. This eliminates the distasteful characteristic of most published programs, total dependence on technology to teach. Students will be more motivated when personally interacting with a live teacher than when impersonally interacting with a machine. In addition to this, teachers can continually adapt and adjust their instruction and, thus, maximize its effectiveness for each learner. In published programs, the lock-step sequence built in to them at the factory makes it difficult, if not impossible, for teachers to adapt and adjust a program to individual learners.

Second, teachers can select particular objectives they believe most important for their students rather than having to accept the objectives provided by the producers of the published programs.

Third, teachers are able to define the behaviors they expect for each objective by preparing their own tests. They are not forced to use tests they think are inappropriate. Fourth, and very importantly, by developing their own program, teachers will be thoroughly familiar with it and thus more likely to adapt and adjust it to individual learners. Printed materials produced by nationally-based publishing companies are usually very intimidating. Teachers tend to assume that the published materials are produced by omniscient "experts" whose work should not be questioned or altered by mere classroom teachers.

A continuous-progress curriculum is developed in four steps. *First,* a satisfactory sequence of objectives is identified.[2] The objectives should be arranged progressively from lowest to highest. The list should be as brief as possible because a separate test and instructional task will be designed for *each* objective. Students will be allowed to move through the sequence of objectives at different rates, therefore, a list of 2400 objectives in reading is an almost unmanageable number of separate items for the teacher to keep track of. Also, management becomes even more difficult if another 2400 objectives are identified for language, and still another 2400 for mathematics.

Second, a test is prepared for each objective. The test indicates how a person who has mastered the objective should perform. *Third,* an instructional task is prepared for each objective. The instructional task is intended to help students perform satisfactorily on the test. *Fourth,* record forms covering all objectives are prepared.

The most important characteristic of a continuous-progress curriculum and the one which gives the most difficulty to teachers developing it is *internal consistency. A continuous-progress curriculum is internally consistent when the test and instructional task for each objective are logically related to each other.* Internal consistency is paramount to a continuous-progress curriculum because the entire idea of it is *mastery of identified objectives.* The test for Objective #23 is intended to represent the behavior expected of a person who has achieved that objective. The instructional task for Objective #23 is intended to help the person to exhibit the behavior identified for Objective #23 as exemplified in the test for that objective. The instructional task for Objective #23 will be most effective

---

2. Prepared lists of instructional objectives are available from many sources. Publishers frequently have them for their series. They can be found in many methods textbooks. A complete list of school objectives can be purchased inexpensively from: Instructional Objectives Exchange, Box 24095, Los Angeles, California 90024.

in helping students perform adequately on the test for Objective #23 if both involve the same student behavior.

Internal consistency and inconsistency are shown in Figure 3.5. Instructional Task A is appropriate because it requires the same kind of student behavior as the test. Instructional Task B is not appropriate because it requires a different behavior than the test. Instructional Task A is internally consistent with the test because it has students make *a written response to a spoken stimulus.* On the other hand, Instructional Task B is inappropriate because it has students make *a spoken response to a written stimulus,* while the

---

Objective: *The initial consonant b.*

Test:

Exercise

The teacher pronounces one at a time the following list of words: bit, done, boy, bee, pick, push. Students are to write the first letter they hear in each word. "Write the letter for the first sound you hear in this word, bit. Now write the letter for the first sound you hear in this word, done." And so forth.

Adequate Answer

In order to be considered adequate, a student must write the letter b for the words, bit, boy, and bee. If a student fails to write the letter b for any of those three words, or writes the letter b for any of the three other words, instruction for the objective should be given.

Instruction:

Task A Appropriate Instruction	Task B Inappropriate Instruction
(It is logically related to the test.) *The teacher shows a picture of a bus and asks each student to say the word. The teacher then shows a card with the letter b printed on it. The teacher says that the word bus begins with letter b. The teacher writes the word bus on the chalkboard. The teacher then pronounces other words and asks students to tell whether they begin like the word bus: bus—bit, bus—put. If the second word begins with the letter b students are asked to write b on a piece of paper. Instruction continues until students seem to be able to identify b-words correctly. The test is then given again.*	*(It is not logically related to the test.)* *The teacher shows words written on cards: bus, bone, ball. Beside each word is a suitable picture. The teacher asks students to pronounce the word bus using the picture as a clue. When all students are able to pronounce the word bus, even when the teacher covers the picture, the teacher follows the same procedure with the next word. Instruction continues until all children are able to pronounce the three words. The test is then given again.*

Figure 3.5

test has them make *a written response to a spoken stimulus.* Although Instructional Task B might have some merit, that merit is not in terms of the objective stated for Figure 3.5.

GROUPING

Grouping has been a feature of schools in the United States for over a century. In earlier times, a typical small community had about enough people of school age to fill one classroom. The teacher handled all ages and all subjects as well as janitorial duties. When the student population grew too large for one teacher a second was hired and the students were divided between them. Age was the common selection factor. All students six through twelve years of age were assigned to one teacher; all those from twelve up were assigned to the other. As the population grew, so did the number of classroom groups. Grouping on the basis of age usually made no finer distinction than one year. All six-year-old students were assigned to the first grade, seven year olds to the second, and so on. If there were too many six year olds for one teacher, two first grades were established.

The major purpose for grouping is individualization. Students are grouped so that the range of individual differences, academic and social characteristics, the teacher has to contend with is narrowed. Age was used originally as the only selection factor because it does correlate with social characteristics and was all that was available to indicate academic characteristics until the introduction of standardized achievement testing in the early twentieth century. Age continues to be the major selection factor.

When selection factors other than age came into use, it became necessary to differentiate between two types of grouping, one based entirely on age. The term *heterogeneous grouping* (*heter* meaning different) came into use when the absence of a grouping pattern based on anything other than age was referred to. When all six-year-old students were assigned randomly to the two first-grade classrooms in a school, the classrooms are said to be grouped heterogeneously. Students of widely varying academic abilities are found in each classroom.

The term *homogeneous grouping* (*homo* meaning same) came into use when grouping based on something other than age, or in addition to age, was referred to. When six-year-old students were assigned to the two first-grade classrooms on the basis of their performance on reading-readiness tests, the classrooms were said to be grouped homogeneously. All students below a certain readiness score were assigned to one classroom and all above that score to the other classroom. A narrow range of academic abilities was thus exhibited in each classroom. The grouping patterns discussed in this section are, in most cases, homogeneous because they are based on factors other than age alone.

Common Patterns

Ungraded Grouping

Grade levels are abandoned. The early one-teacher schools were ungraded because they contained students of all grade levels in one classroom. Contemporary ungraded-grouping patterns usually distinguish between lower elementary and upper elementary, *ungraded primary* and *ungraded intermediate.* Students are assigned to an ungraded primary for at least their first three years of schooling. They are promoted to the intermediate group on the basis of age, social maturity, academic ability, or some combination of the three factors. A school might have three or more ungraded primary classrooms. The teacher in a primary classroom might stay with the same group of students for the entire three years, thus assuring that the teacher becomes well acquainted with students.

Interclassroom Subject Grouping

Students are grouped according to the subject they are studying. This is the most common grouping pattern in junior and senior high schools. It is used in elementary schools when teachers trade for different subjects, such as when the two fourth-grade teachers agree that one will teach reading to both classes while the other teaches all the mathematics. During a two-hour period, Teacher A has reading with Class A for the first hour and reading with Class B for the second hour. Teacher B follows the opposite schedule for mathematics. The pattern is also followed when special teachers are hired to teach all the music, art, and physical education.

Interclassroom Ability Grouping

Students are assigned to classrooms according to their performance on intelligence and achievement tests. For example, students might be assigned to one of the two sixth-grade classrooms on the basis of their scores on a general achievement test. All those scoring grade level or higher are assigned to one classroom, while all those scoring from grade level or below are assigned to another. A high school might use placement tests to assign students to different English and mathematics courses, or even to totally different tracks. The assignment to ability groups may be for the entire day or only for special subjects, as when the disabled readers or gifted students are pulled from their classes for instruction by special teachers. The term homogeneous grouping is sometimes used to refer to this grouping pattern.

Students are assigned to a split-day schedule as a means of reducing class size for critical subjects. It is commonly used for reading in the primary grades. For example, half of the class comes to school at 8:30 a.m., and receives reading instruction until 9:30 a.m., when the second half of the class arrives. At 1:30 p.m. the first half of the class leaves school, and reading instruction is provided the second half from 1:30 p.m. until 2:30 p.m; then they go home. By having only half of the class present during reading instruction, the teacher can provide more individual help.

Split-Day Grouping

Within the classroom, students are grouped on the basis of ability. The pattern is most common in reading where students are given a reading achievement test and then assigned to one of three groups according to their performance—a "high group," a "middle group," and a "low group." This grouping pattern has been used at all grade levels from kindergarten through high school.

Intraclassroom Ability Grouping

Students are assigned for short periods and, on the basis of their ability, to a special teacher. For half an hour each day a remedial reading teacher might work with students below a certain reading level and an enrichment teacher might work with students above a certain level. Remedial programs for disadvantaged students may use a number of intellectual, academic, and social factors in selection as might enrichment programs for gifted students.

Special Ability Grouping

Instruction in the classroom is provided for one student at a time. Reading programs called "individualized reading" (Veatch 1966) follow this pattern. The pattern has become more popular in the last ten years because of the availability of published, self-instructional materials. The best use of a continuous-progress curriculum is with this grouping pattern. The factor used in selecting students into individual groups varies widely and sometimes none is used; students just work alone.

Intraclassroom Individualized Grouping

Problems and Solutions

Lack of Data

The school may lack explicit, reliable, and valid data about individual students. The school may not give standardized tests frequently enough. Pupil turnover means that information about new students is fragmentary. When a grade-level curriculum is used, valid achievement tests should immediately be given to all entering students. When a continuous-progress curriculum is used, the separate tests for each objective are selection factors. Using a diagnostic-teaching procedure, the teacher begins with the first objective and continues testing until a student performs inadequately on a test. Instruction for the objective of that test is then provided.

Uneven Developmental Patterns

The uneven and usually unpredictable developmental patterns of individual students makes grouping hazardous if the same group assignment continues for a long period of time. One is never certain how long a student will retain the particular academic characteristics which determined the original assignment to a group. The more frequently selection factors are rechecked the better. In a grade-level curriculum, students should be rechecked more frequently than once a year. In a continuous-progress curriculum, the factor is rechecked every time the test for an objective is given.

Intraindividual Variability

Intra-individual variability makes the identification of valid selection factors difficult. Recall the achievement profiles shown in Figure 2.3. Three students having grade-level-equivalent scores in general achievement of 5.6, 5.7, and 5.8 respectively, varied on subtest scores from a high of 7.8 in word meaning to a low of 4.2 in language. Even in terms of a single subject area, reading, one student varied from 5.8 in paragraph meaning to 7.8 in word meaning. If a grade-level curriculum was being used with that student, the teacher should provide instruction in paragraph meaning from a fifth-grade reading text and instruction in word meaning from a seventh-grade text. The best that usually can be accomplished is a compromise at the reading average 6.8. In a continuous-progress curriculum, intraindividual variability is not a problem because the selection factors, the tests for each objective, cause group assignments to be specific to desired performances. Two or more students who performed inadequately on the same test would be grouped together. The group is disbanded when it is able to perform adequately on the test. (This was discussed in the last section with reference to Figure 3.2, Group Record Form.)

Grouping will not improve the effectiveness of teaching if the cur- *Inadequate*
riculum does not provide for individualization. For example, in some *Curriculum*
schools which have used interclassroom ability grouping in reading,
teachers made the mistake of teaching everyone assigned to one
group at the same time and with the same materials. The teacher
used a form of recitation to teach as many as thirty or more students
together. Reading instruction would have been much more effective
if the students had simply remained in their regular classrooms and
been assigned to ability groups. At least each group would contain
no more than ten to twelve students and, so, they would have
gotten more individual attention.

Grouping assignments can affect students' self-concepts, which in *Negative*
turn can affect their motivation and success in school. The negative *Self-Concepts*
affects that grouping can have is eloquently described by Robert
Hutchins, a former president of the University of Chicago and
long-time advocate of high academic standards:

> As every educator knows, people do what they are expected to do and
> become what they are expected to be. Children on the high plains of
> Africa are shepherds at the age of ten. Young people on the high plains
> of Colorado are in college at the age of twenty-one. Both groups are where
> they are because that is where they are expected to be. If the traditions
> and resources of Kenya were the same as those of Colorado, the African
> children would go on to college and do about as well there as the Ameri-
> cans do. This is why the system of "tracking" in the American schools,
> by which the "bright" students are separated from the "dull," perpetu-
> ates racial discrimination and poverty. The children in the lower tracks
> are put there early in their educational careers. They are labeled stupid
> and officially informed that they are not expected to amount to much.
> They then live up (or down) to these expectations. For them school
> becomes a custodial institution from which they must escape at the
> earliest possible opportunity. Of course the slum child acts stupid when
> he comes to school. He confronts an alien culture. His home, if he may be
> said to have one, is likely to be broken. If he has parents, they are likely
> to have little education; and they will often be hostile, or at best indif-
> ferent, to the school. They will have given the child little of the back-
> ground he needs in order to get off to a good start. A child who can read
> and count by the time he goes to school has an enormous advantage when
> he arrives there. He will be placed in one of the higher tracks, and, since
> he will be expected to succeed, he is likely to do so.[3]

3. R. Hutchins, "People Do What We Expect," *Los Angeles Times,* 27 November
   1967.

Hutchins' concerns are supported by research. Studies reported by Mycock (1967), Roger (1969), and Samuels (1969) indicate that preschool through junior-high students in ungraded grouping patterns develop more positive self-concepts than those grouped by ability. In a review of studies that compared students in ungraded grouping patterns with those in ability grouping patterns, Martin and Pavan concluded that "cognitive outcomes appear to be the same in varied grouping arrangements, but there is evidence of social, and maturational advantages in the vertical or heterogenous arrangement."[4] The likelihood of causing students to form negative self-concepts, and otherwise retard their maturity, is a major weakness of a grade-level curriculum or any curriculum used with permanently assigned ability groups. Permanently assigned, grade-level-ability groups are inevitability labeled "high," "middle," and "low." The students assigned to each group identify with others in the same group and develop certain group views and expectations. Students assigned to the "low" group in the first grade are usually in the same group in the sixth grade. The formation of negative self-concepts is minimized with a continuous-progress curriculum or with any curriculum used with an individualized grouping pattern or ungraded grouping pattern.

Conclusions

When grouping is used as a means of individualizing instruction, three variables to be considered are: (1) selection factors; (2) flexibility of group assignment; and, (3) suitability of curriculum.

Selection Factors   The selection factors should be valid indicators of the abilities for which instruction is being provided. Validity is improved by specificity. For example, in reading, the *average reading score* is more valid than the overall *general achievement score* for all subjects. The *paragraph meaning score* is more valid for paragraph meaning instruction than the *average reading score.* Best of all is the student's performance on the test for an objective that is specific enough so that it can be learned in a brief time ranging from a few minutes to a few days.

Tests used for selecting should be given frequently. The more

---

4. L. S. Martin and B. N. Pavan, "Current Research on Open Space, Nongrading, Vertical Grouping, and Team Teaching," *Phi Delta Kappan* 57 (1976):310–315.

frequently they are given, the better. The optimum frequency is for each objective the same as that for a continuous-progress curriculum.

The potentially negative effects of group assignment can be minimized by assigning students to different groups for different purposes. Even for one subject, like reading, students can be assigned to a number of groups. They might be assigned to one group for skill instruction, another for leisure reading in the library, and still another for presenting a play to the class. Different selection factors should be used for different group assignments so that students have the opportunity of interacting with a wide variety of kinds of people.

    Permanent group assignments should be avoided. Some way must be found to avoid assigning a student permanently to a "low" group. Using only an individualized-grouping pattern, possibly with an ungraded pattern, is one way. Another is to have frequent retesting followed by regrouping.

Flexibility of Group Assignment

Individualization of instruction involves both *grouping* and *curriculum.* Either can cancel out the potentially beneficial effects of the other. Assigning students to different classes according to reading ability, and then using an ineffective recitation method with the whole class of thirty at one time, is undoubtedly worse than keeping them in their original classrooms, having intraclassroom ability groups, and using recitation with groups of about ten. Likewise, assigning students to individual groups and then not providing any individualized skill instruction is worse than carrying out skill instruction with ability groups.

Suitability of Curriculum

INDEPENDENT ACTIVITIES

In order for teachers to make the individual student the working unit of instruction, they must fully concentrate on teaching small groups and individuals. Only if they have organized the program in such a way that other students are fully self-directive, responsible for their own behavior and completion of assignments, however, will teachers be able to concentrate on individual students. *Independent activities* are ones that students do without continual supervision from the teacher. While the teacher is engaged in instructing individuals and small groups of students, the rest of the students are doing independent activities.

The only time independent activities are not necessary is when the teacher ignores individual differences and attempts to teach the whole class the same thing at one time. For example, Figure 3.6 shows a sixty-minute period devoted to teaching the whole class at the same time.

If the teacher utilizes an intraclassroom ability-grouping pattern and has three ability groups which are instructed for twenty minutes each, the organization of the sixty-minute period looks like that shown in Figure 3.7. Notice that in any one twenty-minute period, two-thirds of the students must carry out independent activities in order for the teacher to be able to concentrate on instructing the other one-third. Further, students spend forty of the sixty minutes doing independent activities.

If the teacher uses an individualized grouping pattern and instructs six students for ten minutes each, the sixty-minute period looks like that shown in Figure 3.8. Notice that with an individualized-grouping pattern students spend most of the period doing independent activities. Quite obviously, the more individualized the teaching, the more important independent activities become.

Types of Independent Activities

There are three types of independent activities: *individual assignments, group projects,* and *learning centers.* The major distinctions between them are their variabilities in time and location. For

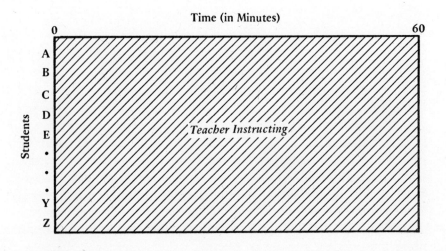

Figure 3.6

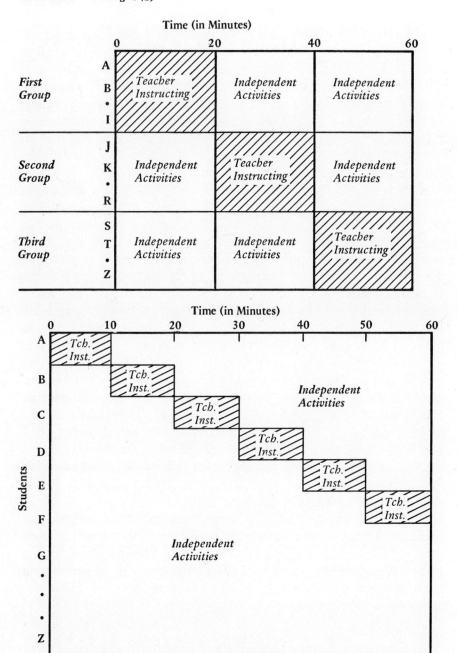

Figure 3.7

Figure 3.8

individual assignments, time and location are variables. For group projects, time is a variable but location is usually fixed. For learning centers, both time and location are fixed.

Individual assignments are tasks students are asked to do by themselves. They may be asked to complete a certain number of pages in the mathematics text or a lesson in the spelling or English text. These tasks can usually be started or stopped at almost any time—after the first math problem, or the fourth, or after the first of three pages. They can also be resumed whenever there is free time available. They can be completed almost anywhere in the classroom— at the student's own desk, at another desk, at a table in the rear of the room, or in the study hall. Individual assignments are variable both in terms of time and location.

Group projects are tasks students are asked to do in groups. Four students may be asked to prepare a large papier-mâché relief map of a country they are studying. They can begin working on the map at anytime they are not assigned to do something else. They can stop working at anytime. The location where group activities are carried out is usually determined by the task. The group doing a mural must work at the bulletin board in the rear of the room where the mural is to be displayed. The papier-mâché relief map must be constructed on a table located by the sink. Group projects vary in terms of time spent on them but fixed in terms of their location.

Learning centers are tasks students do alone or in small groups, and at certain designated locations in the classroom. The Writing Center is located at a table by the windows and a particular student is assigned to be there from 10:15 until 10:45. The student is then assigned to go to the Listening Center and to remain there until 11:15. The time and location of Learning Centers are fixed.

Teachers will want to use all three types of independent activities. Students should be assigned to a variety of individual assignments, group projects, and learning centers.

Nothing more will be said here about individual assignments because they are, and always have been, the most frequently used type of independent activity. The teacher may want to try increasing students' motivation to do individual assignments by combining them with *student contracts* and *incentive techniques*. These are discussed in the next chapter.

Group projects are extremely effective for motivating students while at the same time providing opportunities for varying the content. Students having different aptitudes and interests can be assigned to different projects. Group projects are also very effective in developing a healthy classroom atmosphere, which is the goal of the teacher as a *group leader*. Group projects are discussed as a strategy in section 2 of this book. The remainder of this discussion will be devoted to learning centers.

Organizing the Classroom for Learning Centers

Teachers have been able to make learning centers operate effectively in all types of classrooms ranging from ancient self-contained ones where students' desks fill every inch of available space, to modern ones featuring open pods and having three or more classrooms and teachers. While the physical constraints in a classroom have much to do with the way learning centers are organized and carried out in the room, four factors that must be considered in organizing learning-centers in any classroom are:

1. Continual teacher monitoring
2. Free traffic flow
3. Varying noise levels
4. Clear student assignments

Teacher Monitoring

The physical organization of the classroom should allow the teacher to view everything going on at all times. Obstacles to the teacher's vision should be avoided. When screens and other types of dividers are used to separate learning centers from each other—dividers are important because they give people in the center an important and calming sense of territoriality—they should be placed so they are *in line* with the teacher's vision rather than across it. The two situations are shown in Figure 3.9.

In a self-contained classroom, teacher monitoring is provided by locating the teaching station in a section of the classroom where unobstructed vision is assured to all parts of the room. In open-pod classrooms housing ninety to one-hundred students and three teachers, monitoring can be accomplished by keeping the center of the room relatively clear and locating teaching stations, learning centers, and individual assignment areas on the periphery as in Figure 3.10. One of the teachers on the team might be assigned, on a rotating basis, as a roving monitor while the other teachers are working in teaching stations with individuals and small groups.

Traffic Flow

When planning for traffic flow in the classroom, the teacher must think in much the same way as a city traffic manager planning streets and stop signs in terms of people's movement to work, stores, schools, and so on. A major concern of the traffic manager and the teacher is avoiding traffic jams because then people become angry, noisy, and less concerned about safety. In planning how a classroom

Yes   No

Figure 3.9

containing learning centers might be organized, the teacher will find it helpful to prepare a scale map of the classroom on grid paper. In places where students are likely to be moving, avoid placing furniture too close. This is less a matter of just having more space than it is of making the available space fit the activity. For example, in a relatively crowded, self-contained classroom, a teacher placed the students' desks close together and created an open area around the periphery for learning centers as shown in Figure 3.11.

More space was required around the learning centers than around each desk because when students worked at their desks, they did not move around while those in the centers did move, both within each center and between centers. A teacher in a self-contained classroom who was not allowed to have any furniture in the room other than student desks organized portable learning centers. Materials for centers were stored in shelves on the sides of the room. Students took the materials to their desks and carried out independent activities there. The desks were arranged so that students had relatively wide aisles to move through on their way to and from the storage areas.

Figure 3.10

Teachers find that smooth traffic flow is usually more than simply arranging physical space. It also involves helping students use the traffic pattern that has been planned. Teachers often find it helpful to point out to students the "streets" in the classroom and then remind them by posting "traffic signs" such as an arrow taped to the floor or suspended from the ceiling.

Group-leader strategies such as *group discussion* and *role play* are also useful for establishing and maintaining a smooth traffic flow, and are discussed in section 2.

Noise Levels

Classrooms with learning centers can be expected to be noiser than those in which students spend most of the school day sitting at their desks, but the noise should be no more than *busy noise.*

Many teachers have found that the bothersome levels of noise can be avoided by making use of acoustic materials and by locating noisier activities in one area of the room and quieter activities in another. For example, the teaching station and library center might

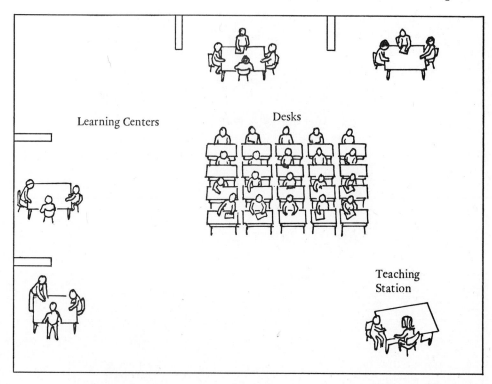

Learning Centers   Desks

Teaching
Station

Figure 3.11

be placed in one corner while the game center and science center, both involving some noisy socialization between children, are located in an opposite corner. The centers are separated by sound-absorbing panels. The panels might be expensive commercial products or inexpensive, paper egg cartons nailed to plywood.

One of the problems teachers often face when initiating independent activities—and thus having self-directed instruction occuring simultaneously with teacher-directed instruction—is adjusting the volume of their own voices to fit the size of the audience being addressed. Teachers accustomed to speaking only to the whole classroom often find that they appear to be shouting when they use the same volume level with one student in the teaching station or when assisting two or three students in a learning center. As the teacher learns to modulate volume, so will most students. Group-leader strategies such as *group discussion* and *role play* are also useful in helping students keep the noise level down.

Assignment Clarity   At all times, students should know what they are supposed to be doing and where they are supposed to be doing it. Teachers have found that an effective way of clarifying students' assignments is by constructing permanent assignment charts. The assignment charts can take many forms but their major characteristic should be *clarity* and *durability*.

A chart like the one in Figure 3.12 was used by a second-grade teacher to make assignments during the one-hour period devoted to reading instruction. The circular chart could be rotated so that the letter indicating a group could be moved from one activity to another very quickly. The teacher changed the center assignment midway during the reading period by ringing a bell and turning the central card showing group assignments to learning centers. While students changed centers twice each period, they stayed with the same group. The teacher assigned students to groups on the basis of expected compatibility and behavioral balance; so that each group had an equal distribution of both quiet and active students.

A chart like that shown in Figure 3.13 was used by a teacher in a fourth grade. Centers are identified by color. The red center has a red tag beside it. Centers were used during four time periods. Students' names were written on tags and placed on pegs located under each column. Each student's name appeared four times, once under each column. The advantage of using color coding for centers is that the chart does not have to be changed every time students change centers. All a teacher has to do to establish a new center is hang a colored tag beside it. In addition, one colored tag could refer to more

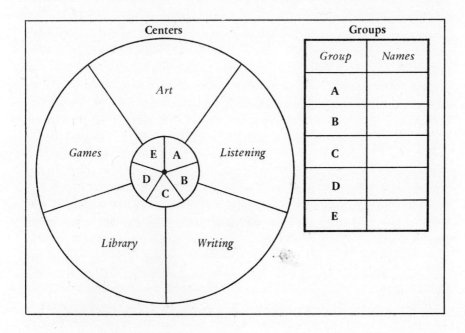

Figure 3.12

	Period			
Center	A	B	C	D
Red	⋮	⋮	⋮	⋮
Blue	⋮	⋮	⋮	⋮
Green	⋮	⋮	⋮	⋮
Yellow	⋮	⋮	⋮	⋮

Figure 3.13

than one activity located at different places in the classroom. While Figure 3.13 has only four centers, it could be expanded to include many more. Notice that these group-assignment charts contain three vital items of information: (1) each student's name; (2) the activity to which the student is assigned; and, (3) the period of time of the assignment. Students' names are written on something durable like a tagboard card or clothes pin.

Some teachers prefer individual-assignment charts. Figure 3.14 shows a chart used in a first grade. The teacher had an individualized-grouping pattern and had students doing independent activities during three twenty-minute time periods. The teacher devoted some time each Monday morning to having students complete their weekly schedules. Students were expected to devote one time period to doing assignment-completion activities and the other two periods to doing learning-center activities. Students were expected to change their activities without any direction from the teacher. The clocks told them when to change.

The chart shown in Figure 3.14 was used in a first grade for one hour a day. A longer version covering the entire day was used in an upper-grade class that had learning centers operating most of the day. Students planned their weekly schedules on Monday morning, and then were expected to follow them faithfully during the rest of the week.

Name _____

Monday   _____   _____   _____

Tuesday   _____   _____   _____

Wednesday   _____   _____   _____

Thursday   _____   _____   _____

Friday   _____   _____   _____   *Figure 3.14*

Operating Learning Centers

Learning centers follow a four-step basic routine:

1. *Selection.* The activity is selected either by the student's choice or the teacher's.
2. *Completion.* All that is to be accomplished in the activity is completed.
3. *Recording.* Students complete some type of record form indicating that the activity has been completed.
4. *Housekeeping.* Students clean up after themselves and prepare the center for its next participants.

Selection

Students are assigned to centers in one of two ways. Either they decide what they wish to do or the teacher decides. This selection may be in terms of *which centers* to do and with *which students.* Often students are expected to work at all centers sometime during the week, but are allowed to select the sequence in which they will do them. Two factors must be considered in the teacher's decisions about how much to involve students in selection—the number of attractive centers available and students' social maturity. Unless teachers are able to prepare or have access to a great variety of activities that can be used in centers, they simply may not be able to let students freely choose the activities they would like, only the sequence in which they would like to do them. Likewise, unless students are sufficiently socially mature to select center partners wisely, the teacher should assign them to groups on the basis of ability, compatability, and behavior.

Completion   The activities carried out in centers must be sufficiently clear and well enough explained so students can carry them out successfully *without asking the teacher for assistance.* Explanations can be provided in a number of ways. With games that students do not know, the teacher may want to give a lesson to the entire class on how the game is played.

A similar procedure might be followed when a manipulative device is used in a center. For example, if students are expected to use a filmstrip projector, instruction on how to operate it should be provided to the whole class prior to the time students start the center activity. Explanations can also be provided by means of written directions, which could also be illustrated. Teachers sometimes prepare directions in the form of job cards or task cards. The cards look much like the recipe a cook follows in that they very explicitly state: "First, you. . . . Second, you. . . ." And so forth. With some activities, the directions might look like those shown in Figure 3.15. This serves as a general set of directions for a center and allows the teacher to change activities without having to change directions by simply assigning each worksheet and filmstrip a number or letter.

The materials in a center should be organized so that students are able to locate them easily, and refile or dispose of them properly. For example, with the series of worksheets and filmstrips used with the directions shown in Figure 3.15, the teacher filed the worksheets behind index cards in a cardboard box that was attractively decorated and labeled *Worksheets.* Beside it stood another cardboard box of a different color that was similarly indexed and labeled *Answers.* Another indexed and labeled box was for filmstrips. Located also at the center was a wire basket labeled *Completed Work.* The arrangement of materials eliminated the need for a student to ask a teacher, "What am I supposed to do?" or "Where is the worksheet?" or "What am I supposed to do with the worksheet when I am finished?" A center should contain all the materials a student will

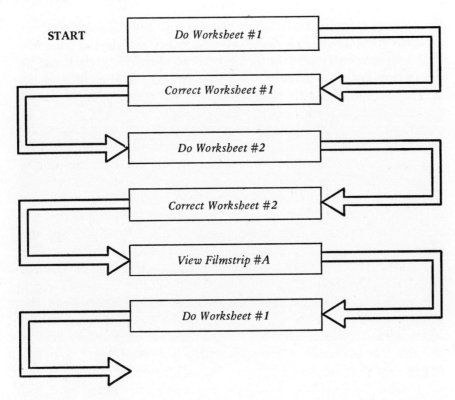

Figure 3.15

need in completing the activity: pencils, paper, erasers, colored crayons, rulers, pins, or whatever.

When centers are initiated with students, many teachers have found that the group-leader strategies of *group discussion* and *role play* are helpful. Students may role play the sequence followed in a center and then discuss the important things to do. A set of rules for centers might be established. (See section 2, Group Leader Role.)

Recording

A record-keeping system for centers serves a number of purposes. It gives students a tangible sense of accomplishment and thus provides intrinsic motivation. The fact that they must record their results causes students to devote more effort to an activity rather than just giving it a quick and surface level of attention. Also, very importantly, it provides a permanent record of which students did which activity. For example, if the teacher lets students choose their centers and only a few people choose a particular activity, the teacher knows by the record that it is time to change the activity. The record is also useful in describing the program to principals, other teachers, and parents.

A recording system should function as a natural part of an activity. For example, the worksheets students complete in a science center could function as both a record of their completion and as an instructional activity. Students make frequent recordings of conditions in an egg incubator. The record serves as the basis of conclusions to be made later in science.

Housekeeping   The only way for learning centers to operate as an independent activity is for students to be *fully responsible* for cleaning up the center when they are finished, and preparing it for the next people to use it. Effective housekeeping can be facilitated by the way the center is organized. For example, in a center where students are making block prints that leave a mess not easily wiped up, the teacher might cover the worktable with layers of paper, much like the layers of table cloths in a restaurant. As the waiter quickly cleans the table by peeling off the top tablecloth to expose a clean one underneath for the next customer, so also students clean the printing table by peeling off the top layer of paper. In an art center where water colors are being used, the teacher might make certain the center is permanently supplied with a bucket and sponge for use in cleaning.

Designing Learning Centers

The kinds of things that can serve as center activities are almost endless. You will want to utilize a greater variety of activities than just games and worksheets. Some activities are suggested here. They are intended to help you think about the centers you might design for your classroom.

1. A *Motor Center* might contain small electric motors, an old engine from a lawn mower, or even an old automobile engine. Students might be allowed simply to play with the engines, or they may be asked to make drawings, or even to produce a simple repair book for other, less mechanical, students to use.

2. A *Library Center* might contain a small rug, an old easy chair, and some comfortable pillows. One teacher even lined an old bathtub with a furry rug. Students might simply be assigned to read, or they might be asked to prepare book reports in the form of pictures that are used both to decorate the center and to inform others about desirable books.

3. A *Mathematics Center* might contain flash cards so that two students can drill each other on such things as the addition facts. It might contain different objects which students are to measure with a yard-stick or tape measure. A game where students use play money could be included. Dominoes and other games where knowledge of the basic facts are used are good.

4. A *Dream Center* might be simply a comfortable place to relax and think. Students might bring their own materials to the center.

5. A *Listening Center* might contain a listening post so that three to six earphones can be connected to one source. Students listen to a tape recorder or record player. They listen to recordings of children's books, dramatic productions and music.

6. A *Reading Center* might contain commercial and teacher-made games. It might have word cards so that a pair of students can drill each other. It might contain manipulative devices to develop visual discrimination and motor coordination.

7. A *Sand Center* might contain a sand box and an assortment of meas-uring devices, small cars, trucks, and houses. Students could simply be allowed to play in the center, or they might be asked to solve some problems by using the measuring devices. They might be assigned to construct a village and then to draw a map of it.

8. A *Writing Center* might contain old typewriters that students use to write stories. It might contain pencils, paper, colored pencils, and crayons that can be used in writing and illustrating stories. Perhaps there might be sample commercials that serve as models for silly commercials students write. The stories and books students write might be posted in the Writing Center, shelved in the Reading Center, or displayed on a board elsewhere in the classroom.

9. A *Woodworking Center* might contain a workbench, a few tools, and some scrap lumber.

10. A *Music Center* might contain earphones and recorded music, an autoharp and music with chords indicated, manuscript paper for students to write tunes, rhythm instruments, and possibly even a piano.

11. A *Creative-Dramatics Center* might contain a box of old clothes for students to dress up in. A small puppet theatre, puppets, and materials to make puppets could be a part of it. Also included could be materials for making pictures of stories students want to share. It might contain a tape recorder on which students record radio dramas.

12. A *Viewing Center* might contain a filmstrip projector and assorted filmstrips. Perhaps there could be a movie projector where sound is heard by means of earphones.

13. A *Science Center* might contain collections of objects to be classified, the complexity of a task depending on the grade level. Also included might be science experiments where students record and prepare reports about things such as plants growing under different conditions. It might contain filmstrips about science. It might contain a circuit board and electrical equipment which students assemble in different ways. It might contain small animals in cages or fish in tanks. A weather station that students maintain could be a part of this. Their weather predictions might be posted in school hallways and printed in the school newspaper.

14. A *Games Center* might contain recreational games, such as checkers or chess, and educational games intended to teach reading, spelling, and mathematics. The games may be both commercial, teacher, and student made.

15. A *Sewing Center* might contain material scraps, large needles, and scissors. A chart posted in the center might show various decorative stitches. Students might sew, do needlepoint, or hook rugs.

16. An *Art Center* might contain materials for working with clay, watercolors, or block printing.

17. An *Interest Center* might contain activities students have selected. An interest inventory is used in identifying activities and materials for the center.

18. A *Social Studies Center* might contain filmstrips and books about social studies topics. Pictures and models could be included.

19. A *Career Center* might feature books, pamphlets and filmstrips about different careers. Each week a different career is featured.

20. A *Reading Enrichment Center* might be established to broaden the reading interests and skills of the advanced readers. It could feature a multicolored wheel divided into different types of literature: science fiction, biography, dreams, and so forth. When students read a book from an area, their names are written on a tag and placed in the appropriate place on the wheel.

21. An *Inquiry Center* might provide students with information and then ask them to draw conclusions. It might ask them to read and then compare two folklore stories, one Indian and one American, and to draw pictures of what they liked about each. It might provide them with information about travel and a map and then ask them to plan a route on the map, much like the travel recommendations made by some service stations.

When designing centers, try to provide as much variety as possible. The activities should be changed frequently, and the activities in different centers operating at the same time should be different.

All should not involve reading or drawing pictures. Not all should be games or use filmstrips.

Initiating Learning Centers

The primary caution about initiating learning centers is to *move slowly.* Both the students and the teacher need time to adjust to centers. Students need time to learn how centers should be used responsibly and with self-direction. Teachers must learn how to prepare clear sets of directions, assign students with minimal disruption, and design centers which students can operate independently. Initially, one or two centers might be organized. As students get used to doing centers and the teacher more able in designing them, additional centers might be added.

The group leader strategies of *group discussion* and *role play* are especially useful in helping students understand and appreciate the problems encountered in operating centers, and then in identifying rules for the behaviors that are necessary if centers are to be used. (See section 2, Group Leader Role.)

TEAM TEACHING

Team teaching basically refers to "a group of two or more persons assigned to the same students at the same time for instructional purposes in a particular subject or combination of subjects."[5] It is the counterpart of solo teaching, where one teacher and a certain number of students are housed in one room and the one teacher has sole responsibility for instruction.

Cunningham suggests four organizational patterns that teachers might follow with teams.[6] The patterns involve different ways of designating leadership.

1. *Team Leader.* One teacher is designated as the team leader when the team is organized.

5. R. H. Johnson and M. D. Lobb, "Jefferson County, Colorado Completes a Three-Year Study of Staffing, Changing Class Sizes, Programming and Scheduling," *National Association of Secondary School Principals Bulletin* 43(1959):57–78.
6. N. L. Cunningham "Team Teaching: Where Do We Stand?" *Administrator's Notebook* 8 (1960): 1–4.

2. *Associate.* No one is designated as the leader. Leadership is expected to emerge naturally in the process of interaction. As the pattern often develops, different teachers assume the leadership of different activities or subjects.

3. *Master Teacher-Beginning Teacher.* This is similar to what occurs in student teaching in that the more experienced teacher is designated as the leader. The team might consist of a supervising teacher, two or three interns, and possibly a few instructional aides.

4. *Coordinated Team.* Teachers coordinate their efforts rather than share a joint responsibility for a common group of students. It may involve team planning, team evaluation, or team coordination of discipline. A grouping pattern mentioned earlier, *interclassroom subject grouping*, involves a coordinated team. For example, teachers in two self-contained classes trade so that one teaches reading to both classes and the other teaches mathematics to both.

Why Team Teach?

A commonly held assumption is that team teaching results in improved student achievement. The assumption is not supported by research. In a review of seventeen studies of team teaching at both the elementary and secondary school levels, Armstrong (1977) found that the majority of them reported findings of no significant differences in the achievement scores of team-taught and solo-taught students.

The reason for the lack of achievement differences between students in the two types of classrooms may be explained by the studies of Rutherford (1975) and Charters and Jones (1974). They concluded that, in terms of the actual patterns of interaction between teacher and student, there were no substantive differences between the two teaching conditions. Team teaching appears to be an administrative arrangement having little connection with the nature of the instructional process.

But if team teaching does not result in improved achievement, why has it spread from secondary schools, where it was originally established in the 1950s, to all grade levels and become a fixture of American education? An answer is suggested in a study by Hall and Rutherford (1975). In a survey of the concerns of 307 teachers who varied in their experience with team teaching from no experience to more than three years, the researchers discovered that regardless of their experiences with teaming, respondents ranked concerns with student achievement low. Teachers were more concerned about organization and working with others.

A major reason for the popularity of team teaching may be that it provides opportunities for teachers to interact with other adults and be less isolated. An educational sociologist, Seymour Sarason, describes the isolation of the typical primary teacher in a self-contained classroom in this way:

> During the course of the average day the teachers spend almost all of the time with small children. Leaving lunchtime aside, during the course of the average day, the amount of time teachers spend in face-to-face contact with each other is extremely small. . . it is unusual for these face-to-face contacts to exceed one minute.[7]

The story is told of a first-grade teacher who was driving home from school when on an icy curve her automobile slipped into a ditch. She got out, walked around to look at the dented fender, and muttered, "Oh, oh, oh! Look, look, look! Damn, damn, damn!"

Team teaching brings teachers together in a collegial relationship that would not otherwise exist in most schools. A study of team teaching by Bears showed that the more team members discussed what they were teaching, the more the question of why they were teaching it began to intrude.[8] The ultimate result, therefore, was substantial curriculum reform, a result that had not been anticipated when the study began.

Teaming also provides numerous opportunities for teachers to observe and learn from each other. They can eventually create a cooperative working relationship where the whole is greater than the sum of its parts.

Team teaching permits team members to take advantage of individual teacher strengths in planning, instructing, and evaluating. The advantages of having teams composed of teachers whose strengths compliment one another can be expected to increase as methods and materials become more complex and require greater teacher knowledge and instructional competence. No one person can possibly keep up with the rapid changes in new math, modern English, reading systems, and laboratory science. Team teaching may be a recognition that the day of the specialist in teaching has arrived.

---

7. S. B. Sarason *The Culture of the School and the Problem of Change* (Boston: Allyn and Bacon, Inc., 1971), p. 105.

8. E. B. Bears, *"Team Teaching"* mimeographed (Lexington, Mass: Lexington Public-Schools).

Making Teaming Successful

Successful teaming occurs when three or four self-contained class-room groups of "my" students and "your" students become one group of "our" students. Three ways of establishing and maintaining successful teacher teams are suggested.

Collaboration   The most important element in establishing and maintaining team teaching is collaboration. The successful team has open communication and a trust relationship based on the notion that team members can help each other grow and increase each other's potential abilities (Bechtol 1976). When members are not able to collaborate, team teaching will not be successful. Jung et al note:

> Innovations such as team teaching, modular scheduling and differentiated staffing increase the need for collaboration at all levels. In the traditional system of self-contained classrooms, most educators have carried out their roles in relative isolation. Many potentially valuable innovations have not been implemented successfully due to issues of influence, polarized conflict and ineffective communication. Increased interpersonal communications skills of school personnel will reduce at least one hindrance to local improvement efforts.[9]

A number of multimedia instructional systems have been developed to help teachers learn to collaborate more effectively. The Northwest Regional Educational Laboratory has developed a very successful system called *Interpersonal Communication* that contains twenty, ninety-minute training exercises.[10] Each unit provides teachers with a different competency. Here are examples of two.

> *Unit 2   Paraphrasing.* This competency involves the ability to re-state what another person has said so that it reveals the understanding received by the individual who is listening. Paraphrasing frequently begins by the listener saying something like, "Let me see if I am understanding you correctly. I think I heard you say that . . . ." The listener then describes his or her understanding of what

---

9. C. Jung, R. Howard, R. Emory, and R. Pino *Interpersonal Communications* (Portland, Oregon: Northwest Regional Educational Laboratory, 1971), p. xi.

10. The multimedia program *Interpersonal Communication* is available from the Northwest Regional Educational Laboratory, 500 Lindsay Building, 710 S.W. Second Avenue, Portland, Oregon. This program requires a trained leader. Training is provided through the Laboratory. It can also furnish names of people in different parts of the country who have already been trained as leaders.

was said. The speaker can respond by acknowledging that the listener understands what was intended, or the speaker can try to explain it another way.

Unit 4   Describing Feelings. This competency involves the ability to describe one's feelings, as distinguished from expressing them. An expression of feelings can abort the communication process. Instead of expressing a feeling by saying, "You talk too much," the person describes feelings by saying, "I'm getting bored and beginning to tune out." Instead of expressing feelings by saying, "You don't care about me," the person describes feelings by saying, "It hurt my feelings when you forgot my birthday."

A less complex multimedia instructional system that does not require trained leaders has been developed for schools wishing to initiate Individually Guided Education (IGE).[11] The system describes and shows exercises that develop "team-building skills."[12] Two examples of team-building exercises are described here.

Nonverbal Blind Trust Walk. People are divided into pairs and one is blindfolded. The pair walk around outside for ten minutes. They then switch roles. Throughout the blind walk the pair may not talk. They communicate by touching. When the blind walk is over, the pair talk about how they felt. A feeling of cooperation and trust is the desired outcome of the exercise.

We Agree. Team members write on a chalkboard or newsprint as many statements as possible that they can agree on. The exercise is intended to help each team member build and internalize the team philosophy.

Most school counselors are familiar with exercises that are intended to develop teachers' ability to collaborate, and will be glad to assist interested teacher teams. Many school administrators have also had experience with collaboration exercises.

Teachers on teams have the same problems of clarifying roles as others in close working relationships. They must solve the problem of dominance-subservience. In any close relationship, in order for one person to be dominant, the other must be subservient. The most mutually acceptable solution is by establishing a system of trade-offs: I will follow your lead in reading and you will follow

Roles and Responsibilities

---

11. References to IGE are given at the end of this chapter.

12. Team-building exercises are described in the book: W. M. Bechtol, *Individualizing Instruction and Keeping Your Sanity* (Chicago: Follett, 1973), 117–126. The skills are shown in the 16 mm film, *Making Unit Meetings Effective* (Reading, Mass.: Addison-Wesley, 1976).

mine in mathematics. Unless I have an emotional need for sub-
servience, I will not be happy following your lead in everything,
and may react by letting you do more of the work and take more
of the responsibility. Quite unconsciously, I find subtle ways to
undercut you, perhaps by using the art supplies you had intended
to use, or by allowing my students to become noisy enough that
they disturb your lesson. Successful teams have usually found it
helpful to identify the areas where *each* will be the *lead teacher,* and
then strive hard to be *good followers* in the other areas.

The number of bodies physically present under one roof at one
time make clear, written communication very important in open-
space classrooms. As school districts which grow from having one
school to having twenty schools soon find out, the larger the group,
the more important written policies become. Using *group discussions*
to establish rules for all activities, and then writing and posting these
rules, is more critical in team-teaching situations than in solo ones.
Which door is used to go to recess? How does one get permission
to go to the bathroom? How does one move from one learning
center to another, or from a learning center to a desk? Everyone
in the room, teachers and students alike, will avoid conflicts if they
have agreed on the answers to these questions *ahead of time.* (*Group
discussion* is explained in section 2, Group Leader Strategies.)

Gradual Change   Much of the general uneasiness that many teachers and students
feel initially in open-space classrooms where team teaching is taking
place is cultural shock caused by change in accustomed time and
space arrangements. (Recall the discussion of time and space arrangements in the last chapter.) The room is uncomfortably large;
they long for the security of closer walls. The daily schedule is so
complex; they long for the one where *everyone* does reading from
nine until ten and mathematics from ten until eleven. Getting over
cultural shock requires time, patience, and a certainty that it is
worth the effort.

One of the most helpful ways for teachers new to team teaching to adjust is to recreate initially in the open-space classroom
the time and space arrangements found in self-contained classrooms.
The self-contained grouping within an open-space classroom might
have a seating arrangement like that shown in Figure 3.16. Teachers are assigned a group of students which they are largely responsible
for instructing, and operate their own schedules.

Change should come slowly by things such as introducing one
or two learning centers that are used by all classes, by dividing

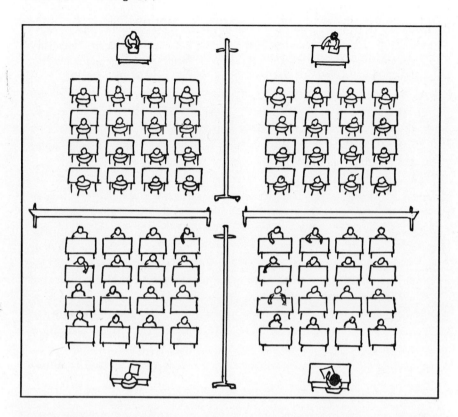

Figure 3.16

all students in the room according to reading ability and having different teachers work with different groups, and by having students share with each other the activities they have participated in such as a puppet play or mural. Bit by bit, the portable walls should be removed and the room treated as a whole. Teachers have found that it usually takes almost three years before they feel really satisfied with team teaching. The first year they find out what it is all about; the next year they work at refining it; and, in the third year it finally begins to "jell."

REFERENCES

Armstrong, D. G. 1977. Team teaching and academic achievement. *Review of Educational Research* 47: 65–86.

Bechtol, W. M. 1976. In J. S. Sorenson; M. Poole; and L. H. Joyal, eds., *The unit leader and individually guided education.* Reading, Mass.: Addison-Wesley Publishing Co.

Charters, W. W., Jr., and Jones, J. E. 1974. *On neglect of the independent variable in program evaluation.* Project MITT Occasional Paper. University of Oregon, Eugene Center for Educational Policy & Management, Eugene, Oregon.

Hall, G. E., and Rutherford, W. L. 1975. *Concerns of teachers about implementing the innovation of team teaching.* University of Texas at Austin Research and Development Center for Teacher Education, Austin, Texas.

Mycock, M. M. 1967. A comparison of vertical grouping and horizontal grouping in the infant school. *British Journal of Educational Psychology* 37:133–137.

Roger, R. P. 1969. *Heterogeneous versus homogeneous social class grouping of preschool children in head start classrooms.* Detroit: Merrill-Palmer Institute. (Available in ERIC as EDO45176).

Samuels, S., et al. 1969. *The influence of team teaching and flexible grouping on attitudes of junior high school students: final report.* Albany, N.Y.: New York State Experimental and Innovative Programs, New York Board of Education, Division of Research.

Rutherford, W. L. 1975. *Team teaching—how do teachers use it?* University of Texas at Austin Research and Development Center for Teacher Education, Austin, Texas.

Veatch, J. 1966. *Reading in the elementary school.* New York: The Ronald Press Company.

FOR FURTHER READING

For additional reading about the rationale, materials, and procedures that characterize a continuous-process curriculum at both the elementary and secondary school levels see:

Glaser, R. "Adapting the Elementary School Curriculum to Individual Performance." In *1967 Invitational Conference on Testing Problems* (October 28, 1967, New York City). Princeton, N.J.: Educational Testing Service, 1968.

_____. "Individuals and Learning: The New Aptitudes." *Educational Researcher* 1 (June 1972): 5–13.

_____, and Cooley, W. M. "Instrumentation for Teaching and Instructional Management." In *Second Handbook of Research on Teaching,* R. M. Travers, ed. Chicago: Rand McNally & Company, 1973, chap. 26.

Hillson, M., and Bongo, J. *Continuous-Progress Education.* Chicago: Science Research Associates, 1971.

Hull, R. E. "Selecting an Approach to Individualized Education." *Phi Delta Kappan* (November 1973):169–173.

Neill, G. W., "The Reform of Intermediate and Secondary Education in California." *Phi Delta Kappan* (February 1976):391–394.

The research on published programs having a continuous-progress organization indicates that students using them achieve as well or better than those using the more traditional programs. See:

Progress Report II: Individually Prescribed Instruction. Philadelphia: Research for Better Schools, Inc., March 1971.

Quilling, M. R.; Fischback, T. J.; Rendfrey, K. H.; and Frayer, D. A. *Individual Goal Setting Conferences Related to Subject Matter Learning: A Report on the Field Test.* Madison, Wisc.: The Research and Development Center for Cognitive Learning, University of Wisconsin, Technical Report No. 190, 1971.

The most encouraging achievement results were obtained with disadvantaged, rural, special education, Indian, and Mexican-American students. See:

Scalon, R. G., and M. V. Brown. "Individualizing Instruction." In *Planned Change in Education,* D. S. Busnell and D. Rappaport, eds. New York: Harcourt Brace Jovanovich, Inc., 1971.

For a discussion of some of the disturbing factors of instructional technology see:

Miller, G. A. "Assessment of Psychotechnology." *American Psychologist* 25 (1970): 991–1001.

For further reading on Individually Prescribed Instruction see:

Individually Prescribed Instruction. Philadelphia: Research for Better Schools, Inc., 1971.

Lindvall, C. M., and Bolvin, J. O. "Programmed Instruction in the Schools: An Application of Programming Principles in 'Individually Prescribed Instruction'." In *Programmed Instruction,* P. C. Lange, ed., Sixty-Sixth Yearbook of the National Society for the Study of Education, Part II. Chicago: University of Chicago Press, 1967.

For further reading on Individually Guided Education see:

Benson, W. W. *A Focus on Change: Individually Guided Education Multi-Unit School—Secondary (IGE/MUS-S).* Madison, Wisc.: The Research and Development Center for Cognitive Learning, University of Wisconsin, 1973.

Klausmeier, H. J.; Quilling, M. R.; Sorenson, J. S.; Way, R. S.; and Glasrud, G. R. *Individually Guided Instruction and the Multi-Unit Elementary School, Guidelines for Implementation.* Madison, Wisc.: The Research and Development Center for Cognitive Learning, University of Wisconsin, 1971.

Individually Guided Motivation. Madison, Wisc.: The Research and Development Center for Cognitive Learning, University of Wisconsin, 1973.

Otto, W., and Askov, E. *The Wisconsin Design for Reading Skill Development.* Minneapolis, Minn.: National Computer Systems, Inc., June 1970.

Romberg, T. A., and M. E. Montgomery. *Developing Mathematical Processes: A Different Kind of Individualized Program.* A Report from the Project on Analysis of Mathematics Instruction. Madison, Wisc.: The Research and Development Center for Cognitive Learning, University of Wisconsin, 1973.

For further reading on Program for Learning in Accordance with Needs (PLAN) see:

Description of Project Plan. New York: Westinghouse Learning Corporation, 1969.

Lipe, D., and Steen, M.T. *Assessment of PLAN Teacher Development Program.* New York: Westinghouse Learning Corporation, final report, Spring 1970.

For further reading on computer-assisted instruction see:

Atkinson, R. C., and Hansen, D. N. "Computer-Assisted Instruction in Initial Reading: The Stanford Project." *Reading Research Quarterly* 2 (Fall 1966): 5–25.

Cooley, W. W., and Glaser, R. "The Computer and Individualized Instruction." *Science* 166 (1969):574–582.

Sass, R. E. *A Computer-Based Instructional Management Program for Classroom Use.* Pittsburgh, Penn.: Learning Research and Development Center, 1971.

For further reading on team teaching see:

Boyes, M. P. "A Comparative Study of Pupil Achievement and Adjustment Using Instructional Teams Composed of Teachers, Teacher Assistants, and Teacher Aides." Doctoral diss., University of Georgia, 1967. *Dissertation Abstracts* 28 (10-A): 3873–3874 (1968). University Microfilms No. 68-5034.

Cooper, D. H. and Sterns, H. N. "Team Teaching: Student Adjustment and Achievement." *Journal of Educational Research* 66(1973):323–327.

Corrigan, D. and Hynes, R. "What Have We Learned From Team Teaching?" *Social Education* 28 (1964): 205–208.

Gamsky, N. R. "Team Teaching, Student Achievement, and Attitudes." *Journal of Experimental Education* 39 (1970): 42–45.

Klausmeier, J. J. and Wiersma, W. "Team Teaching and Achievement." *Education* 86 (1965): 238–242.

Rhodes, F. "Team Teaching Compared with Traditional Instruction in Grades Kindergarten Through Six." *Journal of Educational Psychology* 62 (1971): 110–116.

4

Strategies *(2)*

Four instructional manager strategies are explained in this chapter: (1) instructional aides; (2) student contracts; (3) incentive techniques; and, (4) parent communication.

INSTRUCTIONAL AIDES

There are four compelling reasons for using instructional aides. The first and most obvious reason is because they *reduce the teacher-student ratio.* The more instructors there are in a classroom, the easier it is to individualize instruction.

Secondly, using instructional aides is *good public relations.* Most people outside of school have erroneous conceptualizations of teaching based on faulty memories and what they see on television. Some think teaching is a cushy job with marvelous hours. Those who serve for awhile as instructional aides, however, better understand and acquire a more sympathetic appreciation of the job, and even begin to wonder how teachers are able to stand the pace. Also, teachers tend to feel less threatened by outsiders who are willing to come in and help than by those who just come to sit and stare. Visitors who assist soon become so busy and involved that they have little time or inclination to find fault.

The third and not sufficiently appreciated reason for using aides is that they *provide students and adults with opportunities to become meaningfully involved in helping relationships with other human beings.* The lack of opportunities for meaningful involvement with people is one of the serious defects of our highly technical society which depends on specialization, large impersonal organizations, machines, and mobile and nuclear families. Children spend a lot of time in the passive, lonely activity of watching television. Since one-room schoolhouses are virtually extinct, few older students have the opportunity to help younger students learn. In the nuclear, highly mobile family, grandparents and other kin are separated from students. Being an instructional aide gives students an opportunity to help each other, as well as giving parents an opportunity to become more involved in the education of their children. Concerned people in the community are given an opportunity to participate in schooling, and senior citizens find renewed vigor by assisting the young.

The fourth reason for using aides is that it *results in increased learning.* Research reviewed by Devin-Sheehan et al[1] indicates that "tutoring programs can effectively improve the academic performance of tutees and, in some cases, that of tutors as well."

Kinds of Aides

Principals and teachers contemplating the use of instructional aides usually make the mistake of seeking out only people like themselves, adults trained as teachers, for these positions. They despair when the school district cannot afford to hire more certificated teachers. Recent research indicates that under certain conditions, people other than certificated teachers can be as effective as certificated teachers, and sometimes even more effective. *The essential condition is that the instructional program used by the aide be prescriptive;* That is, it should be a "cookbook" program where the aide does exactly what the directions say. Here are some illustrative examples of that research.

Robertson had low-achieving fifth graders tutoring first graders in reading with a highly prescriptive system of pictured flash cards.[2] Robertson found that the first-grade students who were tutored

---

1. L. Devin-Sheehan, R. S. Feldman, and V. L. Allen, "Research on Children Tutoring Children," *Review of Educational Research* 46 (1976), p. 363.

2. D. Robertson, "Intergrade Tutoring: Children Learn from Children," in *The First R: Readings in Teaching Reading,* S. Sebesta and C. Wallen, eds. (Chicago: Science Research Associates, 1972), pp. 277–283.

made significantly greater progress in reading achievement than other first-grade students who received all their reading instruction in regular classrooms. Further, the attitudes about reading, teachers, and school held by the low-achieving, fifth-grade tutors improved significantly as a result of the experience. Durrell found gains in general academic achievement in a program of *team learning* where students in the fourth, fifth, and sixth grades worked in groups of two or three.[3]

Untrained adults from the community can also be effective teachers. A study by Greenleigh Associates compared the effectiveness of four reading programs and three types of teachers in teaching reading to welfare recipients who were eighteen years old and older and reading below the fifth-grade level.[4] The four reading programs were highly prescriptive. The three types of teachers were certificated teachers, college graduates not trained as teachers, and high school graduates. The comparative effectiveness of the reading programs and teachers was determined by measuring the achievement-test score gains made by students; the greater the gains the more effective a program or type of teacher. The four programs were found to be equally effective. On the other hand, the most effective type of teacher was the high school graduate. Schoeller and Pearson found that untrained volunteers from the community, working under the close guidance of a reading specialist, could effect significant improvement in students' word-recognition skills.[5]

The research indicates that many persons can function effectively as instructional aides: students in the classrooms, students from other classrooms, and volunteers from the community. Here are some examples:

1. *Team Learning.* Students of equal abilities are assigned to groups of two or three for the purpose of drilling each other on things such as the week's spelling words or the addition facts.

2. *Discussion.* Students of varying abilities are assigned to groups of three to five to discuss their reactions to points brought up by the teacher in an earlier presentation.

3. *Intraclass Peer Tutoring.* More able students in the class are assigned to tutor the less able in reading, language, arithmetic, or almost any

3. D. Durrell, "Differentiated Instruction in Elementary School," *Journal of Education* 142 (December 1959).

4. Greenleigh Associates, Inc., *Field Test and Evaluation of Selected Adult Basic Education Systems* (New York: Greenleigh Associates, Inc., 1966).

5. A. Schoeller and D. Pearson, "Better Reading Through Volunteer Reading Tutors," *The Reading Teacher* 23 (April 1970):625–636.

subject. The more able student might be assigned to drill a number of less able students on the spelling words. In a class project to produce a newspaper, the more able student might be assigned as the editor for a number of less able students; the editor assists with spelling, punctuation, sentence construction, and so forth.

4. *Interclass Peer Tutoring.* Robertson's intergrade tutoring project could be adapted to other skill areas besides reading. The older students might come from this school, as with Robertson's study, or from other schools, like when high-school students tutor in a second grade.

5. *Equipment Specialists.* Students might be trained to operate audio-visual equipment and then assigned to operate it for their own classroom or for the entire school.

6. *School Monitor.* Older students can assist with younger students on the playground before school, at lunch, and after school. They can wear "Helping Badges" to signify their duties and the honor of being selected. Older students can also be assigned to a school patrol which is responsible for helping students cross streets before and after school.

7. *Community Volunteers.* Persons in the community, ranging from recent high school graduates (or mature elementary school dropouts) to senior citizens, are assigned to carry out certain designated, prescriptive, instructional tasks.

8. *Parents.* Parents can be assigned to certain instructional tasks either in the classroom where their children are enrolled or in another class.

9. *Paid Aides.* Any of the above mentioned types of people, from students working after regular school hours on up, might be paid for carrying out instructional tasks.

Program Elements

A successful instructional-aide program contains three important elements: selection, training, and simple, clearly defined tasks.

Selection Selection involves two steps, *interview* and *trial period*. For example, one school had what they called a Parent Participation Program. Parents were informed at the beginning of the school year about the voluntary, nonpaid program and were asked to submit a short and informative application if they were interested. Each parent was then interviewed by a teacher, usually the one with whom the parent would be working. The teacher explained the tasks and responsibilities. Instructional aides would have to commit themselves to a scheduled time for being in the classroom. They would have to *be there* when scheduled or call ahead of time. They would have to treat their own children the same as the others insofar as possible. During the two or three hours a week they were in the classroom, they would have to keep actively involved; there were to be no casual observers.

If the parents agreed to the conditions and the teacher considered them acceptable, they entered into a required one-month trial period, a type of student teaching. Many parents who thought they would like teaching found that they did not. Other parents proved to be unsatisfactory because they were too impatient, lazy, had unsuitable personalities for working with children, or could not discipline themselves to keep to the schedule.

The same two-step selection procedure of *interview* and *trial period* should be used with all kinds of instructional aides and for all kinds of tasks, whether it is drilling, spelling words or operating the motion picture projector. The two steps and their purpose should be explained to the potential instructional aides when they originally volunteer.

Robertson's study, described earlier, suggests a model for training instructional aides. Robertson trained fifth-grade students in three twenty-minute sessions. Periodic reviews where conducted later during the year. The students were trained to use a highly prescriptive "look-say" procedure for teaching the pronunciation of words. They used cards having a word printed on one side and a picture representing the word on the other as shown in Figure 4.1.   *Training*

Tutors were to show the person they were teaching the word on Side 1. If the person could not pronounce it, the tutors were to turn the card to Side 2 and ask the person to name the picture. When the person named the picture, the tutors informed the person that the word and picture were the same. The person was asked to pronounce the word a number of times. Then, the tutors were to turn the card back to Side 1 and ask for the pronunciation again. The tutor then placed the card on a practice pile for later review. Periodically, tutors would drill their students on the words in the review

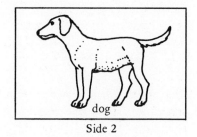

Side 1   Side 2   *Figure 4.1*

pile. If a student pronounced a word correctly when it was originally shown or after being given it in a number of practice reviews,
tutors recorded the word on a record form. In addition to using the
"look-say" procedure, Robertson wanted the tutors to use only
positive comments; they were never to criticize. They were to say
things like, "You did very well on that word," or "Well, almost,
let's try again."

Robertson's three training sessions were conducted like this.
In the first session he explained the two procedures, "look-say"
and positiveness. He then demonstrated the procedures with one
student. In the second training session, he divided the students into
pairs and they role-played using the two procedures. While they
role-played, Robertson walked around and made suggestions. In the
last training session, the tutors practiced with actual first graders
while Robertson observed and made suggestions.

Robertson's training program had three important characteristics.
First, the two instructional procedures were simple, clearly definable.
Second, he moved through a training sequence of *theory to practice* by explaining the procedures, demonstrating them, having students role-play them, and then having the students practice carrying
them out with actual first graders while he observed and commented
on their performances. Third, students did not even begin a trial
period until Robertson had officially certified them. While Robertson did not issue a formal written certification, another teacher
who trained students to operate audiovisual equipment did. The
certificate is shown in Figure 4.2.

This Certifies That

_____

has gone through training and is authorized to operate

_____

Date _____   Teacher _____

Figure 4.2

The certificate serves to inform others of the students' comppetencies. The certificate also provides the student with tangible evidence of achievement and, thus, is very motivating. In addition, the formalness of having a certificate makes the job seem more important than it might otherwise.

The more the instructional task an aide is asked to perform approaches the simplicity and clarity of the "look-say" and positive-comment procedure Robertson used, the greater will be the aides' effectiveness. An aide would be much less effective if the instructional task were defined vaguely as, "Help them with reading."

Simple, Clearly Defined Tasks

Teachers have tried different ways to make tasks clear for aides. Some teachers identify a worksheet they want students to do and they write directions for the aide on how the worksheet should be used. The written directions state in clear language, "First, you. . . . Second, you. . . .", and so forth. The directions are placed in a folder with a supply of worksheets. All the teacher then has to do is hand the folder to the aide and identify the students to be instructed. Other teachers have found that the manuals accompanying some published series in reading, language, and mathematics are written in a simple, clear way that is ideal for an instructional aide. The manual states the questions to be asked, gives words or problems to write on the chalkboard, and sometimes even suggests what to do if the student has difficulty:

> If the wording of the last question fails to help a child with the new word *care,* encourage him to read to the end of the sentence in which the meaning gives another clue.

When an aide is to follow written directions in carrying out instruction, it is often necessary to study the lesson a day ahead of time.

The best instructional tasks for aides are those that can be used all year long, such as Robertson's "look-say" procedure, or a procedure for memorizing the weekly spelling words, or a procedure for learning the addition and subtraction facts. The "look-say" procedure can be used for all words students are to learn. The procedure for memorizing spelling words can be used each week. The procedure for learning the addition and subtraction facts is useful until those facts have been acquired and then adapted easily to the learning of the multiplication facts.

The Teacher's Role

The teacher's role obviously changes when instructional aides are used. The teacher spends less time working directly with students and more time designing lessons others will use. The teacher becomes more of a diagnostician who prepares prescriptions which aides will administer. The teacher spends more time as a trainer and supervisor of instructional aides.

STUDENT CONTRACTS

Student contracts are an obligatory agreement negotiated between the student and the teacher for the completion of a certain task by a specified date. The tasks usually involve an independent activity. A student might contract to satisfactorily complete three pages in the arithmetic text by next Tuesday, prepare and present to the class next week an illustrated talk on a specified topic in social studies, or read and write a review of five books by one month from now.

Student contracts help with a number of concerns teachers express about classroom management: developing self-direction, increasing motivation, and reaching disruptive children. Student contracts help because they focus instruction on the learner and learning rather than on the teacher and teaching, create a situation where students share in the responsibility for their own learning, and provide opportunities for teachers and students to work cooperatively and show mutual respect for one another. The result of this refocusing is the development of greater self-direction, an increased interest in learning, and a more positive attitude about school and teachers.

Characteristics

Student contracts have two critical characteristics. *First, the student has a major role in negotiating the conditions of the contract.* The student decides whether to read and review five books or fifty. While the teacher is certainly an active participant in the negotiation process, the student is allocated fifty-one percent of the vote. If the student wants to read and review ten books and the teacher cannot convince him to read more than that, the contract is made for ten books. Student contracts should be used only with those instructional experiences where the teacher feels willing to negotiate the conditions.

Second, the conditions of the contract are clearly specified in writing and in sufficiently operational terms that the participants will be able, later, to agree when the conditions have been met. The conditions should include a completion date. They should describe exactly what the completed task will look like. With something like completing satisfactorily three pages in the arithmetic text, the only conditions needing clarification are the date of completion, the pages to be accomplished, and the percent of correct responses which constitutes "satisfactory work." With something like a talk to be given on a topic in social studies, the conditions might include the name of the topic, the length of the talk, the day it is to be given, and possibly the sources to be searched and audiovisual materials to be used. The more clearly the conditions of a contract are stated, the less room it allows for unpleasant arguments later about whether the task has been satisfactorily completed.

Procedures

Student contracts are carried out in three steps: negotiation, execution, and evaluation.

The teacher and student hold a conference and agree on the contract's conditions. The process of negotiation should be as personalized as possible, preferably on a one-to-one basis. When the teacher and student can agree on the written description of the conditions, the contractual document is signed by both parties. Separate copies should be prepared, one for the teacher's file and one for the student's. *Under no conditions should a teacher unilaterally alter the conditions of the contract once it has been signed.* If the teacher has second thoughts after the contract has been signed, those should be saved for the next negotiation conference. *Negotiation*

The student performs the contracted instructional task. The teacher provides whatever assistance is requested. If the student is having difficulty completing the contracted task, a renegotiation conference might be held. If the conditions are changed from what was originally contracted, a new contract should be prepared. *Execution*

Evaluation   On the contracted deadline date, the teacher and student hold a conference for the purpose of evaluating the task. If the student has satisfactorily completed the task, he may wish to begin negotiating another contract. If the student has failed to complete the conditions of the contract, he may wish to renegotiate the original contract. For example, if the student very ambitiously contracted to read and review ten books and then completed only three another contract might be prepared for the remaining books.

The teacher should never punish a student for failing to meet the conditions of a contract. To do so would have the effect of absolving the student from responsibility for learning. As soon as the teacher administers punishment, the responsibility becomes the teacher's. This is directly contrary to a major purpose of student contracts, which is to have students share responsibility for their learning. With students who are chronic violators of contracts, the closest thing approximating punishment might be to take away the privilege of making contracts.

Whenever a student fails to meet the conditions of a contract, the teacher will want to examine the contract carefully. The fault may lie with the contract rather than the student. The conditions might have been stated unclearly. The expectations might have been unrealistic for the student. There may have been insufficient resources available to the student.

Teacher Success

A teacher's success in using student contracts is dependent on three factors: respect, systematic evaluation, and provision for reward.

Respect   The teacher should display a genuine respect for the student's ability, good intentions, and willingness to take on responsibility. Displaying respect will be much easier for the teacher if student contracts are not used in those areas where the teacher has already decided what each student will accomplish. For example, if the teacher has already decided that Mary *will* do pages 41, 42, 43, and 44 in the arithmetic text, it would be inappropriate to go through the farce of having Mary contract to do those pages. She may insist on doing only three pages. Likewise, the teacher should not have students contract for the number of spelling words they will study if the teacher has already decided that they will do all of them. One student may insist on doing only half. Student contracts should be used only in those areas where it does not matter to the teacher how much a student does and so feels perfectly free to talk about one page of math or three, ten spelling words or twenty.

Being respectful does not mean that teachers should avoid hard bargaining. Teachers should not hesitate to tell a student that in their opinion only completing five books is way below the level of expectation the student should be setting for himself. However, if that is what the student wants and cannot be talked out of it, okay. The honest and forthright stating of the teacher's opinion, coupled with a willingness to accept the goal the student finally sets, displays a genuine respect for the student and the student-teacher relationship. Perhaps in future contracts the student will set higher goals.

Many teachers give a minimum non-negotiable assignment in a subject and then encourage students to contract for additional work in that subject. For example, the teacher may identify three ability groups in spelling. Students in each group are assigned a different minimum number of spelling words to study. The low-ability group may have five words while the high-ability group has all the words. Students in the low-ability group are then encouraged to contract individually for additional words from the spelling list. Students in the high-ability group are encouraged to contract individually for additional words from other sources, such as social studies or science, or words they select to challenge them.

The teacher should have a systematic procedure for monitoring students' completion of contracted tasks. The first step in being systematic is limiting contracted work to what can realistically be evaluated on schedule. For example, if everyone contracts to complete three pages of arithmetic by next week and the teacher will determine whether the papers are satisfactory, that means about ninety pages have to be corrected *prior* to holding the evaluation conferences. Also, if the teacher does not manage to complete the papers by the time contracted, the teacher will have violated the contract's conditions. A teacher violation is obviously much more serious than a student violation because it works against the very goals of student self-direction and motivation which the teacher is trying to achieve.

Systematic Evaluation

The next step in being systematic is developing simple ways of processing contracts. The teacher can have an *In-Basket* for papers to be checked, and an *Out-Basket* for papers needing further work. Students might be given access to correct answers and made responsible for checking their own papers, although they will likely miss many incorrect answers. Some of the more able students in the room may be selected as proctors and assigned to check papers. Instructional aides could be asked to check papers. A planned schedule for holding negotiation and evaluation conferences might be set. Monday morning might be designated as the time for negotiation conferences and Friday afternoon for evaluation conferences.

Provision for Reward

The teacher should make certain that a student feels rewarded for successfully completing a contracted task. If the task provided intrinsic motivation, simply completing it is rewarding. If the teacher makes enough of a show of recognizing students' completion of contracts, students may have a satisfying feeling of *self-actualization,* of completing a task they set out to do. Feelings of self-actualization are enhanced by the formality of negotiation and preparation of written contracts. The feelings are further enhanced when formal procedures for recognizing successful completion are used such as putting a gold seal on the written contract, or giving a printed certificate of completion, or placing the students' names on a chart that shows when contracts have been completed.

The teacher can also use incentives. The incentive used most frequently in school is grades. Some teachers have students contract for the grade they wish to receive, with different grades being given for different tasks. Contracts will be more effective if incentives other than grades are made available, and if they are used in a systematic way. The systematic use of *incentive techniques* is the next topic discussed in this book.

How rewarded a student feels when completing a task will usually be in direct proportion to how frequently student contracts are used. The more frequently they are used, the less rewarding completion is likely to be. Students' contracts should not be expected to carry the full burden of motivation.

INCENTIVE TECHNIQUES

Before reading this section you may want to review the discussion of incentives in chapter 2.

Examples of School Incentives

Grades are the most frequently used school incentive. However, they are ineffective with many children. Candy, gum, raisins, and small gifts are also used. The teacher will want to consider other incentives, perhaps in the form of activities suggested here.

Some activities that might be used as incentives at the primary school level are: *Primary Activities*

    painting or drawing
    playing with toys
    choosing your own seat
    leaving the room first at recess time
    sitting in a special chair
    daydreaming; looking out the window
    studying the subject of your choice
    talking to a classmate
    playing in the puppet theater
    using clay
    listening to the record player or tape recorder
    walking around the room
    doing drawing or painting outside the classroom
    playing a favorite game
    watching a motion picture.

Some activities that might be used as incentives at the intermediate school level are: *Intermediate Activities*

    playing a favorite game
    getting first choice of athletic equipment
    leaving first at lunch time
    being selected as a monitor to take attendance, clean the room, help the
        teacher, etc.
    doing art work, such as painting, drawing, working with clay.
    watching a motion picture
    recording a story on the tape recorder and playing it for the class
    working outside
    having extra time for such enjoyable activities as P.E., art, recess
    helping in other classrooms or the principal's office.

Some activities that might be used as incentives at the upper elementary and high school levels are: *Advanced Activities*

    making up a game or quiz for the class
    playing a game such as chess
    reading
    going to the library

sitting at the teacher's desk or in other special areas
doing extra-credit problems
decorating a bulletin board
being an instructional aide in this classroom or others
being first for recess, lunch, and so forth
writing letters.

Types of Incentive Techniques

Incentive techniques are of two types: contingency management and token economy. *Contingency management* refers to using *primary reinforcers,* things that directly meet a person's physiological or psychological needs. The example of vegetable and dessert used in chapter 2 to illustrate Grandmother's Rule is contingency management because the person gets dessert as soon as the vegetable has been eaten.

Token economy refers to using *secondary reinforcers,* tokens that are redeemable for things that directly meet a person's physiological or psychological needs. Money is the familiar token. It is redeemable for things that satisfy needs. The contingency coupling of vegetables and desserts could be adapted to a token economy if the person received a ticket for each vegetable he ate and then was allowed to trade them in, later, for dessert. For three tickets the person could have pie, his favorite, and for one ticket jam on a cracker.

Contingency Management School activities are thought of as being of two kinds, nonpreferred *Tasks* and preferred *Rewards.* The two activities normally occur in different parts of the classroom. A room organized for contingency management is shown in Figure 4.3. With the room shown in Figure 4.3, the tasks consist of worksheets which students do at their desks.

A lesson using contingency management would follow these steps. First, all students are seated at the desks in the Task Area. Each desk has a large card with the word *Task* printed in red on one side and the word *Reward* printed in green on the other. The teacher makes certain that all students have the task side of the card facing up. Second, the teacher gives the students two worksheets and tells them to begin. When a student finishes both worksheets, he or she raises one hand and the teacher walks to the desk. The teacher examines the papers and indicates errors which should be corrected.

Third, if a teacher finds no errors on the student's papers, the teacher turns the card over so that the reward side is up. This indicates

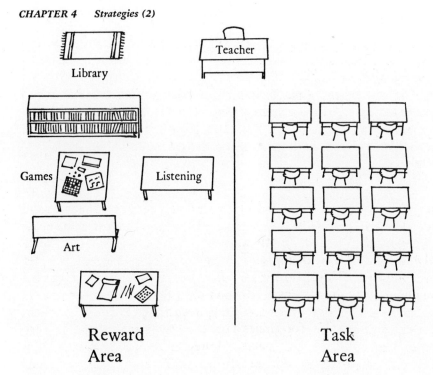

Library

Teacher

Games

Listening

Art

Reward Area

Task Area

Figure 4.3

that the student is free to move to the Reward Area. The first students in the Reward Area get their choice of activities. Fourth, when everyone has finished, the teacher allows the last student to spend five minutes in the Reward Area. Fifth, the teacher calls students back to the Task Area and begins another lesson.

A major advantage of contingency management over token economy is the fact that the reward is provided immediately after the nonpreferred activity has been completed. As soon as the students complete their worksheets correctly, they get to do the rewarding activities of drawing or playing games; they do not have to wait. Grandmother's promise of dessert has the most powerful effect when the pie is visible and can be eaten as soon as the vegetables have been consumed. The pie will have a much less powerful effect if it cannot be eaten until next week. Can you imagine Grandmother saying, "You eat your vegetables today, and next week you may have pie?"

Providing immediate reward becomes very difficult to manage, however, when the entire class is involved at the same time. As more and more students move into the Reward Area, the noise level increases, disturbing those still in the Task Area. There are probably not enough highly rewarding activities for everyone, and students are dissatisfied when they do not get the activity they want. Students complete their papers more quickly than the teacher can correct them and the ones waiting become impatient.

Contingency management works best with small numbers of students. In the regular classroom, the teacher can use it effectively in conjunction with instruction given to a group of ten students, or less. The rest of the class is doing an independent activity at their desks. The Task Area is a table in the corner with chairs around it. The teacher discusses a principle and gives students a worksheet intended to provide practice in using the principle. When a student completes the worksheet, it is checked by the teacher. If it is satisfactory, the student is allowed to move to the Reward Area.

Contingency management works best when students have a task that they will complete at different rates. One student will finish in one minute, another in a minute and a half, and so forth. The teacher then has time to check one person's work before the next person is finished. It is critical that the teacher carefully check each person's work for reward should be forthcoming *only* after successful completion of the task.

Token Economy

As with contingency management, school activities are thought of as being two kinds, *tasks* and *rewards*. Unlike contingency management, though, they need not take place in different parts of the room with reward following immediately after task completion. Students perform the task at one time and if it is satisfactory they receive a token redeemable later for a reward. For example, students might collect tokens during the week and trade them for rewarding activities during a special events period on Friday. One special event, a motion picture, costs eight tokens. A chance to play a favorite game costs four tokens. Working with clay costs three tokens. Students purchase whatever rewards they can afford. Those without tokens remain at their desks and do assigned tasks, perhaps more worksheets.

The more tangible and distinctive tokens are, the more effective the token economy will be. Some teachers use play money either commercially produced or teacher made. Money is distinctive and tangible. Some teachers place marks on a student's record sheet, like that shown in Figure 4.4. The student may redeem marks for rewards daily or once a week. The marks may be gold stars, smiling faces, or simply a checkmark. The marks on the record are tangible and distinctive. Things that are tangible but not distinctive are, for example, colored strips of construction paper. Marks on the chalkboard are even less tangible and distinctive.

A major advantage of a token economy over contingency management is that a token economy is easier to organize in the classroom.

Name					*Date*	to	

Monday	
Tuesday	
Wednesday	
Thursday	
Friday	

Figure 4.4

Students do the tasks at one time and receive the rewards at another time. The classroom does not have to be organized into formal Task Areas and Reward Areas as with contingency management. The teacher does not have to worry about an insufficient number of rewarding activities because students can be given their rewards over a longer period of time. Today the student earns a token which can be redeemed at any time tomorrow when someone else is not at the game table which is the desired reward for this student.

Another advantage of a token economy is the flexibility it offers in adjusting for the value of rewards and tasks. A particularly difficult task may be worth three tokens while a less difficult one is worth only two tokens. The same task might be assigned different values for different students depending on their ability. Rewards can also be given different values. Viewing the motion picture costs ten tokens, playing a favorite game five tokens, playing in a puppet theater three tokens, and so forth.

Another advantage of a token economy is the range of choice in rewards that can be offered. The student is free to weigh the relative value of one motion picture versus two favorite games. The student can, in effect, be presented with a "reward menu" from which selections are made. The limiting factor in the selection is the student's pocketbook.

A token economy is sufficiently flexible so that it can be used with only two or three students in the classroom; those who are particularly unmotivated, discouraged, or disruptive. For example, a teacher has two students with emotional and learning problems. They are not responding well to the same strategies as the rest of the class. One student has a very short attention span. The other is severely discouraged after years of failing in school and has simply stopped trying—a sort of intellectual dropout. They are the only students in the class with whom reward strategies are being used. The rest of the class is aware of this but has accepted the fact that teachers do different things for different students, and they are satisfied with the things they are doing in class. The rewards are things the teacher can hand out privately, such as candy, small toys, and special weekend outings previously arranged with the students' parents.

The teacher arranges a different token system for each student. With the student having the short attention span, the teacher gives a token at the end of every thirty-second period that the student has been attending to the lesson. As the student's attention span increases, the token system is changed to one after every forty-five-second period of paying attention; and then later, after every minute. When the student's attention span is more normal, the reward strategy is dropped. The student does the same instructional tasks as the rest of the class.

The severely discouraged or depressed student is given individual attention with a continuous-progress curriculum. The teacher gives one or more tokens after each objective has been accomplished, as indicated by the student's adequate performance on a test for the objective. The reward strategy will be dropped when the student becomes self-confident enough so that he can feel rewarded by a normal compliment from the teacher or by a sense of self-actualization upon successfully completing an objective.

Important Factors

Five factors will determine how successful the teacher is in using incentive techniques.

Reward Only, No Punishment   This technique should be used in only one direction—reward. *The student is never punished by losing rewards earned earlier.* Once a student has earned tokens, they should never be taken away. For example, if the student with the poor attention span has an especially bad day and his attention span never reaches the minimum level of thirty seconds required for a token, the teacher simply does not give a token. Teachers can destroy the great effectiveness of incentive techniques by mixing punishment and reward.

Rewards Are Rewarding   Activities and objects which students actually find rewarding must be identified and provided. Students might be given an interest inventory to determine what things they would like as rewards. A variety of alternative activities can be prepared on a "reward menu" so that students may select what they want. The activities intended for reward should be changed frequently so they do not become stale.

The tasks must have a sufficiently specific terminal point so that both the teacher and the student know when it has been reached and can look forward to its completion. When a worksheet is the task, the terminal point is obvious. It is when all the problems have been completed satisfactorily. When the task is something less obvious, like attention span, indicators of task completion must be developed. The teacher might use a stop watch or even a large clock with a second hand. Everytime the second hand passes a certain point, a token is earned. With the poorly motivated child, the test and record sheet used with the continuous-progress curriculum provide indicators of satisfactory task performance, but the teacher might want to use something more eye catching such as a large chart and comic figures.

Tasks Have Terminal Point

The more promptly the teacher gives the reward or the token redeemable for a reward, the more effective the incentive technique will be. A major problem in using either type of incentive technique in classrooms is devising ways of issuing rewards and tokens promptly. When the entire class is doing a worksheet that the teacher must correct, the teacher is seldom fast enough so that students do not have to wait. The longer a student has to wait to have a paper corrected and receive the reward or token, the less effective the reward strategy will be. Correction can be speeded up in a number of ways: instructional aides might assist with correction; the task might be made self-correcting by providing answers; or the students bring the paper to the teacher only for confirmation.

Reward Promptly

The distribution of tokens can be speeded up if the teacher carries around a supply at all times. In some classes, instructional aides are responsible for promptly distributing tokens. The aides might be adults or students from outside the classroom or designated students from within the classroom.

The coupling of preferred and nonpreferred activities must be consistent. The teacher should not haphazardly initiate an incentive technique this week, forget about it next week, and then expect to pick it up the third week. Incentive techniques should be introduced with suitable pomp and circumstance along with a commitment to try it out for a given period of time. Consistency is important because

Reward Consistently

it affects the students' view of the teacher's credibility. The more credible the teacher is, the more effective incentive techniques will be.

PARENT COMMUNICATION

Many an excellent educational program has "bitten the dust" because school personnel did not realize that they must educate parents and other people in the community as well as children. The strategies explained here can be done by individual teachers, groups of teachers, and by the principal. Two levels of communication are discussed, the school and the classroom.

Communicating at the School Level

Be Active Go to the parents and community rather than wait for them to come to school. The principal and groups of teachers might offer to participate in teas or neighborhood gatherings given in homes by parents. A pamphlet explaining the program and answering the most common questions and criticisms might be prepared and distributed. Other means of actively communicating might be parent-school meetings, conferences, workshops, and television programs.

Be Child Centered The esoteric rhetoric of educational philosophy, psychology, and methodology may be meaningful and interesting to professional educators but to parents the use of it is often seen as evasive. Parents want to know what is happening to their children, and they want to be told in a simple and straight-forward way. If parents feel their children are happy and learning, then they will be happy about the school program.

Be Realistic Do not promise perfection. In fact, it is not a bad idea to promise just a little bit less than you know can be delivered. This makes for a happy client. For example, upon being assigned to a new school to organize an open-classroom program, a principal made the error of promoting the program as a new and utopian method that would solve all of the children's problems. Like all utopias, it was never fully achieved and now the principal is in trouble and a noble and exemplary program is in jeopardy.

The principal, particularly, should be sensitive to conflicts that arise between the parents and the teacher and should move quickly to resolve them. The resolution might come through parent-teacher conferences or even by moving the student to another teacher.

Be Sensitive to Conflicts

Teachers should feel responsible for *knowing well* the students assigned to them. They should feel responsible for knowing each one personally and for knowing what each is doing and the difficulties and successes each is encountering. Also, they should feel responsible for communicating this knowledge to parents.

Be Responsible

Communicating at the Classroom Level

Teachers should try to establish contact with the parents of their students within the first week of school. Some teachers make home visits in the first few weeks. Some invite parents to orientation meetings held after school or in the evening. Some tell parents both their school and home telephone numbers and encourage them to call. Some invite parents to participate as instructional aides. Teachers should not wait until the time of the first grading period to establish some type of contact.

Establish Contact Early

Teachers should be ready to explain to parents, either by conference or in writing, just what they hope to accomplish with their students this year. The objectives communicated to parents should be more specific than saying something as obvious and general as, "Be better in reading, writing, and arithmetic," and yet less specific than a hundred page list of behavioral statements. The objectives might identify the general areas of skill in reading and arithmetic. For example, "This year in reading we will work especially hard on helping the students make justifiable conclusions about what they read and to be more critical readers."

Have Clearly Defined Objectives

Maintain records on children's performance and keep data which support and explain the records. For example, in language arts, teachers might keep papers that illustrate a student's performance on different objectives. With something less tangible like not paying attention in class, teachers might keep anecdotal records that objectively describe sample incidents where the child was being inattentive. When the illustrative data is collected over a period of time, the teacher can use it to demonstrate the student's progress.

Collect Illustrative Data

Be Goal Oriented   Teachers should be goal oriented rather than procedure oriented. The purpose of school is to help a child accomplish goals that he or she might not have accomplished if the child had not attended school. The purpose is not to use open-classroom procedures, make murals, or use a certain phonics textbook. Teachers should use illustrative data to demonstrate children's progress toward the goals. In conferences with parents, the student's present level of attainment should be identified, as well as the next steps. The record forms used with a continuous-progress curriculum are excellent for reporting student progress to parents in goal-oriented terms.

Help Parents with   Most parents are the best kind of parents they know how to be.
Parenting   They want to help their children succeed but they usually possess little knowledge of child development. They are confused by the continual bombardment of stories and articles that blame parents for a child's problems and, particularly, the "overly" permissive parents. They also tend to overreact to criticism and praise of the children because a child is naturally an ego-extension of the parent. A number of helpful things a parent might do are:

1. Spend time talking with the child and sharing the child's activities.
2. Read with the child. This should be done in a pleasant atmosphere, by both parents, where the emphasis is on enjoyment.
3. Let the child be a meaningful contributor to the home by having a reasonable set of work responsibilities.

Many teachers provide sources of information about parenting, often by providing a list of suggested books. Some schools have a library of books on parenting which parents are encouraged to check out. The books can also be used in workshops, conferences, and discussed in parent-teacher meetings.[5]

Summary

The instructional-management strategies are summarized in the form of observation guides that can be used in evaluating your use of

---

5. Some books you may wish to recommend are: Stella Chase, Alexander Thomes, and Herbert Birch, *Your Child Is a Person* (New York: The Viking Press, 1965); Rudolph Dreikurs and Vicki Soltz, *Children: The Challenge* (New York: Hawthorn Books, Inc., 1964); Haim Ginott, *Between Parent and Child* (New York: The Macmillan Company, 1965); and Eda LeShan, *On How Do Your Children Grow?* (New York: David McKay Company, Inc., 1972).

the strategies. The observation guides could be used by one teacher for self-evaluation, or by two or more teachers working as a team and evaluating each other.

I. CONTINUOUS-PROGRESS CURRICULUM

			Rating	
Subject	Date	Yes	So-So	No
(reading, arithmetic, etc.)				

A. *Materials*

1. *Components.*   A continuous-progress curriculum contains four components: (check each)

   a. *Objectives.* There is a defined sequence of progressively arranged objectives that represent the full range of abilities desired in that subject.

   b. *Tests.* There is a *separate* test exercise provided for *each* objective listed. The performance of each student can be interpreted in terms of the student's attainment of the objectives for which the test was designed.

   c. *Instructional Tasks.* There is a *separate* instructional task for *each* objective listed. The task is organized so that it can be used *only* with those students who perform inadequately on the test.

   d. *Record Form.* The record form provides a means of recording each student's attainment on each objective listed.

2. *Essential Characteristic: Internal Consistency of Materials.* The test and instructional task for an objective are logically related to each other. The student carries out the same essential activity in each.

   Suggestions: _____

B. *Procedures.* The following steps are followed: (check each)

   1. The teacher calls a student to the teaching station or goes to the student's desk.

   2. The teacher examines the student's record in order to determine what the objective should be for today's lesson.

   3. The teacher identifies and administers a test for the objective identified as being appropriate.

   4. If the student performs adequately on the test, the teacher *either* records the performance on the record form and excuses the student from further instruction *or* identifies another objective for which to test.

   5. If the student performs inadequately on the test, the teacher identifies and begins the instructional task for the objective tested.

Rating

Yes   So-So   No

6. Instruction continues until the student is able to perform the instructional exercises without the teacher's help or until the student performs adequately on a post-test.

7. The teacher records the student's performance on the record form.

    Suggestions: _____

II. GROUPING

Subjects
                                                                    _____
                                                                       Date

A. *Grouping Patterns.*   Note the subject in which each grouping pattern is used. Commonly, different grouping patterns are used in different subjects.

1. *Ungraded Grouping.* A primary unit and an intermediate unit replace grades one through six or eight.

2. *Interclassroom Subject Grouping.* One teacher takes two or more classes for a subject, such as social studies; could occur with team teaching.

3. *Interclassroom Ability Grouping.* Students are assigned to classes on the basis of their performance on intelligence and achievement tests.

4. *Split-Day Grouping.* The first and last periods of the day are staggered. Half of the students come an hour early and leave an hour early.

5. *Intraclassroom Ability Grouping.* Students are grouped in the classroom on the basis of ability.

6. *Special-Ability Grouping.* Students are assigned for short periods, and on the basis of their ability, to a special teacher.

7. *Intraclassroom Individualized Grouping.* Instruction in the classroom is provided for one student at a time.

8. *Interclassroom, Heterogeneous Grouping.* Students are assigned to classrooms solely on the basis of age.

9. *No Intraclassroom Grouping.* The same subject matter is taught to all students in the classroom at the same time.

    Suggestions: _____

B. *Factors Considered in Grouping*

Rating

Yes   So-So   No

1. *Selection.* Factors used in selection should be valid indicators of the abilities for which instruction is being provided. Validity is increased by specificity.

2. *Flexibility of Group Assignment.* Students should be assigned to different groups for different purposes.

3. *Suitability of Curriculum.* The curriculum should be suitable for the *degree of individualization* involved in the grouping pattern.

Suggestions: _____

III. INDEPENDENT ACTIVITIES
    A. *Types of Independent Activities*
        1. *Assignment Completion.* Activities that students do independently, at no special location and with no definite time assignments. Usually consists of exercises in textbooks, worksheets, and workbooks. They may be commercially produced or teacher made.
        2. *Learning Centers.* Activities that students do independently at a designated location and at an assigned time.

Suggestions: _____

        3. *Group Projects.* Activities that students do in groups, at certain locations, but with no definite time assignments.
    B. *Learning Centers*
        1. *Organizing the Classroom*
            a. *Continual Teacher Monitoring.* The physical organization of the classroom allows the teacher to view almost everything going on in the classroom at all times.
            b. *Free Traffic Flow.* The physical organization provides the greatest amount of space in the areas of greatest traffic flow. The teacher guides students in following the planned traffic patterns by having traffic signs and using such other strategies as *group discussion* and *role play.*
            c. *Noise Levels.* The room is organized to minimize the effects of noise. Acoustic materials are used to separate areas of the classroom and the noisier activities are placed in one section and the quieter in another.
            d. *Assignment Clarity.* The teacher uses group and individual assignment charts so that students know at all times what they are supposed to be doing and where they are to do it.

Suggestions: _____

        2. *Operating Centers*
        A four-step routine is followed:
            a. *Selection.* The activity is selected either by students or the teacher.
            b. *Completion.* The activities in centers are explained clearly enough so that students can carry them out successfully without asking the teacher for assistance.

      c. *Recording.* A record system is maintained that identifies which students did which centers and what they accomplished at the center.

      d. *Housekeeping.* Students are fully responsible for cleaning up after themselves and preparing the center for the next to use it.

Suggestions: _____

3. *Designing the Centers.* A greater variety of activities are used in the centers than just games and worksheets.

Suggestions: _____

4. *Initiating the Centers.* The use of centers has been introduced rapidly enough to that students' enthusiasm is maintained and yet slowly enough so that the teacher can learn to design suitable centers and students can learn to adjust to the decentralization involved.

Suggestions: _____

IV. TEAM TEACHING

    A. *Collaboration.* Team members have open communication and a trust relationship based on the notion that team members can help each other grow and increase each other's potential abilities.

    B. *Roles and Responsibilities.* Classroom rules have been developed and written down. Other strategies such as *group discussion* and *role play* are used in helping students accept and follow the rules. The rules that have been prepared are specific enough that there is little misunderstanding in their use.

    C. *Gradual Change.* Teachers just starting team teaching get over the cultural shock by moving into the program slowly.

Suggestions: _____

V. INSTRUCTIONAL AIDE

    A. *Selection*

      1. *Interview.* People interested in being an aide are interviewed for the purpose of informing them of the roles and responsibilities and determining their suitability.

      2. *Trial Period.* Aides go through a mandatory period of trial that is intended to determine their interest and suitability. They can be dropped at the end of the trial period.

    B. *Training.* Aides go through a training program intended to prepare them to carry out their tasks. They attend meetings and receive supervised practice.

C. *Simple, Clearly Defined Tasks.* The tasks are kept simple. Teachers prepare specific directions on carrying out tasks. When a new task is to be done, aides are given time to become acquainted with it.

Suggestions: _____

IV. STUDENT CONTRACTS

A. *Steps*

1. *Negotiation.* The terms of the contract are agreed upon by the teacher and student in an individualized conference. The student has the larger role in determining the conditions but the teacher contributes actively.
2. *Execution.* The student carries out the conditions of the contract. The teacher does not unilaterally change the conditions of the contract.
3. *Evaluation.* On the deadline date of the contract the teacher and student evaluate the completion of the contract and may plan the next contract.

Suggestions: _____

B. *Characteristics*

1. *Respect for the Student.* The teacher *displays* a respect for the student's ability, intentions, and willingness to take responsibility.
2. *Monitoring the Contract.* The teacher carefully oversees the student's attainment of the contract's conditions. The keynote of this monitoring is consistency.

Suggestions:_____

VII. INCENTIVE TECHNIQUES

A. *Types* (check one)

1. *Contingency Management.* Primary reinforcers are used. When students satisfactorily complete a Task activity they are allowed to begin immediately a Reward activity.
2. *Token Economy.* Secondary reinforcers are used. When students satisfactorily complete a Task activity they receive a token that entitles them to carry out a Reward activity at a later date.

Suggestions: _____

B. *Characteristics*

1. *Reward Only.* The student is never punished by losing rewards earned earlier.
2. *Rewards Are Rewarding.* The program is organized so that

Rating

Yes   So-So   No

students actually *feel* rewarded by doing the Reward activities.

3. *Task Has Terminal Point.* The task has a sufficiently specific and observable point of termination so that the teacher and student know when it has been accomplished and can look forward to its completion.

4. *Prompt Reward.* The primary or secondary reinforcement is issued *immediately* after the student has satisfactorily completed the Task activity.

5. *Consistency.* The teacher uses incentive techniques consistently. Students are given the rewards promised and the technique is not arbitrarily started and stopped.

Suggestions: _____

VIII. PARENT COMMUNICATION

A. *Communicating at the School Level*

1. *Early Contact.* Contact with the parent is established at the beginning of the school year.

2. *Objectives.* The program objectives are clearly enough defined so that parents can understand them.

3. *Illustrative Data.* Teachers collect and communicate to parents objective data that show the progress of their students toward the school's objectives.

4. *Goal Oriented.* Communications deal with the students' progress toward the objectives identified rather than with the procedures the teacher is using.

5. *Parenting.* Parents are helped with parenting.

Suggestions: _____

Assessment

The purpose of an assessment is to determine whether or not educational goals are being attained. When an assessment is used in the instructional-manager role, it is intended to measure how effective instructional-manager strategies are in accomplishing the school's instructional objectives. Was the use of student contracts effective in increasing the students' learning of mathematics? Was the reading center effective in increasing the students' volume of leisure time reading? Was the group project devoted to making a relief map of South America effective in causing students to learn the major geographical features of South America?

ASSESSMENT LEVELS

Assessing the effectiveness of instructional-manager strategies can be done at two levels, *student behavior* and *management strategy*. The discussion which follows is intended as an illustration of assessment at the two levels. It explains how the effectiveness of student contracts for increasing students' learning of spelling words can be assessed at two levels.

Student Behavior

At the level of student behavior, the average spelling test scores of students would be obtained for the five weeks preceding the use of contracts. The average score might be 80 percent. If during the six weeks that contracts were being used the average score for all students rose to 85 percent, the difference between 80 and 85 percent indicates how effective contracts were in increasing students' learning of spelling words.

The effectiveness of contracts can also be determined for individual students. Here are spelling scores for three students:

STUDENT'S NAME	PERCENT AVERAGE PRIOR TO CONTRACTS	PERCENT AVERAGE DURING CONTRACTS
John S.	55	95
Mary J.	100	100
Larry F.	75	70

Contracts were quite effective with John; his spelling scores rose from 55 percent to 95 percent. Contracts were of no benefit to Mary, but then again, they did not hurt her. Her scores remained at 100 percent. Contracts seemed to be somewhat counter-productive with Larry; his scores dropped from 75 percent to 70 percent. The teacher will probably want to continue using contracts with John, seriously question whether they are worth the time and effort with Mary, and consider either revising or dropping them with Larry.

Teachers too often assess only a narrow range of student behaviors, usually those related to skill in language and mathematics, and possibly knowledge in literature, science, and social science. However, very satisfactory measures also exist for measuring such other student behaviors as problem-solving ability, self-direction, and willingness to risk failure.[1] Teachers interested in locating such tests should contact the district psychologist or school counselor.

Management Strategy

Prior to dropping the use of contracts with Larry, the teacher may want to assess them in terms of how she and Larry *feel* about them. This is assessment at the level of the management strategy. Larry's feelings could be informally assessed by having him talk about what he likes and dislikes about contracts, and about any suggestions he might have. Larry's feelings could be more formally assessed

---

1. These tests are viewed in J. W. Atkinson, *The Psychology of Motivation* (Princeton, N.J.: Van Nostrand Co., Inc., 1964).

by the use of a written test having multiple-choice responses. (Instruments of this sort are suggested later in this chapter.) The teacher's feelings might be assessed by a self-examination of how well he is *actually* doing what he *intends* doing. Other instruments useful for assessing the teacher's feelings are suggested later in this chapter.

TYPES OF MEASURES

Two types of measures are available for assessing at the level of student behavior, *norm-referenced tests* and *criterion-referenced tests*. Norm-referenced tests provide a way of measuring the student's performance *relative* to that of other students who took the same test. Criterion-referenced tests provide a way of measuring the student's *absolute* performance in terms of a standard or criterion.

Norm-Referenced Tests

The student performances reported in Figure 2.3 were from a norm-referenced, standardized achievement test. The achievement profile given there reported, among other things, these grade-equivalency scores for *word meaning:*

> Student A — 7.8
> Student B — 6.0
> Student C — 5.9
> Student D — 4.8

The scores do not indicate the actual number of words these students know the meaning of, rather only the *relationship* between their knowledge and that of the students in the norm group with whom they are being compared. Student A knows as many words as the average student in the norm group who is in the eighth month of the seventh grade. Student D knows as many words as the average student in the norm group who is in the eighth month of the fourth grade.

Criterion-Referenced Tests

The spelling test scores of four students are reported below in a criterion-referenced way:

NAME	PERCENT CORRECT	NUMBER CORRECT
Arnie	100	10 out of 10
Betty	80	8 out of 10
Carlos	60	6 out of 10
Debra	50	5 out of 10

The test consisted of ten words. Arnie spelled all the words correctly or 100 percent; Betty spelled eight words correctly or 80 percent; and so forth. The percentage and raw scores are both criterion-referenced because they identify the student's *absolute* performance in terms of the standard or criterion which is 100 percent or 10 out of 10.

The Difference

The difference between norm-referenced and criterion-referenced tests lies in their interpretations of student performance rather than in the organization of the tests themselves. Tests can be interpreted in either a norm-referenced or criterion-referenced way. Student performance on the standardized word-meaning test would be reported in a criterion-referenced way if the percent of words known by each student were reported as they were with the spelling test. The spelling test could be interpreted in a norm-referenced way if the scores were ranked.

NAME	NORM-REFERENCED: RANKING	CRITERION-REFERENCED: PERCENT CORRECT
Arnie	First	100
Betty	Second	80
Carlos	Third	60
Debra	Fourth	50

The norm-referenced scores do not indicate how many words each student spelled correctly, only the relative position of the four students to each other. The norm-referenced scores would be the same even if the criterion-referenced scores were different.

NAME	NORM-REFERENCED: RANKING	CRITERION-REFERENCED: PERCENT CORRECT
Arnie	First	40
Betty	Second	30
Carlos	Third	20
Debra	Fourth	10

While it is possible to interpret all tests either way, tests intended to assess general abilities and capacities lose their validity if interpreted in other than a norm-referenced way. Standardized achievement and intelligence tests are designed to be interpreted only in a norm-referenced way. For example, the test for word meaning shown earlier is designed to indicate general word-meaning ability. If the teacher identified some words that Student D missed on the test, taught them to her, and then tested her again, her score the second time would probably be raised. As the result of learning only four words she might move from a score of 4.8 to a score of 7.8. Quite obviously, though, the learning of only four words does not logically constitute a *real* three-grade improvement in her word-meaning ability. By teaching the specific four words on the test—"teaching for the test," so to speak—the teacher invalidated it as a test of general reading ability.

On the other hand, tests intended to be criterion-referenced are not invalidated by "teaching for the test." The most logical thing for Betty to do is to identify the two spelling words she missed, study them, and then take the test again. If she now scores 100 that is validly equal to Arnie's 100.

INCREASING USEFULNESS OF ASSESSMENT

How useful particular instruments are in assessing the effectiveness of instructional-manager strategies depends on three factors: *validity, frequency of administration,* and *specificity.*

Validity

Test validity refers to the extent to which a test measures what it purports to measure. A test that is valid for one purpose such as measuring mathematical computation ability, may be invalid for another purpose—measuring mathematical problem-solving ability.

Teachers can avoid incorrectly assessing the effectiveness of their instructional-manager strategies if they make certain that the purpose for which the strategy was designed is the same purpose for which the assessment instrument is valid. A learning center intended to develop students' mathematical problem-solving abilities should not be assessed with a test valid only for measuring mathematical computation ability.

The purpose for which a test is valid may not be discernable from its title. A test called "Understandings in Social Studies" may be valid for the purpose of rotely memorizing names and dates but invalid for the purpose of gaining a conceptual understanding of certain major principles. Teachers will want to examine carefully the items on the test in order to determine whether the behavior assessed in the items is really what the teacher is trying to develop with the strategy.

Frequency of Administration

Standardized tests of achievement are more useful if they are administered twice during the school year, at the beginning and end, than if they are administered only once. The teacher who is provided with students' grade equivalency scores for word meaning at the beginning of the school year and is also provided scores from a different form of the same test at the end of the school year has some basis for evaluating the effectiveness of the instructional-manager strategies used during the school year to develop students' word-meaning abilities. If the tests are designed to be given monthly their usefulness is increased still further. Sometimes tests are available for units of work that can be completed in about a week. If the teacher developed a learning center intended to help students attain the objectives of that unit, the test provides a basis for evaluating the effectiveness of the center. Likewise, more useful information will be gained if student motivation is assessed monthly than if assessed only twice a year. (Tests of student motivation are suggested later in this chapter.)

Specificity

A major distinction between norm-referenced and criterion-referenced tests is specificity. The norm-referenced scores for word-meaning ability, shown earlier, did not list the specific words tested. The criterion-referenced spelling scores shown earlier are more specific because spelling scores are normally related to a certain lesson and, thus, a particular list of words. The scores for the spelling test would be even more useful if the specific words missed by each student were also identified. The teacher, for example, might find that Betty, Carlos, and Debra all missed the word *interrupted*. They misspelled it as *interupted.* That common error might be caused by something other than poor motivation, which is the condition the teacher is attempting to assess. That error might result from a misunderstanding that no amount of motivation by itself is likely to remedy.

A strength of the tests used with a continuous-progress curriculum is their specificity. By having a test for each specific objective, the teacher has a basis for evaluating the strategies used in achieving each objective. The teacher, for example, might decide to organize an instructional aide program to help students learn the addition facts. If the teacher has tests for a few specific addition objectives, he can test students' knowledge of the facts, introduce the aide program, and then assess students' knowledge of the facts a week later. If they have learned as many facts as he had hoped, he can continue the aide program as it is with other mathematics objectives. If they have not learned as much as he hoped, he can try another strategy, modify this one, or reconsider the reasonableness of his expectations.

INDIVIDUAL DIFFERENCES

Two contemporary approaches available to the teacher desiring to provide for students' individual differences were identified in chapter 2, *vary the rate* and *vary the content.* The teacher *varies the rate* when all students move through the same content but at different speeds. For example, they all are expected to learn the addition facts. Some will have learned them early in the first grade; some not until the third grade; some will still be working on them in junior high school.

The teacher *varies the content* when activities intended to lead to different instructional objectives are provided for different students. A library center might be set up solely for those with exceptional reading abilities and it might consist of experiences in reading and responding to literary material. Teachers can also vary the content by allowing students opportunities to select or modify an activity on the basis of interest. For example, students might be given an individual assignment, to read a story of their own choosing and then present it to the class in the form of a mural, puppet play, radio show, or any other way they wish.

Assessment with either approach can occur at two different

times, *prior* to the organization of the strategy and *after* the strategy has been used. For example, with the library center mentioned above, the teacher should have reading achievement information about students prior to setting up the library center and identifying the students who will do it. After using the center for awhile, the teacher will want to determine its effect on student reading achievement and motivation.

Organizing Strategies on the Basis of Assessment

Five factors that might be considered in organizing particular management strategies and selecting students to do them are:

Learning rate (intelligence)
Present achievement
Interests
Social situation (discipline pattern, status, group membership)
Personality (self-concepts and coping style)

Social situation is discussed in the second section of this book. Personality is discussed in the third section.

Learning Rate　Intelligence tests are designed to measure how much a person is likely to benefit from experience if all other things, such as motivation, are equal. Thus, a student of average intelligence, 100 *IQ*, will likely learn more of a given subject in a certain period of time than will a student of below-average intelligence, say 90 *IQ*.

The more information the teacher has about a student's learning rate, the more appropriate the management strategy can be made. For example, before negotiating a student contract for work in mathematics, the teacher should know how much a student could reasonably be expected to accomplish in the time specified by the contract. A student with an *IQ* of 90 should not be expected to accomplish as much as one with average or above-average intelligence.

Present Achievement　The teacher who is using a continuous-progress curriculum as a way of *varying the rate* will benefit at the beginning of the school year from achievement data indicating each student's appropriate placement in the sequence of instructional objectives. When a continuous-progress curriculum has been used by the teacher in the student's previous grade, and that teacher kept a record form like the one shown earlier in Figure 2.2, the present teacher knows immediately the objectives for which testing and teaching should begin.

If no such information exists, the teacher might want to construct a survey test based on the tests used in the continuous-progress curriculum. The survey test could be constructed from the tests for a random selection of objectives, for example, the tests for Objectives 2, 18, 25, 38, and 45. If the student performed adequately on the tests for Objectives 2 and 18, the teacher assumes that the student is also able to perform adequately on the tests for all the other objectives between 1 and 18. If the student performed adequately on the tests for Objectives 2 and 18 and performed inadequately on the tests for Objectives 25, 38, and 54, the teacher would probably want to start testing and teaching at the step of Objective 19.

The standardized achievement tests usually administered at the beginning of the school year provide much valuable information for the teacher desiring to individualize by *varying the content.* As was mentioned earlier, the teacher may identify a group of students having unusually high reading achievement scores and then organize a learning center intended to provide enriched literature experiences for them. Conversely, a group might be created for some students having very low scores in mathematical computation. A special program of instructional aides and student contracts might be organized to help them. Some students in that group might also benefit from the use of an incentive technique.

Interests

Provision for students' individual interests enables the teacher to make many important adjustments in the way management strategies are designed and students assigned to them. The variation might be as simple as having a learning center where students are allowed to select how they will illustrate what they learned in the center; they may draw, paint, or use clay. Less simple is to organize a number of alternative learning centers from which students may choose.

In order to provide for student interests, the teacher must know what they are. An instrument intended to inventory the interests of students in the primary grades is shown in Figure 5.1. Students mark the pictures showing their interests. Also, space is provided for them to picture other interests. An interest inventory for older students might consist of a list of activities which they are to check, or simply have the direction to describe their interests.

Teacher _____   Date _____

I like to:

Paint	Record Player	Science	Sandbox

Games	Puppets	Clay	Projector

Draw	Read	Math	Groups

Writing	Old Clothes	Crafts	Models

Some other things are

_____ _____ _____ _____

Figure 5.1

Revising Strategies on the Basis of Assessment

Information useful in revising or eliminating a management strategy can be gained by assessing the strategy at two levels, student behavior and management strategy. Assessing student behavior was discussed in prior sections of this chapter. The discussion here will be about assessing at the level of the management strategy.

Assessing at the level of management strategy can be done with two sources, teachers and students. Teachers can assess their own use of strategies with checklists like that shown at the end of the last chapter. They can also help assess the way strategies are used by other teachers, either those they work with on a team or those in other rooms. Teachers are a helpful source of information for each other because they are knowledgeable about instruction, and as a visitor they frequently see things that the regular teacher in that classroom has become too accustomed to to notice. Also, the visitor will often be ignored by students and they will behave naturally.

Instruments

An instrument designed for the teacher to use in assessing learning centers is shown in Figure 5.2. It can be adapted for such instructional-manager strategies as *student contracts, instructional aides,* and *incentives* by designing questions appropriate for those strategies.

Two instruments that students can be asked to use in assessing a management strategy are shown in Figure 5.3. Alternative formats are shown, multiple choice and free response. The instruments could be used with most instructional-manager strategies, such as *grouping, independent activities, instructional aides,* and *student contracts.* The instrument could be adapted to the primary grades by using smiling faces to represent rating points as shown in Figure 5.4. Students in the lower grades might also be interviewed by the teacher or an aide.

Student evaluation of learning centers can also be part of the regular system of record keeping which every student is expected to carry out. An instrument designed to elicit student evaluations of three instructional-management conditions is shown in Figure 5.5. (*Learning* and *Difficulty* refer to individual differences, *Interesting* to motivation, and *Directions* to time and space arrangements.) The instrument shown in Figure 5.5 might be handed in by a student once a week. In the lower grades, the four areas to be rated might be explained to the whole class at one time to assure that they know the meaning of the terms and can read them. The rating steps might be in the form of faces, as in Figure 5.4.

_____ _____ _____ _____
Teacher   *Room*   *Assessor*   *Date*

Directions: *Four questions are given. Respond to each question with each*
                    center. Make the response in the form of a rating:
                    1   2   3   4   5
                    Low   High

                    Space is provided for writing comments about each center.

Questions   1. *How appropriate is the difficulty of the task for the students?*
                    2. *How clear are the directions?*
                    3. *How accurately are children keeping records?*
                    4. *How appropriate is the center for its stated goals?*

Responses   *Center 1.* _____
                                                      Name

                    1. ☐   2. ☐   3. ☐   4. ☐   5. ☐

                    Comments. _____
                    Center 2. _____
                                                      Name

                    1. ☐   2. ☐   3. ☐   4. ☐   5. ☐

                    Comments _____

Figure 5.2

Interpretation   Two kinds of interpretation can be made of most test data, *numeri-cal interpretation* and *diagnostic interpretation.*

Numerical Interpretation. The purpose of a numerical interpreta-tion is to derive a number or score which allows comparison over time and between activities and students. Grade equivalency scores such as those shown in this chapter for word meaning are a numerical interpretation of student performance. The overall performance of Student A is interpretated numerically as 7.8. If at the end of the year the score rises to 9.6, the difference between the two scores represents the achievement gain Student A made this year.

   The easiest numerical interpretation is to derive a *modal* score. The mode is the point of the greatest concentration of scores. For example, Figure 5.6 shows data collected from a portion of the instrument shown earlier in Figure 5.5. The ratings are for three learning centers, Reading, Art, and Science. The number of students who chose each rating step are shown below the rating steps. Thus,

Multiple Choice	Free Response
_____	_____
Name	*Name*
1. Today I learned: (check one)	1. Today I learned:
___ *a) not much*	
___ *b) a little*	_____
___ *c) average*	
___ *d) more than usual*	_____
___ *e) a lot*	
2. The purpose of what I did was:	2. The purpose of what I did was:
___ *a) not at all clear*	
___ *b) not clear*	_____
___ *c) alright*	
___ *d) could be clearer*	_____
___ *e) very clear*	

Figure 5.3

twenty-eight students rated the Reading Center as 5, two rated it as 4, and none rated it as 3. The modes for each center are circled. Students overwhelmingly rated the Reading Center as *very difficult* and the Art Center as *very easy*. The scores for the Science Center have too much spread for a clear interpretation.

Because scores will frequently not be as concentrated as they were with the Reading and Art Centers, a second kind of numerical interpretation is often necessary for a clear evaluation of the data. A *mean* number is derived. Figure 5.7 shows the steps in deriving the mean score for students' rating of the difficulty of the Science Center. (The original data were shown in Figure 5.6.) Notice that the *modal* score for the difficulty of the Science Center is 5 while the *mean* score is 3.0.

Name _____

How Clear?

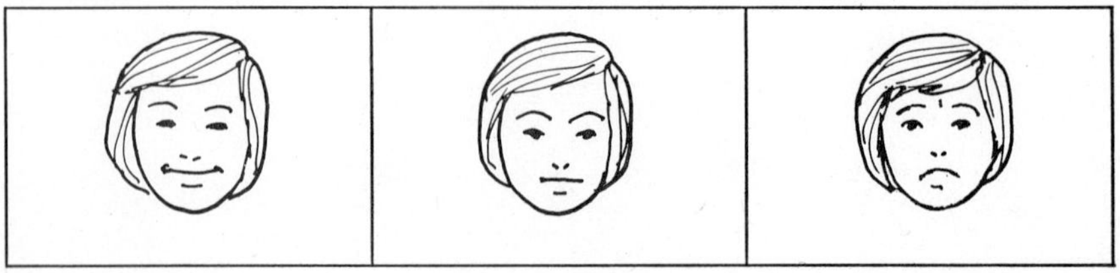

How Difficult?

Figure 5.4

Directions:
Indicate how you feel   Name _____
about each of these things
by giving your rating.

      1   2   3   4   5
    Low   High

Date	Center Title	Interesting?	Learning?	Difficulty?	Directions?

Figure 5.5

Center	Rating–Difficulty				
	1	2	3	4	5
Reading	0	0	0	2	(28)
Art	(21)	7	2	0	0
Science	6	6	7	3	(8)

Figure 5.6

Rating Levels	1	2	3	4	5
Tallies at Each Level	6	6	7	3	8
Weights Assigned Each Level	1	2	3	4	5
Weights Times Tallies	6	12	21	12	40

Sum of Weights Times Tallies   91

Mean Rating (Sum Divided by Number of Students—91 ÷ 30 = 3.0)   <u>3.0</u>   *Figure 5.7*

Figure 5.8 shows the mean scores for the three centers for which students rated the difficulty. (Again, the original data were shown in Figure 5.6.) A comparison of the mean scores indicates that students think the Reading Center is very difficult (4.9), the Art Center is very easy (1.4), and the Science Center is in-between (3.0).

When centers are more or less permanent, the teacher can determine the overall success of the center by recording the mean scores periodically. Figure 5.9 shows a portion of the record sheet where the mean scores for the difficulty of the three centers are recorded once a month. If the teacher collects data from the same instrument in October and finds that the mean score for the difficulty of the Science Center has risen to 3.5 the teacher knows that students are finding it more difficult. That may or may not have been the intent.

Center	*Mean Difficulty Rating*
Reading	4.9
Art	1.4
Science	3.0

Figure 5.8

Rating for Difficulty

Center	Sept.	Oct.	Nov.	Dec.	Jan.	Feb.	Mar.
Reading	4.9						
Art	1.4						
Science	3.0						

Dates

Figure 5.9

The interpretation of the data shown in these figures depends on the teacher's purpose in setting them up. If the teacher intended the Art Center to be an easy experience for everyone, then he has succeeded. If the teacher assumed that the Reading Center would be easy for the better readers and hard for the poorer readers, then he did not succeed. It was apparently difficult for everyone. The Science Center, on the other hand, seems to reflect students' probable range of individual differences. One would expect that if all students in the classroom worked at the Science Center and their range of abilities was normal, then their rating of difficulty should be spread like these scores are.

Diagnostic Interpretation.   The purpose of a diagnostic interpretation is to identify specific areas where problems seem to be occurring and where progress might be made. For example, the numerical interpretation shown earlier raises some questions about the difficulty of the three centers. Students' rating of the Reading Center is puzzling. One would assume that if the Reading Center presented an instructional task suitable for all students in the classroom then their inter-individual variability in reading ability should be reflected in their ratings, as might have been the case with Science. The scores for the Reading Center might have occurred for one of two reasons: (1) the difficulty level was appropriate for all students but the directions were unclear, or (2) the difficulty level was high for even the best students and, thus, the average and below-average readers learned little. Each possibility should be checked out and the necessary adjustments made in the Reading Center.

Both possibilities can be checked out by examining students' performance scores if they are available and by talking with students representing differing reading abilities. If a comparison of students' performance scores (pre- with post-) indicates that only the best readers made any achievement progress, then the Reading Center is too difficult to be of any value for most students. As long as all students are to be assigned to it, the difficulty level should be reduced. An alternative would be to vary the content and assign only the best readers to the Center. If there does not seem to be any correlation between students' reading ability and what they learned in the Reading Center, then the directions are probably confusing and should be clarified.

A diagnostic interpretation of the data collected about the Science Center should be directed at determining whether the spread of scores on ratings of difficulty are correlated with students' science ability. The teacher should sort out student's individual ratings like those shown in Figures 5.3, 5.4, and 5.5 into five piles depending on their ratings. All the papers with a rating of 5 are placed in one pile, all those with a rating of 4 are placed in a second pile, and so forth.

Each pile is then examined in order to determine if it is also sorted by ability. Those with the greatest ability in science should have given ratings of 1 or 2, while those with the lowest ability in science should have ratings of 4 or 5. If the piles do not seem correlated with science ability, then reading ability might be tested. It could be that the Science Center required so much reading that only those with high reading ability were able to learn from it. On the other hand, the differences in ratings might be attributable to the time of day when students worked at the center, or the day of the week. If the teacher can support a reasonable explanation for the differences in ratings, then a way to improve the effectiveness of the center becomes obvious.

While these examples of interpretation have been for learning centers, the same approach can be used with any management strategy. The important thing in diagnostic interpretation is to search for explanations of students' scores and then to suggest logical solutions that might be tried.

TIME AND SPACE

Four questions that teachers should ask about the conditions of time and space were suggested in chapter 2. They were:

1. Given the existing physical structure of the classroom and school, what different time and space arrangements are *possible?*
2. How well do each of these arrangements *facilitate* the attainment of educational goals?
3. What unique *problems* must be solved with each?
4. What are the *solutions* to these problems?

The assessment of time and space arrangements should provide information for answering the second and third questions, and, indirectly, should be a source of ideas for the first and last questions.

Problems can arise in at least four areas when new time and space arrangements are introduced, especially when those arrangements involve greater degrees of decentralization than the teacher and students are accustomed to. Assessment should provide information about the potential problem areas.

1. *Location.* Location affects traffic flow, varying noise levels, access to materials, and housekeeping.
2. *Time Allotment.* For how many minutes should students be assigned to one learning center? How satisfactory is the teacher's schedule for teacher-directed instruction? How long should students' contracts run— one week, two, a month?
3. *Clarity.* How clear are the written directions in learning centers? How clear are the written directions given to the instructional aides? Are the students' contracts sufficiently specific?
4. *Adjustment.* Students' adjustment to the cultural shock involved in new time and space arrangements is evidenced by how comfortable they feel and how self-directive their behavior.

Information about these four areas of potential problems can come from two sources, fellow teachers (including adult instructional aides) and students.

Teacher Assessment

Teacher assessment will be discussed in terms of two elements, the instruments that can be used and the procedures for interpreting data collected with the instruments.

Instruments   In designing instruments for other teachers to use, questions should be formulated which pertain to the four potential problem areas. An instrument for teacher assessment of the provision for individual differences in learning centers was suggested earlier, in Figure 5.2. That instrument could be expanded to include information about the potential problems related to time and space arrangements. Some suitable questions are suggested below. The problem areas to which the questions pertain are given.

AREAS	QUESTIONS
Location	1. How appropriate is the location so that the noise students make does not bother people in other centers or those students are not bothered by noise made by students in other centers?

Location   2. How appropriate is the location in terms of student's access to things they need like books, paper, and so forth?

Location   3. How appropriate is the location for students who are cleaning up the center when they have finished?

Location   4. How appropriate is the location in terms of students moving from one center to another, both during and after beginning work in a center?

Time   5. How appropriate is the time allocated for students to be in the center?

Clarity   6. How well are students able to follow the directions given and use the materials provided? Are they able to begin and carry out the activities without the assistance of the teacher or students from other centers?

Clarity   7. How clear are the directions for students cleaning up the center when they are finished? Is the next group able to use the center without the teacher having to do additional preparation of it.

Adjustment   8. How comfortable do students seem to feel? Are they cooperative and happy?

Adjustment   9. How much responsibility do students seem to be taking for completing their activities. How self-directive are they?

By referring to the four areas of potential problems an instrument can be designed to assess the suitability of time and space arrangements for any instructional-manager strategy. The questions given below might be asked about *instructional aides*. The questions could be used in a format like that shown earlier in Figure 5.2.

AREAS	QUESTIONS
Location	1. How appropriate is the location of the area where instructional aides are working? Are they bothering others, or being bothered by others?
Time	2. How appropriate is the time allocated to work with the instructional aide?

Clarity   3. How clear are the directions given to the instructional
                    aide? Is the aide able to begin instruction without seeking
                    assistance from the teacher or other aides?

Adjustment   4. How comfortable does the aide seem to feel? Is he or
                    she tense?

Adjustment   5. How much responsibility is the aide taking for com-
                    pleting the instructional activity?

Adjustment   6. How much is the student cooperating with the aide?

Questions relating to the four potential problem areas can also be
prepared for *grouping, team teaching, student contracts,* and *reward
strategies.*

Interpretation   A *diagnostic interpretation* should provide information about the
four potential problem areas and suggest solutions. A form for sum-
marizing the suggestions about learning centers is suggested in
Figure 5.10. The form shown in Figure 5.10 is intended to be action
oriented. It suggests solutions.

A *numerical interpretation* could be made if the teacher wanted
to determine the general success of a strategy over time. The average
score for all ratings could be derived in order to determine the overall
success of centers. Or, a score could be derived for each of the potential problem areas by averaging the ratings that relate to each
area.

Student Assessment

Student assessment will be discussed in terms of instruments and
interpretation.

Instruments   In designing instruments for students to use, questions can be formulated which pertain to the four potential problem areas. A multiple-
choice instrument for assessing problems in the four areas is suggested in Figure 5.11. The areas are identified. The instrument is
designed for use with learning centers.

The questions could be made into free-response items by leaving
off the alternative answers. (How quiet were the people in other

Suggestions for Learning Centers

Center 1   _____
                                    Name

1. *Location:*

_____

2. *Time Allotment:*

_____

3. *Clarity:*

_____

4. *Adjustment:*

_____

Center 2   _____
                                    Name

Figure 5.10

centers?) The instrument could be adapted for use in the lower grades by having a picture for each of the questions. A picture of people fighting could be used for Question 4. Students could have an answer sheet with faces like that shown earlier in Figure 5.4. Somewhat more complicated would be a picture for each of the five levels of cooperation identified in Question 4, or at least the first, middle, and last. Students would check the picture that best illustrates their group.

An instrument for having students evaluate centers as a regular part of the record keeping carried out in centers was suggested

Name_____

LOCATION   1. The people in other centers were: (*check one*)

_____*a*) *so quiet I hardly heard them.*

_____*b*) *not quiet, but I was not bothered.*

_____*c*) *somewhat noisy, but it only bothered me a little.*

_____*d*) *were so noisy I had trouble doing anything.*

_____*e*) *were so noisy that I did not do anything.*

TIME   2. I finished: (*check one*)

_____*a*) *just when the period ended.*

_____*b*) *just before the period ended*

_____*c*) *about halfway through the period*

_____*d*) *soon after the period began.*

_____*e*) *immediately after the period began*

CLARITY   3. I felt lost, and needed help: (*check one*)

_____*a*) *never.*

_____*b*) *only once.*

_____*c*) *sometimes.*

_____*d*) *often*

_____*e*) *all the time.*

ADJUSTMENT   4. The people in our center: (*check one*)

_____*a*) *help each other a lot.*

_____*b*) *sometimes help each other.*

_____*c*) *do not help each other, but do not fight.*

_____*d*) *fight sometimes.*

_____*e*) *seem to fight all the time.*

Figure 5.11

earlier in Figure 5.5. That instrument identified only one of the four potential problem areas, clarity (It asked the child to rate: Directions?). That instrument could be expanded to include location, time, and adjustment.

The instrument shown in Figure 5.11 could be rewritten in such a way that would make it suitable for assessing any instructional-manager strategies.

A *diagnostic interpretation* of the data collected about time and space arrangements could be carried out at the same two levels as that collected about individual differences, discussed earlier in this chapter. At the first level of interpretation the purpose is to look for areas of wide agreement. Agreement is indicated by the *modal* number. (See Figure 5.6). If twenty-eight out of the thirty students who worked at one center give a rating of *d* (the people in other centers were so noisy that I had trouble doing anything) then either this center or the other noisy center should be relocated.

Interpretation

A second level of diagnostic interpretation would be carried out when students do not agree in their ratings. (See the rating for Science in Figure 5.6.) If a similar range of ratings was found for something like *adjustment* in the *Science Center,* the teacher might search for the reasons by looking to see whether there was agreement between the students assigned to a center at the same time. What the teacher would probably find is that one group fights and one group does not. An examination of the children's perceptions about norms and group structure might give some indication of why they fight. (See section 2, Group Leader Role.) For example, groups consisting of all stars or all isolates will sometimes not work well together. If the groups that fight also reports much difficulty with the task, their frustrations with the task could cause the fighting.

A *numerical interpretation* of the data provides some evidence of the general success of a strategy over time. The procedure that can be followed in making a numerical interpretation of data relating to time and space arrangements is identical to that followed with individual differences. The procedures were explained in Figures 5.6 and 5.7.

MOTIVATION

Motivation will be discussed in two parts, Introduction and Assessing Student Feelings.

Introduction

Motivation can be assessed at two levels, *student behavior* and *management strategies.*

Student Behavior   Assessing motivation at the level of student behavior is accomplished by measuring student learning gains that can be attributed to motivation. For example, a teacher might wish to assess the use of student contracts done in conjunction with a self-instructional program organized like a continuous-progress curriculum. The program provides a series of worksheets which enables students to test and teach themselves. They move to a new objective only when they have performed successfully on a test for the previous objective. The teacher is dissatisfied with the slow progress students are making through the program and hopes that student contracts will speed them up.

Before beginning contracts, the teacher collects information about the average number of objectives each student has attained each week during the last three weeks. That becomes the *before* rate. When negotiations for contracts are being conducted, students are shown their *before* rate and encouraged to specify a slightly faster rate. The contracts are for two weeks. After using the contracts for one month, two contract periods, the teacher assesses the effectiveness of the contracts by comparing students' *before* rate with their rate during the month contracts were used. The data for three students are shown in Figure 5.12.

An examination of the scores shown in Figure 5.12 indicates that student contracts appeared to be effective in motivating Mabel and Carol and ineffective in motivating Luis. In fact, contracts seemed to be counterproductive with Luis. Student contracts should probably continue to be used with Mabel and Carol and dropped immediately with Luis.

		Objectives Completed			
Name	*Before*	*Week 1*	*Week 2*	*Week 3*	*Week 4*
Mabel	2	4	4	5	6
Luis	4	5	5	3	2
Carol	1	4	4	5	5

Figure 5.12

Increased motivation caused by student contracts is the probable cause for the increased learning rate in the example just described because the only thing changed was the introduction of contracts. The instruction provided by the self-instructional system of worksheets remained unchanged.

The more alternation that is made in an instructional task during the time the instructional manager strategy is being used, the less clearly any changes in learning can be attributed directly to the motivational effects of the strategy. If, for example, a learning center is organized to help students learn something that they would normally have learned by reading a chapter in the textbook, any marked increase in learning cannot be attributed to the motivational effects of the learning center. The substitution of the learning center for the assignment to read a chapter constitutes a significant alternation of the instructional task. However, after all, if learning appears to have improved as a result of the use of the learning center, who cares whether it is actually caused by the motivational effects of the learning center or a more facilitative organization of the instructional task.

As was mentioned earlier in this chapter, assessment at the level of the management strategy can occur in two ways. Teachers can assess how well they are *actually* doing what they *intend* doing. The second way is to assess students' feelings about an activity. The more they like an activity, the more motivated they probably are to do it. The remainder of this chapter deals with assessing students' feelings. *Management Strategy*

Some words of caution are in order at this point. The teacher should not confuse students' *feelings* about an instructional activity with their actual *learning* as a result of doing that activity. The two variables are not always related. If Mabel, Luis and Carol (Figure 5.12) were asked how they *felt* about student contracts they might have responded less than enthusiastically, but the data collected on their actual *learning* indicate that student contracts were quite effective with Mabel and Carol. A major reason for collecting information about students' feelings is that suitable measures of their actual learning is often not available. For example, a learning center intended to facilitate students' inquiry skills was suggested in chapter 3. Students' actual learning of inquiry skills as a result of having the center cannot be assessed because no suitable measures exist. All that can be assessed is student feeling.

Assessing Student Feelings

Assessment of student feelings will be discussed in terms of instruments and interpretation.

Instruments   An instrument suitable for assessing students' overall motivation is given in Figure 5.13. It measures their feelings about the school and the classroom. An instrument that can be used in assessing specific strategies is given in Figure 5.14. Students are assessing learning centers with the instrument shown in Figure 5.14, but any activity could be included, such as instructional aides, student contracts, group projects.

Student feelings can be assessed in the primary grades by using pictures and having three rating steps, as shown in Figure 5.15.

Interpretation   The interpretation of data collected about student feelings can be done in two ways, *numerical interpretation* and *diagnostic interpretation.*

---

*Name*_____

Directions:

Check the statement that tells how you feel. No one but you and the teacher will see your responses.

1. This school is:

    _____ *a) my idea of a really good school.*

    _____ *b) pretty good, but it could be better.*

    _____ *c) sort of so-so; could be better, could be worse.*

    _____ *d) not very good.*

    _____ *e) is terrible.*

2. The things we are doing in this class are:

    _____ *a) usually very interesting.*

    _____ *b) interesting sometimes.*

    _____ *c) alright, could be better.*

    _____ *d) sometimes boring.*

    _____ *e) usually very boring.*

Figure 5.13

Name _____   *Date* _____

Directions: *Indicate how you feel about each of these activities by making a check in one of the boxes under each statement.*

Activity	Usually Very Interesting	Sometimes Interesting	Alright, Could Be Better	Sometimes Boring	Usually Very Boring
Reading Center					
Art Center					
Listening Center					
Creative Center					

Figure 5.14

Name _____   *Date* _____

Figure 5.15

Numerical Interpretation.   The purpose of a numerical interpretation is to derive a number or score which allows for comparison over time and between students and activities. Numerical interpretations are particularly useful for assessments of instructional-manager strategies that are continued for long periods of time. The information collected with the instruments shown in Figures 5.13 and 5.14 will be very useful if interpreted numerically. Also, a numerical interpretation of information collected with the instrument shown in Figure 5.15 would be useful if the activities identified are carried on for most of the school year such as a Reading Center and instructional aides.

The simplest kind of numerical interpretation is to derive a *modal* score. Figure 5.16 shows the modal scores of data collected with the instrument shown in Figure 5.13.

Another kind of numerical interpretation is to derive a *mean* score. The steps in deriving a mean score from ranked instruments like those shown here was described earlier in Figure 5.7. Figure 5.17 shows the mean scores of the data given in Figure 5.16. In deriving the mean scores shown in Figure 5.16, students' choices are weighted with 5 for *a* and 1 for *e*. With that instrument the most positive rating is *a* and the least negative is *e*. While scores can be weighted in any way the teacher wishes, the means scores are clearer if the heaviest weight is assigned to the most positive ranking.

Figure 5.18 shows a record form for keeping monthly scores for school and classroom motivation. By keeping a record like this,

		Rating				
Question		**a**	**b**	**c**	**d**	**e**
School		0	1	6	(14)	9
Class		6	3	(9)	5	7

Figure 5.16

Question		Mean Rating
School		2.0
Class		2.9

Figure 5.17

Motivation Level	Mean Ratings							
	Dates							
	Sept.	Oct.	Nov.	Dec.	Jan.	Feb.	Mar.	Apr.
School	2.0	1.9						
Class	2.9	3.4						

Figure 5.18

the teacher is aware of being successful in increasing students' motivation to participate in activities in the classroom. Unfortunately, motivation at the school level is not increasing. Perhaps strategies for increasing school motivation might be discussed with the principal or with other teachers.

While mean scores are more difficult to compute than modal scores, their greater precision makes them more useful. For example, the modal scores shown in Figure 5.16 are from the same set of data as the mean scores shown in Figure 5.17. Now, examine Figure 5.18. It shows data collected over a period of two months with the same instrument. Note the mean scores for *Class Motivation* for the months of September (2.9) and October (3.4). There is obviously progress being made, but that progress does not show up if only the modal scores for those two months is examined. The modal scores for both months are the same, *c*.

Diagnostic Interpretation. The purpose of a diagnostic interpretation is to identify specific areas where problems seem to be occurring, and where progress might be made. For example, important clues as to how class motivation might be increased can come from an examination of the differences between students who gave different rankings. To do this, the individual response sheets of students, like the instrument shown in Figure 5.13, are sorted into one of five piles. Those papers with a ranking of *a* are placed in one pile, those with a ranking of *b* in another, and so forth.

When all papers have been sorted into piles, the teacher examines the names of those in each pile in an attempt to identify common elements. Are most of those who gave a ranking of *a* the better students while those who gave a ranking of *e* the poorer students? Are most of the *a*'s girls while most of the *e*'s are boys? Do the differences run along race or ethnic lines. Overall class motivation can be increased by attending to the characteristic which differentiates the piles. If the difference is sexual, then activities need to be designed for whichever sex seems to be least motivated. If the difference is academic, then the teacher might want to consider providing different activities for students of differing academic abilities so that all have opportunities to do things they find personally motivating.

The procedure of sorting student papers into piles will also provide clues about increasing motivation in specific activities when it is used with data collected from instruments like those shown in Figures 5.14 and 5.15. It would be helpful to determine the characteristics that differentiate those students who find the Reading Center to be *usually very interesting* from those who find it to be *usually very boring.* If all students are assigned to do the same thing at the Reading Center, and the difference is found to be reading ability—those with high ability find it boring while those with low ability find it interesting—then the teacher should probably consider designing different instructional tasks for students of differing reading abilities. Students with higher reading abilities will probably be more motivated if given more difficult instructional tasks and they will probably learn more.

For Further Reading

For discussions of norm-referenced and criterion-referenced tests, see:

Glaser, R. "Instructional Technology and the Measurement of Learning Outcomes." American Psychologist 18 (1963):519–521.

Prescott, G. A. "Criterion-Referenced Test Interpretation in Reading." *The Reading Teacher* 24 (January 1971):347–354.

6

Situational Examples

These examples are provided to assist teachers in analyzing the specific management problems they might have. A relationship can then be drawn between the situation and the teaching strategies described in this book.

SITUATION 1

Miss L. teaches a sixth grade that has a wide range of ability. She realizes she is not meeting the needs of each pupil because she is unable to individualize or teach small groups.

Teacher: How can I manage a classroom and have order when I want to group for ability? It seems the only time I have control of the class is when I am speaking to the total group. Then I can demand attention because I focus on everyone.

Comment: It might be interesting to learn this teacher's definition of "control."

Teacher: It sounds easy when I read about individualizing, but somehow I can't carry it off when I try it for real. The activities that I plan for independent work don't keep the children quiet. They talk and fight among themselves and the room soon

becomes chaotic. I find myself yelling at them all to stop whatever they're doing and put their heads down on their desks.

Comment: Habits of independence and self-direction are not something pupils are likely to learn on their own. They are goals toward which
teachers and pupils must work on together over a period of time.
Perhaps the independent activities are not highly motivating.

Teacher: I have an art corner, a science area, and a library area. As I
try to work with individuals or small groups, these learning
center corners become bastions for fights, giggling, and general
disruption so that I must leave what I'm doing to quiet things
down. By the time I get back to my original teaching I have
lost the pupils' attention and my own thoughts.

Comment: Independent activities must be carefully planned. They must
be properly introduced and the rules for use thoroughly understood. There must be some means of control—either by can-
celing that activity or denying the people who disrupt it
the privilege of participation.

Possible Solutions

1. The materials must be thoroughly introduced and the children must
    know how to use them. The rules for the center must also be clear. The
    rules might be posted by the center and periodially discussed.
2. If a center is misused, it perhaps is not a place children see as desirable.
    Therefore, it should be temporarily put out of use and evaluated.
    Perhaps it should be replaced by something else.
3. Let a few people use the centers at first and provide work at the desks for
    the rest of the class. Only allow a limited number at the center at a time.
4. Make children accountable for their time at the centers. They can keep
    a log of what they did during the independent study time.
5. Enlist the help of volunteer aides. Friends of the school (mothers,
    retired citizens) can help run the centers. An adult who cares can be
    the magic ingredient in solving the needs of those children who seek
    attention in antisocial ways.

SITUATION 2

Mrs. W., a first-year teacher, is enthusiastic about her class and
thoroughly enjoys her new career. She has one problem. There aren't
enough hours in the day.

Teacher: I love to teach, and it's a real thrill for me to try out for real all those things we learned in college. The only thing I have to complain about is that one has to be some sort of superwoman to get everything accomplished. Perhaps if I worked twenty hours a day at my job I would get all the lessons prepared, the learning centers set up, the papers graded, and the records kept. Frankly, I find it all impossible and frustrating.

Comment: This is probably one of the complaints most often expressed by teachers, and a most legitimate one it is.

Teacher: I have all kinds of ideas I want to try out with my fourth graders. Sometimes when I have had a particularly good session of math and feel real accomplishment, I suddenly realize that I have recess duty next and I'm totally unprepared for my science class that is scheduled to follow. For that reason it is easy to just pass out the books and have the children take turns reading aloud.

Comment: Teachers of elementary-age children are expected to be proficient in many subjects. As the knowledge base grows larger year by year, this becomes ever more an impossibility. In sheer exasperation, teachers turn to group-oriented materials rather than organize the individualization they know to be more satisfactory.

Teacher: The teacher in the next room is very helpful to me. She has been teaching for five years and has given me many constructive suggestions. She has a good science program, in fact, that is her favorite subject. Our philosophies are similar and we share many ideas about teaching.

Comment: This teacher still has that fresh idealistic view of teaching that so often wears off after a few years leaving a callousness toward education and children.

Possible Solution

1. Play to teacher strengths. The two teachers seem to have a rapport that makes team teaching a possibility. Could Mrs. W. teach both classes of math and her helpful neighbor science? That way, each could use the same lesson techniques for both classes and yet have only one preparation to make.

2. Don't feel that all things must be accomplished at once. One learning center, well-planned and executed, is better than a hurried version

of all those promising ideas listed in the current teachers' magazine or college text.

3. Enlist volunteer aides. The mothers who come in to help can be used to free the teacher from some of the simpler tasks and enable her to do the individualization she would like to have time for.

SITUATION 3

Mr. H. has a sixth grade that he describes as, "just plain lazy." They are a group of youngsters who seem to lack motivation and do very few or none of the assignments that Mr. H. gives to them.

Teacher: I have a class of slow learners. They all scored at or below grade level on the standardized tests of math and reading. They seem to have that, "I don't care" attitude. If I give an assignment they have to be threatened before they turn it in and then inevitably it is poorly done.

Comment: By the sixth grade, children have pretty well established a pattern of behavior and attitudes toward academic subjects. It is somewhat of a self-fulfilling prophecy: "My teacher and my parents think I'm stupid. I'll not disppoint them." With a room full of self-proclaimed failures, it is difficult but certainly not impossible to build enthusiasm for learning.

Possible Solutions

1. Introduce a contract system to those students who are interested. Use it for math and, later on, include the other subjects as well. Negotiate realistically with students on the conditions where contracts seem to be less than you would expect. Always remember that the student makes the final decision. Because the class lacks incentive, start with a short time period for completion of the contract—perhaps two days. This can be extended, as independence grows, to a weekly contract.

   Those not involved with contracts will be given regular daily assignments. Interest will inevitably grow among those not using contract systems and soon those not involved will ask to do so. Gradually, the contract system can be expanded to include the total class, to various subjects, and on an extended time basis.

2. Organize a reward system to encourage greater efforts. Use such incentives as a movie for those who have completed a productive afternoon or a fifteen-minute game time at the end of the day. Let students suggest incentives they would like.

SITUATION 4

Mrs. R. teaches a fifth-grade group whose tests have shown a wide ability range. With thirty-three in the class, it is difficult to teach the children individually at their various levels of ability.

Teacher: I have one boy in my class whose reading-test results show that he is at the high first-grade level. Three children are at the second-grade level. On the other hand, three children's scores are at the eighth-grade level, and one is at the ninth-grade level. The rest of the class is scattered between the two extremes.

Comment: This is a particularly wide range and, of course, the wider the range of ability, the greater the challenge to meet individual needs.

Teacher: Sometimes I have the four most advanced readers read with the four really slow ones.

Comment: This is a good technique but one that should not be overused. Too often teachers rely on this for keeping children busy. Both groups have their own needs.

Teacher: I have been having this same group of eight play word games. The children have had conflicts with this activity. The low group is rebellious and the top readers give up and come to me with their problems. This, of course, disturbs the group or individual that I'm reading with.

Comment: The slow readers are no doubt embarrassed about their inabilities. They know that their classmates can see their inadequacies in ability so it is easy to "goof off" and hope that the reading time will soon elapse.

Teacher: I gave up on the small groups and I now let the top readers read on their own. They go to the library and choose books on various topics about which to make reports. Now I have worked the slow readers into a special group.

Comment: The low group can benefit most from knowledgeable instruction by the teacher. The high ability readers need more than independent reading, which they are more likely to do on their own anyway.

Possible Solutions

1. Enlist the cooperation of the first-grade teacher. Train the low readers to be tutors for her. They will gain prestige for in the eyes of a first

grader all fifth graders are very wise. Of course, it will take some training sessions on the part of the teachers to make certain the tutors know their jobs. During this time of tutoring, the reading skills of both age groups will grow.

2. Let the four top readers work together on special reading assignments. Don't forget that high-ability readers usually need instruction from the teacher, too. Many are lacking skills in the area of critical reading.

3. Rather than always letting the "top" students read with the low-ability students, it might be better to let an isolate of average ability have a one-to-one relationship with a slow reader. This will provide reading help for the slower student and prestige for the isolate.

4. Continuous-progress curriculum offers freedom in the classroom for children to develop a wide range of abilities at their own rate. When children are taught individually they do not have to display their inadequacies publicly.

SITUATION 5

Mrs. J. found herself in a less than ideal open-classroom situation. She is having difficulty working with her team members.

Teacher: When I interviewed for this job I was asked if I had ever taught in an open classroom. I said that although I hadn't been involved in one as a teacher, I had done my student teaching two years ago in such a setting and that I was enthusiastic about it and most anxious to participate in one again. Little did I know what I was in for!

This wing of the school is for grades one through three and contains one hundred and seven students and four teachers. Two of the teachers, Mrs. R. and Mrs. K., have been teaching in this school for ten years and know each other well, both professionally and socially. They agree on all decisions. In fact, they agree so well that it seems like a conspiracy against the other two team members, Miss A., a first-year teacher, and myself. They set up the program and schedule, and then assume that the two of us will go along with it. Occasionally, we make a token decision, yet it is very frustrating to never have a say in what really is taking place. While Miss A. seems satisfied with the arrangement, I feel very rebellious.

Comment: This sounds like a combination of two strong-willed people teamed with two who are rather insecure. Children are not the only ones who form cliques. Adult teachers on teams do too.

Teacher: It seems that my "home" group (together at various times during the day for announcements, roll call, and routine dismissal) is blamed for all the offenses that occur in the classroom. For instance, one or two of my students are always held responsible for disrupting the learning centers. They're always being blamed by the other three teachers for being noisy and destructive. I feel that my students are no more at fault than anyone elses. The other children just try to get my children into trouble.

Comment: Is this teacher overreacting because of unresolved frustrations stemming from her lack of participation in planning the teaching schedule? Team teaching in an open-classroom situation demands some of the same skills that any team requires, cooperative effort. With any group, one person usually emerges as the leader. If, however, this person is truly a good leader and committed to the team, decisions are jointly made and there is general accord. The success of the open-education program depends on teachers who mutually accept responsibility and leadership.

Possible Solutions

1. Open communication between teachers is a key to the success of open education. An expression of feelings by these teachers in a group can often bring about some understandings and behavior change. It is possible that the other teachers are unaware of this teacher's feelings. Or, perhaps they have antagonistic feelings toward her that need to be honestly expressed.

2. Have students spend a greater portion of the day with their "home" teachers. Possibly, the "home" rooms may be created by isolating areas with folding doors or screens. This should be done only as a last resort for it does not really solve the main problem—it only puts it behind barriers.

3. A personality conflict requiring personnel changes may be at the root of the problem. Someone outside the situation should listen with an open mind and attempt to bring about changes. This teacher might work better with another team or, on a more limited scale, in a semi-team situation.

SECTION 2

Group Leader Role

7

Conditions

Help One Another

Most of us have been students in the first grade in the Roosevelt School District at Martin Luther King School, Roosevelt School and Jorgensen School. The classes that we have been in have been Mexican-American, Negro, Oriental and White students

Yes, we have fights but the people who do fight aren't thinking very well. And we think that they should learn to talk it over first and learn to cooperate and to not fight. We learn to read together and talk together. At P.E. time we all "pitch in" and help each other.

We hope that students at other schools play games together, and get to know each other and understand each other better.

We hope all of us have good thoughts about each other.

Signed by twenty-seven students
Third and fourth grades
(Letter to the Editor, The Arizona
Republic, September 29, 1975)

Members in "healthy" groups, such as those who wrote the letter to the editor, work harder, make more sacrifices for the group, more readily extol the group's virtues, are more satisfied, interact more often, and agree with one another more often than do members of "unhealthy" groups.[1]

A democratic society derives its strength from the effective functioning of the multitude of diverse groups which it contains. In this way the maintenance of our democratic society depends on students experiencing "healthy" groups, because only by active participation in such groups will they learn to function effectively in society.

Groups function effectively *only* if their members are able to:

1. Participate effectively in decision making.
2. Adjust differences with others in a cooperative and peaceful way.
3. Maintain an open-minded attitude.
4. Develop a capacity for trust and solidarity.
5. Be willing to accept the leadership of others, and to accept responsibility for leadership themselves.

The primary goals of the school are more likely to be attained in "healthy" classrooms. The goals are for students to develop cognitions and attitudes. Students should *know* how to read, write, and compute. And, they should *value* themselves and what they know how to do, others and their contributions, and the institutions in a democratic society. Cognitions and attitudes are usually interrelated. For example, the student who comes from a home where reading is not valued by the parents probably will not value it himself, and he will be likely to respond poorly to reading instruction. He may become a disabled reader unless the teacher succeeds in altering his attitude toward reading. The teacher will be most effective in changing the student's attitude in a "healthy" classroom.

Students in "healthy" classrooms will be more likely to possess adequately developed personalities. Healthy groups contribute to:

1. The feeling of belonging and status.
2. The protection from real or fantasied threat.
3. The enhancement of self-esteem.
4. The loosening of the facade of defensive mechanisms and the opportunity for testing these against the reality.

---

1. See D. Cartwright and A. Zander, *Group Dynamics: Research and Theory* (Evanston Ill.: Row, Peterson and Company, 1953).

5. The proper conditions for sublimating basic drives.
6. The curbing of infantile desires and behavior.[2]

Teachers in "healthy" classrooms achieve their goals of *individualization, developing self-direction, motivation,* and *reaching disruptive children* (see chapter 1). The instructional-manager strategies by which these goals can be achieved operate best in healthy classrooms. When students have the feelings of responsibility about self and others that were expressed by students who wrote the letter to the editor, they will be able to carry out with less supervision and better results such strategies as *independent activities, student contracts,* and *tutoring.*

Finally, teachers in "healthy" classrooms are happier with themselves and their jobs because students are supportive of their efforts and discipline presents few problems. They do not have to enforce compliance, to press students into submission. Cooperation and support cannot be gained through humiliation and suppression of the students. A classroom has become "unhealthy" when the teacher—often without realizing it—becomes more interested in his or her own power and authority than in the welfare of students. At that point the teacher has stopped being an educator and has become a threatened human being, fighting for rights, position, prestige, and superiority. The teacher is past the point of being able to recognize that the actions of the teacher may be the cause of the students' misbehavior.

TEACHER AS A GROUP LEADER

Many teachers consider their assignment to be to teach individual students and, when necessary, to correct the misbehavior of individual students. Yet the fact that these individual students have been assigned to classrooms means that the psychological dynamics of the classroom group will affect the teachers' success. Teachers have to learn to work *with* groups rather than against them. Unless the teacher can use the group to advantage, it functions as an obstacle.

For example, recall that one of the major concerns teachers expressed about classroom management (see chapter 1) was reaching

---

2. Ibid., p. 57.

disruptive children, those who don't seem to care to learn or to cooperate. The research on social psychology of teaching suggests that teachers' difficulties are often caused by their own lack of knowledge of the psychological dynamics of the classroom group. Bidwell, in reviewing the research on the social psychology of teaching, concludes that low-status boys receive more negative sanctions from the teacher, even though their lack of status with the group causes them to be more in need of teacher approval than students with higher status.[3] Continuing negative sanctions from the teacher eventually become counterproductive in terms of the students' learning and formation of attitudes. In addition, the low-status boys may react by forming subcultures in opposition to both the teacher and the group standards accepted by other students. In other words, they become disruptive and are unmotivated to learn.

As every teacher knows who has taught more than one group of students, classroom groups are not merely a collection of individual personalities; each class has a personality of its own.

Many teachers mistakenly assume that the group personality, or group atmosphere, is something they have to learn to live with because there is nothing they can do about it. Ms. Jones just has to accept the unpleasant fact that by the luck of the toss she has a wild bunch that will not settle down long enough to learn much, and will generally make her life miserable this year. The best she can do is buy tranquilizers and long for June. But group atmosphere can be changed by teachers, just as students' reading and writing skills can be. Unhealthy classrooms can be made healthy. And the results of change, both in terms of the students' learning and the teachers' mental health, justify the time and effort involved. Changing group atmosphere requires an understanding of the conditions that determine it and competency in utilizing appropriate teaching strategies.

Getzels and Thelen suggest that one might "conceive of the classroom as a miniature society or social system with differentiated role and personality relationships linked to differentiated educational goals."[4] Further, they note that classroom groups are unique in that: (1) learning is the goal or purpose for which the group is

3. C. E. Bidwell, "The Social Psychology of Teaching," in *Second Handbook of Research on Teaching*, R. Travers, ed. (Chicago: Rand McNally and Company, 1973), pp. 413–449.

4. J. W. Getzels and H. A. Thelen, "The Classroom Group as a Unique Social System," in *The Dynamics of Instructional Groups*, N. Henry, ed., Fifty-Ninth Yearbook of the National Society for the Study of Education, Part II (Chicago: The University of Chicago Press, 1960), pp. 53–82.

brought together; (2) participation in the group is mandatory, and so are the goals; and (3) the members of the group have no control over the selection of the leader, and no recourse from his leadership.

Some of the conditions that determine the health of the class-room group are determined by the *direct personal influence* of the teacher, and some the teacher alters *indirectly* by affecting *group influence.*

PERSONAL INFLUENCE

Personal influence is the capacity to affect another person's behavior. The teacher initiates a certain action with the intention of affecting the behavior of students. The teacher may ask students to pay attention to the lesson or to complete an assignment. The greater the teacher's influence, the more likely students are to comply quickly and enthusiastically with the teacher's request. (For reviews of research on personal influence see Lippitt, Polansky and Rosen (1952), Thibault and Kelly (1959), and Bidwell (1973).

Conditions that Determine Personal Influence

There are four conditions that determine the personal influence teachers have with their students.

A teacher's influence will be positive if the teacher is liked by students and negative if the teacher is not liked by the students. The positive effect of liking the teacher is particularly strong in influencing students to adopt the teacher's attitudes. For example, a situation was described earlier of a boy who comes from a home where reading is not valued and thus, the boy does not value reading himself. The boy may become a disabled reader if the teacher cannot influence the boy's attitude toward reading. The more the boy *likes* the teacher, the better the chances are that he will change his attitude and, thus, improve his reading ability.

Student Affection

Conversely, if students dislike the teacher, their original attitudes are strengthened and their rate of cognitive achievement declines. The negative attitude of a boy who comes to school with a dislike for reading will be strengthened if he also dislikes his teacher. And, the teacher will not be able to improve his reading skills, no matter how enlightened the methods and advanced the competence of the teacher are.

Student Perception   Teachers' personal influence is affected by the way their *knowledge, teaching competence,* and *status as adults* are perceived by the students. The higher students regard the teacher's knowledge and teaching competence, the greater will be the teacher's personal influence. One measure of the teacher's personal influence is the incidence of student complaints about assignments. Students are less inclined to complain about an assignment given by a teacher whose knowledge and competence they highly respect than by one for whom they do not hold the same respect. Most teachers have faced this difference in influence during their student-teaching days. When student teaching begins, it is often difficult to command students' respect, get them to do assignments, and behave as requested. Toward the end of the period of student teaching, pupils usually show the same respect for the student teacher that they do for the supervising teacher; the student teacher has become more influential because the children have had opportunities to observe that person's knowledge and competence.

Students' perception of the teacher as an adult is a greater source of influence in the early grades than in later ones. First graders hold their teacher in more awe than do fifth graders.

Misuse of Influence   A teacher's overuse of personal influence can be self-defeating. For example, a teacher who gives students a boring assignment usually must resort to personal influence in order to motivate them to do it. The influence may take the form of offering a reward—"When you finish it you may go to the play area"—or the influence may take the form of a threat—"You can't go to recess until you finish it." The more frequently teachers use personal influence to get students to complete assignments, the more rapidly that influence declines. Consequently, teachers must keep giving ever more pleasurable rewards and unpleasant punishments. By organizing as many assignments as possible in ways that are intrinsically motivating, teachers can save their influence for those assignments that cannot be made intrinsically motivating.

Dependence on force as a means of disciplining students is wasteful of personal influence. If Johnny is playing around and not paying attention during a lesson being taught by the teacher, it is less forceful for the teacher to walk over and stand by Johnny, without stopping the flow of the lesson, than it is to stop the lesson and say, in an exasperated way, "Johnny, stop that and pay attention." And the less forceful disciplinary action will usually be just as effective in controlling Johnny's behavior. If it does not, then a slightly more forceful influence can be tried, such as placing a hand on his shoulder in a gentle but firm manner. While the teacher does have to be firm and not allow Johnny to disrupt the lesson, the lower the level of force used, and the less it is exercised in a way which interferes with the flow of the lesson, the less personal influence the teacher has had to exercise.

Overdependence on forceful disciplinary techniques not only becomes progressively less effective in controlling student deviancy, it also has a negative "ripple effect" (Kounin and Gump 1970) on the rest of the class. Emotional threats made to one student produce a great deal of disruption among the others who witness the episode. Nail biting, shifting in seats, chewing pencils, and looking around nervously are behaviors that increase after the teacher uses a rough or threatening action with one student. The teacher's use of force reduces the other students' estimation of the teacher's likability, fairness, and competence, all of which tends to reduce the teacher's personal influence over them.

Degree of Individualization

Individualization affects the teacher's personal influence because it determines the ways by which students can maximize their rewards and minimize their punishments. When a program provides no individualization, all students are taught the same thing and judged according to the same standard. For example, they all hear the teacher's explanation of a certain grammatical rule, and are given the same written exercise to complete. The teacher then collects the completed exercises, and grades them according to the same standard. The best papers get an *A*, the next best a *B*, and the poorest an *F*. Under these conditions, students have two ways by which they can increase their level of performance relative to the rest of the class: (1) they can work harder, or (2) they can join together to exert pressure on high-status students to lower their levels of performance. In other words, they develop a "Gentlemen's Agreement" group standard that makes it wrong to work hard in school and do things that please the teacher. These collective attempts are particularly effective at the upper grade levels when students as a group don't seem to care about learning and the few students who do care are pressured by the group to lower their levels of performance. From the teacher's point of view, the students appear to be unmotivated and disruptive.

When teachers provide no individualization, they can increase their influence by doing things that cause students to like them more, and to respect their knowledge and competence more. If teachers using nonindividualized programs are not successful in becoming more likeable and respected, student attitudes and cognitions are likely to remain unchanged, or grow worse.

By contrast, the formation of oppositional group standards are not so likely to occur in individualized programs. In an individualized program, each student is doing something different and judged according to a different standard. For example, Mary is working on Objective 28, John on Objective 43, and Larry on Objective 106. Larry's effort, or lack of it, will not affect the teacher's judgement of Mary's performance and so Mary has nothing to gain by joining with other students to exert group pressure on Larry to lower his level of performance.

One weakness of individualized programs is that students are not likely to have as many opportunities to observe evidences of the teacher's knowledge and competence as they are with programs having no individualization. When an individualized grouping pattern is used in reading, any one student probably spends no more than ten minutes a week under the teacher's tutelage. That gives the teacher only ten minutes a week to demonstrate knowledge and competence. The more impressed the student is with that demonstration, the greater his attitude change and cognitive growth. A *continuous-progress curriculum* provides concrete and persuasive evidence of the teacher's ability (see chapter 3).

Increasing Personal Influence

Three ways teachers can increase their personal influence with students are to:

1. Use the minimum level of personal influence necessary to achieve results.
2. Build personal influence.
3. Use alternative means to achieve results other than personal influence.

Increasing personal influence is critical because the more influential a teacher is with students, the better their attitudes and the more they learn.

One of the group-leader strategies described in the next chapter is *desist techniques.* Desist techniques are those things the teacher does to change students' behavior. The teacher may want them to walk instead of run in the hallway, stop hitting someone when walking back from the pencil sharpener, or refrain from talking during a spelling test. The desist techniques explained in the next chapter are intended to achieve desired results with the maximum conservation of the teacher's personal influence.

Minimum Level of Influence

Personal influence can be increased by strengthening the sentimental tie between teacher and students. Sentimental ties are best strengthened by being friendly, supportive, and kind. Kindness combined with firmness is the only basis for a good and stable relationship with students. Students want to respect their teachers and be respected in return.

Build Personal Influence

Personal influence can be increased by finding ways to demonstrate knowledge and competence. In an individualized program, *a continuous-progress curriculum* is helpful in demonstrating the teacher's competence. Students take the pretest and perform inadequately. The teacher then instructs them until they are able to perform adequately on the post-test. The student's increased ability is obviously due in some part to the teacher's competence (see chapter 3).

Giving students an opportunity to observe something the teacher can do especially well may be an excellent way to build their respect for the teacher, even if the ability is not directly related to school. For example, a teacher who plays the violin in a city orchestra might give periodic solo concerts in class and arrange for students to attend a regular concert at the civic auditorium. Teachers who are good athletes might play ball with their students. Teachers who are good artists might demonstrate that skill in class. These demonstrations are not "ego trips." Rather, they are specific attempts to increase the students' respect for the teacher's competence.

One of the biggest mistakes teachers can make is to pretend to know something they do not, or hesitate to admit errors. Students have an uncanny ability to spot fakery. If they spot it once, they begin to assume that there exists a facade intended to cover a general lack of knowledge and competence. Admitting to one's own faults and mistakes is one of the best ways of winning students' confidence.

In planning how personal influence can be built, and then checking progress in building it, you will want to make use of group-leader assessment instruments. These instruments enable teachers to determine what their students like and dislike about them. For example, to one teacher's total surprise, it was discovered by using the assessment instruments that the students hated the teacher's bad breath. They were most appreciative when the teacher found ways of improving it.

Use Alternatives   Whenever possible, teachers should use ways of getting students to do things by relying on methods other than the exertion of personal influence. For instruction, the teacher can design tasks so that they are intrinsically motivating by using the instructional-manager strategies of *independent activities* and *student contracts* (see chapters 3 and 4). When the teacher cannot figure out how to make an instructional task intrinsically motivating, *incentive techniques* are effective ways of providing extrinsic motivation, and they waste little personal influence if used properly (see chapter 4).

Another alternative to using personal influence is to lead the classroom group in a way that effectively uses group influence. Group influence and the ways it can be altered are discussed next.

GROUP INFLUENCES

Individuals have become a "group" when they differentiate between themselves and outsiders. They develop an *esprit de corps*. The group becomes a social system that develops its own group standards. The standards tend to influence individual members to standardize their behavior. A group structure develops consisting of differing statuses and subgroups.

The difference between "healthy" and "unhealthy" groups can be accounted for in terms of three characteristics of all groups: (1) *group cohesiveness,* the group's *esprit de corps* and feeling of "oneness"; (2) *group standards,* the group's rules; and (3) *group structure,* the differing statuses and subgroups, each possessing differing influence over an individual member of the group.

The more understanding teachers possess of the dynamics of groups, and the ways that they can change those dynamics, the more effective they will be in working *with* groups rather than *against* them. And, the more successfully the teacher works with groups, the more students will learn and the more positive will be their attitudes. [For a readable and complete explanation of the theory and research on group influences, and their implications for the classroom teacher, see Schmuck and Schmuck (1975)]

Group Cohesiveness

Cohesiveness refers to the feeling of "oneness" among members of a group, meaning that they are more likely to talk in terms of "we" than "I." A cohesive group functions relatively free from discord and dissension because members work together doing group chores. Cohesive groups have much time to work because they spend little time in discord. Cohesive groups are able to operate under stress because members are willing to endure pain and frustration for the good of the group. The ability to operate under stress means that the same interruptions, outside distractions, and changes that cause students in uncohesive groups to become anxious and excited are hardly noticed by students in cohesive groups.

Cohesive groups place an almost ineluctable pressure upon individual members to move toward agreement, to conform. Studies by Krech, Crutchfield, and Ballachey show that cohesive groups of college students have been able to exert pressure to get members to adopt positions that were ideologically repugnant to them when questioned individually.[5] In one sample of college students, 58 percent agreed: "Free speech being a privilege rather than a right, it is proper for a society to suspend free speech when society feels itself threatened."

Pressure on members who deviate from the group is indicated by the number of communications addressed to them. When the whole group agrees on a certain position and only one member does not, then a greatly disproportionate number of communications, in the form of talking, looking, and touching, are addressed to him (Newcomb 1953). This flow of communications continues until one of two things happens; either the deviant stops deviating, or the deviant is rejected by the group (Schachter 1951).

The immense influence that a cohesive group has on deviating individual members is shown by the studies of Bogdonoff and his associates at the Duke University Medical Center.[6] They obtained evidence that there are physiological effects consequent upon deviance. While subjects were working at a perceptual judgement task, where individual judgement was artificially opposed by group opinion, sequential measures were taken of the increase in plasma-free fatty acid level, which is an index of central nervous system arousal,

5. D. Kretch, R. S. Crutchfield, and E. L. Ballachey, *Individual in Society* (New York: McGraw-Hill, 1962).

6. M. D. Bogdonoff et al., "The Modifying Effect of Conforming Behavior Upon Lipid Responses Accompanying CNS Arousal," *Clinical Research* 9 (1961):135.

and is felt by the subject as tension and stress. When a subject opposed group opinion, the level of fatty acids went up. When the subject yielded to the group, the level was reduced; when the subject continued to resist the group, the level remained high.

Increasing Group Cohesiveness

Group cohesiveness does not develop just because individual members are housed in a common area, such as students assigned to one classroom (Festinger, Schachter, and Back 1950). It is, instead, determined by the attractiveness of group membership. The more attractive group membership is, the more willingly an individual member will respond to pressure exerted by others in the group. The attractiveness of the group for an individual member is determined, in turn, by how well the group satisfies needs. Groups which satisfy needs are attractive. The basic psychological needs students can satisfy in groups are: (1) the need to be an active learner; (2) the need to socialize; and (3) the need to feel confident and secure. Students in "healthy" classrooms believe they are able to meet these needs through group participation. Students in "unhealthy" classroom groups believe they are unable to meet these needs through group participation.

Group cohesiveness can be increased in these five major ways (Bany and Johnson, 1964; Cartwright and Zander 1965):

1. *Stress the satisfactions the group offers.* Dramatize the many new and interesting activities they can do in the group. When they complete an activity, discuss how interesting it was and how more like it are to come. A preview of coming events on Monday morning creates excited anticipation about the coming week. A review of the past week's events on Friday afternoon heightens their awareness of how enjoyable the week really was, and whets their appetites for the next week. Often, stressing satisfactions is accomplished by turning negative discussions into positive ones. For example, instead of asking what's wrong with the learning centers, ask what they like best about them. (Stressing the satisfactions of group participation is one purpose of the *morale building* strategy described in the next chapter.)

2. *Increase the person's prestige within the group.* The prestige of group membership can be emphasized by frequently reminding students that they are now *first* graders, *seventh* graders, and *juniors.* Favorable evaluations of *this* group can be given by prestigious persons from outside the group, such as the principal, a visiting specialist, or another teacher. For example, when the class gives a play, invite the principal to come, admire, and give public praise.

   Prestige is also enhanced by raising an individual student's status within a class. A student who is an isolate can be paired in activities with students having high status or given tasks that are desired by other students, such as being ball monitor. The higher the person's status rises in the group, the more attractive group membership becomes. (The identification of student status is discussed in the upcoming section on *group structure.* Instruments for measuring status are suggested in the subsequent chapter on Group-Leader Assessment Instruments.)

3. *Engage students in cooperative activities.* Engaging in cooperative activities with members of a group makes the group more cohesive, while engaging in competitive activities makes the group less cohesive. In fact, groups will sometimes become cooperative in order to reduce competition introduced by the teacher. Recall the discussion earlier of the formation of oppositional student cultures when all students are judged by the same standards and thus, only the *few* best are rewarded. The purpose of the opposition culture is to reduce the levels of performance of the best students to a level attainable by most students. (The major purpose of the group-leader strategy of *group projects* is to engage students in cooperative group activities. The strategy is discussed in the next chapter.)

4. *Increase the frequency of interaction.* Increasing the frequency of interaction within the group makes it more attractive to individual members. Interaction is increased by having students work together on planning and carrying out cooperative projects. (Increasing the frequency of interaction between members of a group is a purpose of three group-leader strategies discussed in the next chapter: *group projects, group discussion,* and *role play.*)

5. *Distinguish between this group and other groups.* The effect on group cohesion of distinguishing between this group and others is most clearly evidenced in school sports. Each school has its own identifying colors, mascots, and cheer leaders; "our" team plays "their" team. Participation in competitive activities builds group cohesion when members participate as a *group.* Competition between different classroom groups can take many very healthy forms, such as whole class spelling bees, yard clean-up, and speech contests and debates. (Distinguishing between this group and others is developed through the use of the *morale building* strategy, discussed in the next chapter.)

Some students are not attracted by group membership, and so cannot be influenced by other members of the group. These students constitute a particularly difficult problem for two reasons. First, because group influence is not effective in motivating them to learn and develop positive attitudes, the only way to affect their behavior is through teacher influence. Second, silent and nonparticipating members have a negative effect on other members of the classroom group. They tend to reduce group productivity and satisfaction,

Students with Low Needs for Group Affiliation

and increase defensiveness (Smith 1957). Students with low needs for group affiliation fall into four categories, each requiring different treatment.

Rejected. These students have been rejected numerous times, and have finally concluded that no one likes them, or could possibly like them. They show up as isolates on a sociogram (discussed in chapter 9). They vary all the way from the completely withdrawn, autistic student who requires special therapy to the quiet and reserved student.

The teacher should concentrate on increasing the status within the group of rejected students. This will place a burden on other students, as the negativeness of the confirmed isolate is contagious. The thoroughly rejected isolate should only be paired with very self-confident students of high status. The teacher should find ways to give the student a feeling of academic success, perhaps by individualizing more. The teacher may also want to use some of the counselor-role strategies discussed in Section 3 of this book.

Egocentric. These students are not able to do anything other than follow their own impulses. They lack loyalty and are self-assertive and narcissistic (Ausubel 1954). They lack the ability to share the learning drives of either the teacher or their peers. They have never grown beyond the egocentric and narcissistic stage of two- and three-year-old children. These students are frequently labeled "predelinquent."

About the best the teacher can hope to accomplish with these students is to minimize the negative effects of their present deviant behavior by using teacher influence in a carefully planned program of *desist techniques* (discussed in the next chapter). At the same time, the teacher can use counselor-role strategies to help these students grow beyond their present egocentric stage (discussed in Section 3). Students with severe egocentric problems should have special psychiatric therapy.

Young "Old-Timer." These students seldom evidence any motivation or learning difficulties; on the contrary, they are frequently excellent students. It is just that they act like "old folks," and they are much too young for that. They seem to find adult relationships more attractive than social peer affiliation. They should be helped to use both sources of encouragement.

The group-leader strategies of *group discussion, group projects, morale building,* and *role play* are all effective in helping the young "old-timers" discover the many pleasures of social peer-group affiliation (see the next chapter).

Anomic Individual.   The personal disorientation, anxiety, and social isolation of anomic individuals is described in detail by Reisman[7] and Harvey.[8] Anomic individuals become the "hippies," and range from simply being peaceably "turned off" to normal society to actively resisting society through participation in violent activist organizations. Unfortunately, we are seeing more and more of this type of person. They have a high need for social affiliation, but somehow the normal classroom setting has not provided the satisfaction they desire. On a sociometric test they do not choose other students in the classroom, and the other students do not choose them.

Their lack of affiliation with the class can come from a number of causes. First, it may be the result of coming from a highly authoritarian family, and then being completely lost when assigned to an open-space classroom with sixty or more other students who are so totally independent that group cohesiveness has never developed in the classroom. A major weakness of some individualized programs is that students never do anything as a *group.* As a result, group cohesion never develops and the satisfactions attendant upon group participation are not available. The class is a "faceless" group of individuals, each doing his or her own thing and affected only by teacher influence.

Second, their lack of affiliation may be the result of a substantial extraclassroom basis for solidarity, such as exists in a local neighborhood or in team sports (Coleman 1961). The student who derives a great deal of satisfaction from participation in a neighborhood gang or Little League team may show little interest in or response to the relationships offered by members of the classroom group.

The group-leader strategies of *group discussion, group projects,* and *morale building* can be used in making group participation more attractive. There is little the teacher can do about the negative influence of a student's family life, neighborhood participation, or membership in extraclass team sports. However, there is much the teacher can do to counteract these influences by making participation in the classroom group more attractive.

---

7. D. Riesman, N. Glazer, and P. Denney, *The Lonely Crowd* (Garden City, N.Y.: Doubleday & Co., 1955).

8. O. J. Harvey, D. E. Hunt, and H. M. Schroder, *Conceptual Systems and Personality Development* (New York: John Wiley & Sons, Inc., 1961).

Why Increase Group
Cohesion?
The more teachers can depend on the *group* to influence individual students, the less the teacher has to use precious *personal* influence. In fact, one symptom of cohesive classroom groups is the *seeming* unimportance of the teacher. In a cohesive classroom, the teacher's physical presence appears to be inconsequential. Students act the same whether or not the teacher is in the room. Centuries ago Lao-tzu characterized the *Best Leaders,* and their *seeming* lack of influence are follows:

> Of the best leaders
> The people do not know that they exist;
> The next best they love and praise;
> The next they fear;
> And the next they revile.
> When they do not command the people's faith
> Some will lose faith in them,
> (And then they resort to oaths).
> But of the best, when their task is accomplished, their work done,
> The people all remark,
> "We have done it ourselves."

For those things where group influence cannot be made effective, the teacher *must* use personal influence. The necessity for personal influence is greatest with those students having low needs for group affiliation. The more things which the teacher can accomplish effectively through group influence, the greater the teacher's influence will be with the deviant students. If the only cross word heard from the teacher all day is directed at one deviating student, that cross word is likely to have a more powerful effect on the deviant than if cross words are heard from the teacher all the time.

Teachers are far more effective in improving students' attitudes when they use group influence than when they rely solely on personal influence. As Scheidlinger says, "Values and attitudes are most readily internalized when they are group values."[9] And the more cohesive a group, the greater its influence will be on individual members to internalize attitudes.

Teachers are far more effective in improving student motivation to learn when they use group influence, because participation in a cohesive group can increase an individual member's motivation to complete instructional tasks. Using group influence for motivation,

9. S. Scheidlinger, *Psychoanalysis and Group Behavior* (New York: W. W. Norton & Co., 1952), p. 186.

rather than relying solely on teacher influence, has even more important long-term consequences. As Hilgard and Russell point out:

> Motivation is important not only as an energizer and director of learning but as a habit-system in itself. Children learn to respond to the set of motives used in the school. This is one reason why a teacher who appeals to fear fails to get results in a situation where the fear element is removed. It is the reason high grades or stars in spelling sometimes produce perfect spelling lessons but also produce incorrect general writing.[10]

Motivation to learn will be strongest and most lasting when it is self-initiating and independent of the teacher. Group influence will be around long after the teacher is gone.

As you read this discussion of group cohesion, you undoubtedly gave some thought to the potentially negative aspects of the phenomenon. The phenonenon of group cohesion, like that of fire, is neither good nor bad; it is neutral. It seems good if it enables you to achieve a desired end, and bad if it keeps you from achieving that end. A negative example of group cohesion was mentioned earlier, in the description of the formation of oppositional student cultures intended to lower the overall level of student performance. The more cohesive that oppositional group, the less effective the teacher's instructional efforts will be. The development of positive group actions is the next topic dealt with, *group standards.*

Group Standards

A group standard exists when there are agreements about the behavior group members should and should not enact. In the larger society outside the classroom, group standards are the foundation of the moral order. It is "morally right" to do some things and "morally wrong" to do others. Individual conformity to a moral code at some level is a sign of group membership, and a chief criterion for the individual's continued acceptance by the group. In civilized societies, group standards are codified in writing. *The Declaration of the Thirteen United States of America* states, "We hold these truths to be self-evident, that all men are created equal, that they are endowed by their Creator with certain unalienable rights, that among these are

---

10. E. R. Hilgard and D. H. Russell, "Motivation in School Learning," in *Learning and Instruction,* Forty-Ninth Yearbook of the National Society for the Study of Education, Part I, N. Henry, ed. (Chicago: University of Chicago Press, 1950), p. 68.

Life, Liberty and the pursuit of Happiness." It is "morally right" in this country to treat all men equally, and "morally wrong" to treat them unequally. The group standards are further clarified in numerous criminal and civil statutes by all levels of governing units, from townships to the federal government. Many group standards of the larger society are not defined in laws, but are nonetheless understood by members of the society. For example, the women's liberation groups are actively seeking to redefine the unwritten group standards which specify the acceptable roles of men and women.

In the classroom, group standards are the behaviors that cohesive classroom groups pressure individual student members to exhibit. Group pressure is usually not necessary because members of the group feel an obligation to adhere to group standards. Group pressure is applied in two situations: (1) when an individual member deviates from the group standard, and (2) when an external force is introduced into the group. The first situation is important to the teacher because group standards in a particular classroom may or may not facilitate the school's goals of cognition and attitude formation. From the viewpoint of the teacher, group standards in classrooms may vary from the altruistic to the immoral. The second situation is important because teachers are perceived as external forces in classroom groups, even when they are very effective group leaders.

Individual Deviation   When a member deviates from the group standard, subtle but powerful sanctions are used against him. If it is a group standard to cooperate with the teacher, then an individual who acts uncooperatively will receive sanction messages from other members of the group. The sanctions may consist of a slight disapproving movement of the eyebrow by a class member with high status, a sudden aloofness on the part of many members, or even open ridicule. On the other hand, if it is a group standard to be uncooperative, an individual who gives a good report in class or acts in any other cooperative way will receive messages of disapproval.

Often the group standard is not really oppositional, just inappropriate for the situation. For example, the teacher might have very successfully established cooperation between students as a group standard. The standard facilitates students' attainment of cognitive and affective goals in most subjects. But it is an inappropriate group standard for a spelling test. That is a time for working alone. In order to conduct spelling tests successfully, the teacher must develop a group standard specifically for that activity.

When the group standard in a classroom impedes the attainment of cognitive and affective goals, each member of the class is caught between two opposing influences, the teacher's and the group's. Teachers must recognize this impasse, and not operate on the mistaken assumption that teacher standards are identical to group standards. While it may be a teacher standard that students should walk in hallways, it may not be a group standard, as evidenced by the fact that students run when a teacher is not present and exercising personal influence. The greater the number of instances where teacher standards and group standards are identical, the healthier the classroom group is, and the happier individuals in the group are. Conversely, the wider the range of disagreement and the more frequently individual members are caught between the teacher and the group, the more unhealthy the group and the less satisfied the individual members. In the latter situation, group members are perceived by the teacher, quite correctly, as trying to undercut almost everything the teacher does. This is very frustrating for both teachers and students.

Group standards affect the way individual members respond to external forces. In the classroom, the most important external force is the teacher. The response is illustrated by two studies. Kelly and Volkert studied the relationship between group influences and individual attitude change in a troop of Boy Scouts.[11] First, they assessed each individual member's commitment to the group standards. A week later an adult gave a talk to the troop in which he criticized many Scouting activities. The experimenters then reassessed individual attitudes. The results indicated that those Scouts who were most committed to Scouting were the least influenced by the commuication from the adult speaker, and those who were least committed were the most influenced.

External Forces

When applied to the classroom, the conclusions of this study indicate that teachers will be ineffective in changing the attitudes of students when those students are committed to an opposing group standard. If the group standard is that a student should reject anything having to do with school, such as reading, the teacher can expect to have little personal influence on those students firmly committed to the standard. Teachers who are unsuccessful in changing

11. H. H. Kelley and E. H. Volkert, "The Resistence to Change of Group-Anchored Attitudes," *American Sociological Review* 17 (1952):453–465.

that group standard will likely be ineffective in helping students committed to it become skillful readers. If the teacher is not successful in altering the group standards, the students will become disabled readers, no matter how competent the teacher is in reading instruction. Even providing highly motivating instructional activities is not likely to be effective because group influence is not thereby reduced.

Not only can teachers expect to be ineffective in changing the attitudes of committed group members, a study by Merei indicates that a group will attempt to get a teacher to adopt the group's standard as the price for the teacher being influential with individual members in the group.[12] Merei made initial observations in free-play situations of children ranging in age from four to eleven in order to determine the natural "leaders" and "followers." Groups consisting of three followers were then formed and allowed to play together. After several sessions each group formed its own distinctive group standards having to do with such things as the division of toys, ceremonies about their use, kinds of games played, and the sequence of games. Then a child who had previously been identified as a natural leader was introduced into each group. In virtually all cases, the group forced its newly formed standards on the leader and the leader was able to exert control and direction only by working within the framework of the group standards. Merei concluded that when the leader is confronted by a cohesive group having standards, the leader proves weak, even though when confronting them singly the leader is stronger than any member of the group.

Teachers meet established group standards at the beginning of the school year when students seem committed to what last year's teacher did. Teachers taking over a class in mid-year often face severe tests of dealing with established group standards. The only time that previously developed group standards become a problem is when they are directly oppositional to the teacher's standards. When group standards are oppositional, teachers can do three things.

The *first* thing teachers can do is use their personal influence to get students to follow the teacher's standards. How successful they are will depend on the strength of their personal influence and the weakness of the group influences. Teachers will want to build their personal influence in every way possible.

A *second* way to deal with oppositional group standards is to reduce the cohesiveness of the group holding them. A group's

---

12. F. Merei, "Group Leadership and Institutalization," *Human Relations* 2 (1949):23–39.

cohesiveness is reduced in the opposite way that it is built. (Refer to the earlier discussion of increasing cohesion.)

1. Stress the dissatisfactions this group offers.
2. Do not increase students' prestige within the group.
3. Engage students in activities where they compete with others in the group.
4. Decrease the frequency of interaction between members of the group.
5. Do not distinguish between this group and other groups, except to comment favorably on the other groups.

The *third* way that teachers can respond when group standards are directly oppositional to teacher standards is to change the group standards. This is the next topic.

Research indicates that under certain conditions group standards can be changed through the use of group decision making. Two variables account for most of the change brought about by group decision making: (1) the group makes a *definite decision* (it does not just talk about the problems); and (2) the group reaches a decision by *consensus* (the greater the number of those that agree with the decision, the stronger the general commitment to it).

Changing Group Standards

Group decision making is most effective in changing group standards when the variables of definite decision and consensus are combined in a three-stage procedure that Lewin has characterized as *unfreezing, moving,* and *freezing.*[13] The *unfreezing* step is a kind of "catharsis" which seems to be necessary before prejudices can be removed. To break open the shell of complacency and self-righteousness, it is sometimes necessary to deliberately bring about an emotional stir-up. In the *moving* step, group members express their opinions in an active and free argument. They state their positions rather than try to persuade one another. The greater the number of members that participate in the discussion, the more firm the group's commitment to the decision.

Finally, the group moves toward a convergence, a *freezing* of their decision. A group has not yet moved toward convergence when minority and majority positions must be resolved by formal voting. The discussion must not be allowed to *freeze* until members achieve a consensus, so that *everyone* feels committed to the final

13. K. Lewin, "Studies in Group Decision," in Cartwright and Zander, *Group Dynamics: Research and Theory* (Evanston, Ill.: Row, Peterson and Company, 1953).

decision. The discussion also must not be allowed to freeze until the standards have been made very clear to all members. A study by Raven and Rietsema indicates that when group standards are not perceived clearly by members, the result is disinterest, hostility, and lower feelings of belongingness.[14]

The research on group decision making indicates that group decisions are far more effective in changing group standards than are exhortations and admonitions by the teacher. Every teacher should make a sign that says "Lectures Don't Change Behavior" and post it where she can see it every time she feels tempted to lecture. Group standards cannot be established by teachers exhorting students to "right actions." About all moralistic lectures accomplish is a sense of relief for the teacher. That may be a necessary escape valve for the teacher to use occasionally, but a sense of relief should not be confused with changed group standards.

Two strategies based on the research on decision making, *group discussion* and *role play,* are explained in the next chapter.

Group Influence and Conformity

Unthinking conformity to the "group" is, quite correctly, a particular concern to many teachers. Much of this discussion has dealt with pressure on students to conform to standards that teachers do not support, such as low work output and doing only what one has to do to get by. However, group influence can be put into the service of high productivity and even of promoting diversity and encouraging individual freedom. Canadian studies in mental health show that the freedom to differ and the right to one's own position can be explicitly built into group standards, with the consequence that group influences are in the direction of promoting individuality.[15]

Group standards can be a critical element in a teacher's attempt to individualize. Individualization does not work when the able student, or the highly motivated one, becomes a captive of group standards which prohibit maximum individual progress. On the other hand, in classes where the group standard promotes individuality and diligence, all students are in a field of force that tends to induce maximum learning effort.

---

14. B. H. Raven and J. Rietsema, "The Effects of Varied Clarity of Group Goal and Group Path Upon the Individual and His Relation to His Group," *Human Relations* 10 (1957): 29–45.

15. See *Promotion of Mental Health in Primary and Secondary Schools: An Evaluation of Four Projects,* Report No. 18 (Topeka, Kansas: Group for the Advancement of Psychiatry, January 1951), p. 15.

Group Structure

Groups are characterized by a system of social stratification where individual members have a certain status and are involved in definite patterns of interaction. The same criteria that determine "liking" and "disliking" affect status: sex, age, personality, size, looks, material posessions, athletic ability, academic ability, race, ethnicity, and social class. Status determines an individual's influence with other members of the group. Persons of higher status influence those of lower status, but persons of lower status do not influence those of higher status.

Status affects the way a person is judged, both by other members of the group and by the teacher. The same academic or social behavior that teachers and other students consider acceptable when done by a student of high status is considered by them to be unacceptable when done by a person of low status. Persons of low status are more likely to be poor students, become ill, and display discipline problems. The health of the classroom group is affected by the openness of the structure, by the possibility for persons to raise their status. Classroom health is also negatively affected by the presence of subgroup rivalry. Improvements in group structure can result in a healthier classroom group, with its resulting beneficial effects. It can also bring marked improvements in the academic and social performance of the deviants who possess very low status in the group.

A person's location in the structure of the group is of decisive importance. It determines what the person can do, space for free movement, degree of autonomy, and vulnerability to arbitrary control by others. Students of lower status behave in a deferential manner toward those of higher status, are influenced more by those of higher status, and tend to imitate those of higher status even when the higher status individuals make no overt attempt to bring this about (Lippitt, Polansky, Redl, and Rosen 1952). An individual's location in the group structure determines how attractive the group is to him, and thus the influence the group has over him (Jackson 1952). The higher a person's status in the group, the more attractive group membership is for that person and thus the more willing the person is to be influenced by the group.

Students that teachers perceive as "deviant" are usually of low status. Their deviancy is partially the result of the unattractiveness of group membership, and their unwillingness to be influenced by the group. It is also the result of the tendency of groups to eventually reject members of low status who persistently deviate. When students are rejected by the group, the members of the group stop trying to influence them, as indicated by a decrease in the number of sanctioning communications directed at the rejected persons (Schachter 1951). When a person is no longer influenced by the group, then the only influence that remains is that of the teacher. In addition, low-status students can be expected to behave in an essentially ego-defensive manner (Hurwitz, Zander, and Hymovitch 1953), which is manifested as attention-getting behavior.

Status determines the way a student's behavior is judged by both the teacher and other students in the group. The group tends to judge low-status students to be failing even when their performance is satisfactory, while mistakes of high-status students are ignored (Zillig 1928). In fact, the lower a member's status in the group, the more his performances are underestimated by others in the group. The higher the status, the more his performances are overestimated (Harvey 1953). Teachers seem to judge student's behavior in terms of both sex and status. Low-status boys have been shown to receive teacher criticism while low-status girls receive support (Lippitt and Gold 1959). The learning attainments and social behaviors of low-status students, especially if they are boys, may be evaluated lower than they deserve to be. A low-status student has a difficult time gaining acceptance from either the teacher or group.

While the exact causal relationship cannot be identified, it is clear that status is correlated with a student's health, discipline, and academic performance. Low-status students are usually low in energy, listless, and low in social effectiveness (Northway and Rooks 1956). The lower a person's status, the lower his reading achievement. And this relationship seems to hold true irrespective of the socio-economic level of the school community (Porterfield and Schlichting 1961). The lower a person's status within the group, the more prone he is to become ill and display disciplinary problems (French 1951). The poor health, academic achievement, and discipline of low-status students is not surprising since the vast amount of energy expended in maintaining group relations is energy channeled away from learning activities. Raising their status in the group will reduce the diversion of energy and will result in improved health, academic achievement, and discipline.

The formation of subgroups affects group cohesion, and, consequently, group influence over individual members. When three or more people choose each other exclusively, a *clique* is formed. The presence of cliques makes a less cohesive total group. (Festinger, Schachter and Back 1950). The more cohesive subgroups are, the less cohesive the total classroom group is. The more often subgroups get involved in rival feuds for power and prestige with other subgroups and members of the classroom group, the more the unity of the total group suffers.

The more cohesive the subgroups become, the more the teacher must depend on personal influence. When subgroups are fully *cleaved* from each other, so that there are no friendship choices across subgroups, they feud continuously for prestige and power. Members in one subgroup try to make themselves look good and members in other subgroups look bad. The feuding is not unlike rival street-gangs battling for control of a neighborhood. The normal resentment of the teacher's authority is augmented by an even fiercer resentment of any teacher attempts to interfere in the feud. The teacher must therefore use personal influence *both* to keep peace between rival subgroups *and* to maintain general classroom discipline and affect student motivation and learning. In these classrooms, teachers must depend so much on personal influence that rebuilding it becomes a continual problem.

Subgroups are organized around the same criteria that determine "liking" and "disliking": sex, age, personality, looks, material possessions, athletic ability, race, ethnicity, and social class. Subgroups based on sex have formed when the friendly flirting between boys and girls develops into a feud between mutually exclusive subgroups—all boys on one side and all girls on the other. A full *cleavage* between the subgroups has developed when there are no friendship choices between members of different subgroups. The more cohesive the sex-based subgroups become, the more the teacher must use personal influence in settling arguments between the boys and girls. Cleavage along lines of race, ethnicity, and social class are even more destructive than when along sex lines because they are usually reinforced by the society outside the classroom.

In healthy classrooms, subgroups are really no more than loosely organized "friendship clusters." The friendship clusters are not cohesive because friendship choices are directed both toward people in the cluster and people outside the cluster. The major allegiance of students is still to the classroom group. The existence of *friendship clusters, cliques,* and *cleavages* becomes very obvious to the teacher when a sociometric instrument is used.

Group structure can be altered in two ways: (1) by providing opportunities for *social mobility,* and (2) having *cooperative group activities.*

Altering Group Structure

Social Mobility.   Social mobility refers to the possibilities for raising one's status in the group. Research shows that where there is no perceived opportunity for social mobility, low-status individuals develop hostile feelings towards themselves and the group. A major deterrent to social mobility in classrooms is rigid grouping patterns. Rigid grouping patterns have the effect of reducing motivation and lowering the self-esteem of those students in the permanently low groups (Martin and Pavan 1976). A teacher can increase students' possibilities for social mobility by moving from ability-grouping patterns to patterns such as individualized and nongraded (see chapter 3).

The social mobility of low-status students can be encouraged by increasing their *positive visibility,* meaning that they are placed in situations where other students become more *aware* of them doing *good things.* For example, studies by Bavelas show that the more centrally located people are in the communication system, the higher their status in the system.[16]

In Figure 7.1, the person indicated by the letter *A* will have a higher status in Communication Pattern II than in Communication Pattern I. A student can be placed in Communication Pattern II by having him hand out papers or collect them. The student is given an opportunity to behave in a positive way, and in a situation where others have to interact with him. The positive visability will raise his status in the classroom group.

The social mobility of low-status students can also be encouraged by placing them in work groups with students of high status. A low-status student might be assigned with two high-status students to prepare a bulletin board for the classroom.

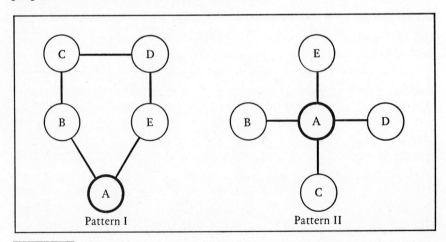

Figure 7.1

Pattern I   Pattern II

---

16. A Bavelas, "Communication Patterns in Task-Oriented Groups," *Journal of the Acoustical Society of America* 22 (1950):725–730.

Cooperative Group Activities. Cooperative group activities refers to situations where individual members of a group come together to work toward a common goal. Research indicates that participation in cooperative group projects and group discussions leads to improved group structures. The strategies of *group projects* and *group discussion* are explained in the next chapter. Studies also show that role-playing techniques lead to improved group structures. (The strategy of *role play* is also explained in the next chapter.)

Activities intended to improve students' peer relationships should be started in the early grades because at later times the changes require personality alterations (Laughlin 1954).

CONCLUSION

Your goal as a group leader is to organize group conditions in such a way that a "healthy" classroom atmosphere is created. That goal is characterized by the letter entitled "Help One Another," at the beginning of this chapter. Healthy groups work harder, make more sacrifices for the group, more readily extol its virtues, are more satisfied, interact more often, and agree with one another more often than do members of unhealthy groups. Students in healthy groups develop more positive attitudes about themselves and others. They are likely to learn more. They are more pleasant to be with and, only in healthy classrooms will teachers be successful in using the instructional-manager strategies that are intended to enable them to individualize more, to improve students' ability to be self-directive, to increase student motivation, and to deal with deviants more adequately.

Two types of group conditions were identified, those the teacher alters directly by *personal influence* and those the teacher alters indirectly by affecting *group influence.* Your personal influence with students is determined by: (1) their affection for you; (2) the perception they have of your knowledge, teaching competence, and status as an adult; (3) your over use of personal influence; and (4) the degree of individualization in your program. You can increase personal influence by using the minimum level of personal influence necessary to achieve results, by building your personal influence, and by using alternative means to achieving results other than personal influence.

Three types of group influences were identified: (1) *Group cohesiveness,* the group's feeling of "we-ness"; (2) *group standards,* the group's rules; and (3) *group structure,* the differing statuses and subgroups, each possessing differing influence over individual members of the group. The more understanding you have of these group influences, the more effective you will be in working *with* groups rather than against them. The characteristics of each type of group influence was explained, as well as general ways that they could be improved.

Strategies for beneficially altering teacher and group influences are explained in the next chapter. Instruments for assessing how effectively they are being altered are suggested in the subsequent chapter.

REFERENCES

Bidwell, C. E. 1973. The social psychology of teaching. In *Second Handbook of Research on Teaching,* R. Travers, ed. Chicago: Rand McNally and Company, pp. 413–449.

Lippitt, R; Polansky, N.; Redl, F.; and Rosen, S. 1952. The dynamics of power. *Human Relations* 5:37–64.

Thibault, J., and Kelley, H. 1959. Power and dependence. In *The Social Psychology of Groups.* New York: John Wiley & Sons, Inc.

Kounin, J. S., and Gump, P. V. 1970. *Discipline and group management in classrooms.* New York: Holt, Rinehart and Winston.

Newcomb, T. M. 1953. An approach to the study of the communicative arts. *Psychological Review* 60:393–404.

Schachter, S. 1951. Deviation, rejection, and communication. *Journal of Abnormal and Social Psychology* 46:190–207.

Festinger, L; Schachter, S; and Back, K. 1950. *Social pressures in informal groups: a study of human factors in housing.* New York: Harper.

Bany, M. A., and Johnson, L. V. 1964. *Classroom group behavior.* New York: The Macmillan Company, pp. 72, 73.

Cartwright D., and Zander, A. 1953. *Group dynamics: research and theory.* Evanston, Ill.: Row, Peterson and Company.

Smith, E. E. 1957. The effects of clear and unclear role expectations on group productivity and defensiveness. *Journal of Abnormal and Social Psychology* 60 (September 1957):213–218.

Ausubel, D. P. 1954. *Theory and problems of adolescent development.* New York: Grune & Stratton, p. 357.

Coleman, J. S. 1961. *The adolescent society.* New York: The Free Press.

Jackson, J. 1952. Analysis of interpersonal relations in a formal organization. Ph.D. diss., University of Michigan.

Hurwitz, A.; Zander, L.; and Hymovitch, B. 1953. Some effects of power on the relations among group members. In Cartwright and Zander, *Group Dynamics: Research and Theory*. Evanston, Ill.: Row, Peterson and Company.

Zillig, M. 1928. Einstellung and Aussage. *Zeitschrift für Psychologie* 61:58–106.

Harvey, O. J. 1953. An experimental approach to the study of status relations in informal groups. *American Sociological Review* 18:357–367.

Lippitt, R., and Gold, M. 1959. Classroom social structure as a mental health problem. *Journal of Social Issues* 15:40–49.

Northway, M. L., and Rooks, M. M. 1956. Creativity and sociometric status in children. In *Sociometry and the Science of Man*, J. L. Moreno, ed. New York: Beacon House, Inc., pp. 194–201.

Porterfield, O. V., and Schlichting, H. F. 1961. Peer status and reading achievement: *Journal of Educational Research* 54 (April):291–297.

French, R. L. 1951. Sociometric status and individual adjustment among naval recruits. *Journal of Abnormal and Social Psychology* 46:64–72.

Martin, L., and Pavan, B. 1976. Current research on open space, nongrading, vertical grouping, and team teaching. *Phi Delta Kappan* 57:310–315.

Laughlin, F. 1954. *The peer status of sixth- and seventh-grade children*. New York: Bureau of Publications, Teachers College, Columbia University.

Schmuck, R. A., and Schmuck P. A. 1975. *Group processes in the classroom*. Dubuque, Iowa: Wm. C. Brown Company Publishers.

FOR FURTHER READING

For reviews of the theory and research on group cohesiveness see:

Cartwright, D., and Zander, A. *Group Dynamics: Research and Theory*. Evanston, Ill.: Row, Peterson and Company, 1953.

Brown, R. *Social Psychology*. New York: The Free Press, 1965, pp. 663–687.

For reviews of the theory and research on group standards see:

Cartwright, D., and Zander, A. Group Dynamics: Research and Theory. Evanston, Ill.: Row, Peterson and Company, 1953., part 3, "Group Pressures and Group Standards."

Morse, W. C. "Diagnosing and Building Relationships Between Group and Individual Class Members." In *The Dynamics of Instructional Groups*, N. B. Henry, ed., The Fifty-Ninth Yearbook of the National Society for the Study of Education. Chicago: The University of Chicago Press, 1960.

Thibault, J., and Kelley, H. "Power and Dependence." In *The Social Psychology of Groups.* New York: John Wiley & Sons, Inc., 1959.

For further reading on changing group standards see:

Bennett, E. B. "The Relationship of Group Discussion, Decision, Commitment, and Consensus to Individual Action." Ph.D. diss., University of Michigan, 1952.

Horwitz, M. "The Effects of Group Goal-Setting and Locomotion on Motivational Processes in the Individual." Ph.D. diss., University of Michigan, 1950.

Kostick, M. M. "An Experiment in Group Decision." *Journal of Teacher Education* 8 (1957): 67–72.

Lewin, K. "Group Decision and Social Change." In *Readings in Social Psychology,* Newcomb and Hartley, eds. New York: Holt, Rinehart and Winston, 1947.

Pennington, D. F., Harary, F., and Bass, B. M. "Some Effects of Decision and Discussion on Coalescence, Change, and Effectiveness." *Journal of Applied Psychology* 42 (1958):404–408.

For reviews of the theory and research on group structure see:

Bany, M. A., and Johnson, L. V. *Classroom Group Behavior.* New York: The Macmillan Company, 1964, chapters 4 and 8, and part IV.

Cartwright, D., and Zander, A. *Group Dynamics: Research and Theory.* Evanston, Ill.: Row, Peterson and Company, 1953, part 5, "The Structural Properties of Groups."

For reviews of the theory and research on social mobility see:

Kelley, H. H. "Communication in Experimentally Created Hierarchies." *Human Relations* 4(1951):39–56.

Thibault, J. "An Experimental Study of the Cohesiveness of Underprivileged Groups." *Human Relations* 3 (1950):251–278.

For further reading on cooperative group activities see:

Cook, L. A. "An Experimental Sociographic Study of a Stratified Tenth-Grade Class." *American Sociological Review* 10 (1945):250–261.

Cunningham, R. *Understanding Group Behavior of Boys and Girls.* New York: Teachers College, Columbia University, 1951.

Fox, R. S. "Better Human Relations Through the Social Studies." *Grade Teacher* 75 (April 1958): 100–104.

Lippitt, R., and Zander, A. "Reality-Practice as Educational Method." *Psychodrama Monographs* 9 (1947):3–23.

Shaftel, G., and Shaftel, F. "Role Playing: The Problem Story." An Intergroup Education Pamphlet, National Conference of Christians and Jews, 1952.

8

Strategies

Healthy classroom atmospheres can be created by teachers who competently use group-leader strategies that alter the teacher's personal influence and the influence of the group in a beneficial way. Five group-leader strategies are explained:

1. Group projects
2. Group discussion
3. Role play
4. Morale building
5. Desist techniques

The first four strategies are intended to alter group influence, which reduces the necessity for the teacher to use personal influence. The fifth strategy uses the teacher's personal influence.

GROUP PROJECTS

Student participation in cooperative group projects has a powerful effect on the group atmosphere in a classroom. The key ingredient in this strategy is *cooperation.* When students are given an opportunity to achieve their basic needs (for action, socialization, and security) by participation in activities involving cooperative effort, the standards the group develops emphasize the cooperation of the students with each other and with the teacher. As standards emphasizing co-operation develop and influence students, the teacher can become less dependent on personal influence. In addition, activities involving cooperative effort provide a means of changing the group structure by breaking down cliques and reducing the number of isolates.

The teacher should not confuse cooperation with an absence of competition. A lack of competition can be achieved in solitary activities, where each student's success or failure depends on his own efforts. Some examples of solitary activities are programmed readers, worksheets, and games or art projects done individually. A healthy group atmosphere will usually not be developed through the use of solitary activities because interaction between students is unnecessary, and even detrimental, to successful completion of the activity.

Characteristics

Activities that are suitable for group projects have three character-istics: (1) they require the cooperative effort of two or more stu-dents; (2) they are intrinsically motivating; and (3) they are mean-ingful.

Cooperative Effort The cooperative effort of two or more students is necessary for a group project. The activity should be organized so that it can be successfully completed only if the participating students apply the motto, "All for one, and one for all." A play wherein each student has a part is an activity that requires cooperative effort. The play will be a success only if the participating actors work together as a closely knit team.

Some examples of projects requiring cooperative effort follow this paragraph. The size of the group doing each project can vary from two students to the entire class. As a rule, the teacher should assign the minimum number of students to a project and then or-ganize parallel projects. It is better to have the class do four dif-ferent plays, giving each student a part, than it is to do one play and have some students who are not involved.

Examples of Group Projects

1. A play is prepared that will be presented to other members of the class, to other classes, and to parents. The play might be intended solely for

entertainment, or it may be part of a social studies unit and intended to illustrate life in such places as Jamestown, the community, or a factory.

2. A set for a play is prepared. The set may be for a play this group is producing, or for one that some other group is doing. The set should be sufficiently portable to enable it to be moved to different classes.

3. A motion picture or television program is produced. The production might be completely simulated, or actually shot on inexpensive 8mm film or with a small video-tape recorder. The program is shown to other members of the class, to other classes, and to parents.

4. A large mural is prepared that covers one wall of the room and requires the efforts of many people. The mural might illustrate agriculture, from the farm to the consumer's table. It might show the sequence of industrial development or the history of flight.

5. A newspaper for the class or school is produced. As part of a study of newspapers, students can assume the roles of editors, artists, and so forth. The newspaper can deal with current events in the school (*Note:* A newspaper is not a group project if students write stories individually and then submit them to the teacher for editing and approval. When the teacher assumes the key roles, interaction between students is eliminated, and the effort becomes a solitary activity.)

6. Large objects are measured, such as a baseball diamond or a school building. The objects are so big that a number of students must cooperate in holding the tape measure and recording the results. This activity may be part of a study of metric measurement.

7. Students in the early grades conduct dramatic plays with large objects that can be moved around. As part of a study of the community, they might set up a part of the room as a city and play that they are shopkeepers, shoppers, police officers, and so forth. As part of a study of transportation, they might set up a seaport or an airport and play the various appropriate roles.

8. A choir or a band is formed that performs for other members of the class, for other classes, and for parents and community groups. Teachers with musical talent may want to consider forming their own class choir or band even though the school may have a special music teacher.

9. Illustrative newspapers are prepared. As part of a study of early America, two newspapers might be produced (one revolutionary and one loyalist) that report on one event of the American Revolution. As part of a study of modern China, an American newspaper and a Chinese newspaper might be produced that record an event that will likely be viewed differently in each country.

10. A papier-mâché object is constructed that is so large that the cooperative efforts of many students are required. As part of a study of ancient reptiles, a three to six foot dinosaur might be built.

11. Students learn to play games as part of their social studies unit. A group is assigned to identify suitable games, and to teach these games to other members of the class. Games played in Colonial America, modern Japan or ancient Mexico might be taught.

12. A city council, state or national legislature, or a United Nations General Assembly is studied and acted out. Different participants and their positions are identified, and they are given current issues to make decisions about.

13. A diorama is constructed that will be used later as a learning center. For example, after reading about an archaeological dig, a group constructs a model of the dig. Students then prepare a job card that requires an observer to identify the objects, interpret them, and then explain how the observations support the conclusions. Observers prepare a short written report that they later share at an "archaeologists' convention," where they may debate their conclusions. Similar dioramas could be constructed as part of a study of the location of factories on a topographical map, crops to plant, and the identification of suitable routes of transportation and the location of cities.

14. A research project is conducted that requires the cooperative efforts of a number of people. For example, as part of a study of weather and wind currents, a group fills balloons with helium, attaches notes asking people who find a balloon to send a postcard telling where they found it, and then the group records the location of balloon discoveries on a large map. A group might also maintain a weather station and record the results.

15. A corporation is formed to produce earrings, bracelets, pendants and rings and sell them to other students and to people in the community. In order to raise money to purchase supplies, the group incorporates and sells stock. Every month or so, dividends are computed and paid.

16. A diorama is produced that illustrates something being studied in science, mathematics or social studies. A group might do a model of an industrial process, from raw material to finished product. A model might be constructed to show the processing of one food in different times, such as grinding corn in the early Southwest and in modern flour mills.

17. The group role plays conflicts between people with different viewpoints as part of a social studies unit. They might portray a conversation in a tavern between two colonists, one a revolutionary and one a loyalist. They might enact a conversation between people representing a labor union and the management of a company about how to settle a strike. The role play does not use a script; it is extemporaneous.

18. A model of the solar system is constructed by hanging scaled globes from the ceiling by wires. They are arranged to show distance.

19. A picture file is developed as part of a unit of study. The file might consist of drawings made by students, pictures taken from old

magazines, and photographs. The pictures might be of manufacturing processes, world leaders, community workers, past and present transportation, or natural resources and their uses and misuses.

20. A large chart is constructed that shows roles and tasks of people, in various organizations, such as community workers, city and state officials, national officials, various international bodies, or companies and educational institutions.

21. Money is raised for the school or class by making art objects that will be sold at a school fair. Students staff the booths on a rotating basis and count and report the money collected. They make decisions about the price of items, and the conducting of a special close-out sale.

22. Field studies are conducted. Students interview various people in the community, in a company, or government offices, and prepare written and oral reports. As part of an ecology study, the group collects, catalogues and displays samples and written information about the natural vegetation and wildlife in an area.

23. Food is prepared as part of a social studies unit; it might be served as part of the unit culmination.

24. The group plays a commercial educational game. Educational games are characterized by two basic features. First, they usually simulate real life situations—they are essentially a simplified slice of reality wherein players are able to try different methods of solving problems. Second, educational games are seldom competitive activities wherein one person wins and others lose. The cooperative and competitive features of real life situations are built into the game, and winning is usually a relative thing.

25. A large relief map of salt and flour or papier-mâché is constructed. It shows the topographical features and locations of rivers and lakes. The map could be used in reports given by different people. In a study of South America, the map could be used by one group reporting on transportation in South America, another reporting on natural resources, and a third reporting on urbanization. At the lower grade levels the map might be of the school or a community.

Intrinsically Motivating

Activities that are used as group projects should be sufficiently interesting that just doing them is reward enough. The teacher should not have to use extrinsic incentives such as grades or points to induce students to participate. An activity will usually be intrinsically motivating if it provides students with an opportunity to be active, to socialize and to feel confident. One test of the intrinsic motivation of activities is whether students are influenced by the threat of losing the chance to do them. Students will quiet down very quickly when they know that their misbehavior will result in not being allowed to measure the baseball diamond or work on the mural. On the other hand, few students are influenced by the threat of not being able to do pages in the spelling workbook. They are more likely to be influenced by the threat of having to do spelling pages and workbooks if they don't quiet down.

Meaningfulness   The group project should not be just entertainment the teacher includes in the schedule to lighten up the day. Meaningfulness can be achieved by relating the activity to regular school subjects such as social studies, science or literature. It can be related to a school project such as beautifying the school by planting trees or painting murals. Sharing the activity with other children in the class, children in other classes, parents and community groups also helps to make an activity meaningful.

Delegate Responsibility

The major mistake of teachers presenting group projects is their failure to delegate full responsibility to the group's participants. Group projects will only be effective in changing the group atmosphere when the participants feel full responsiblity for the outcomes and when they know they must function cooperatively in order to make the project successful. The teacher will be able to delegate this feeling of responsibility only if he allows the group participants enough freedom so that they will enjoy or suffer the natural consequences of their behavior. If the students preparing the newspaper spend so much time fighting with each other that the paper is not completed on schedule, then they should be expected to explain its lateness. The teacher should not feel that he has to apologize. The worst thing a teacher could do would be to step in and protect the participants from failure. While the teacher obviously does not want students to fail, and will support and encourage them so as to avoid failure, he must still realize that the only way students will learn to be responsible for their actions is to have been irresponsible and to have suffered the consequences.

GROUP DISCUSSION

Group discussion has four purposes:

1. It provides a means for establishing and maintaining group standards that facilitate the attainment of educational goals.

2. It helps students understand themselves and each other and realize ways that they can work together cooperatively.

3. It encourages students to be more responsible for their actions because they are sharing with the teacher and other students in finding solutions to mutual problems.

4. It permits all students an opportunity to participate, listen, express opinions and find out what others think.

Group discussion is a process whereby a group solves a group problem. The teacher's role is to guide the discussion and help everyone participate in an orderly and rational way. Group discussion strategy has two phases: (1) the Initial Phase where a problem is encountered and discussed, and a solution is suggested; and (2) the Continuing Phase where the suggested solution is tested and possibly altered.

Initial Phase Strategy

The Initial Phase is intended to move students through the decision-making stages of unfreezing, moving, and freezing. These stages are necessary if group standards are to be altered. The unfreezing stage is a kind of "catharsis" that seems to be necessary before prejudices can be removed. To break open the shell of complacency, it is often necessary to deliberately arouse students. In the moving stage, group members engaged in an active and free argument of their opinions. The purpose is for them to state their positions rather than try and persuade one another. The more members that participate in the discussion, the more firm the group's commitment to the final decision. Finally, the group moves toward a convergence, a freezing of their decision. A group can not move toward convergence while minority and majority positions need to be resolved by formal voting. The discussion should not be allowed to freeze until members achieve a consensus; everyone must feel committed to the final decision.

In the Initial Phase of group discussion, decision making occurs in five steps. In summary, they are: *Summary*

1. *Problem Experienced.* This is the unfreezing stage. The group experiences a situation that they find uncomfortable, but are not able to resolve. The more uncomfortable the students are, the greater the chances that their shell of complacency will be broken, and the more

effective group discussion will be in altering present group standards, or in establishing new ones.

2. *Problem Defined.* The group decides on the reason for their inability to achieve the goal. This is the beginning of the moving stage.

3. *Alternatives Identified.* The group considers alternative courses of action. The moving stage continues.

4. *Consequences of Alternatives.* The group identifies the probable consequences of each alternative action. This is the end of the moving stage.

5. *Solution Proposed.* The group decides on the best alternative solution. This is the beginning of freezing.

Illustrations   The Initial Phase of group discussion will be illustrated with two activities, one related to a group project in a fifth grade and the other to the care of art materials in a first grade.

Fifth Grade. The students are doing a group project as part of a science unit. They are working in groups of five. Each group will prepare a diorama and present a report to their classmates and parents. After the topics have been assigned, the teacher sends each group to a different area of the room so they can begin work. After ten minutes the groups become extremely restless and argumentative. Many of the students come to the teacher asking what they should be doing. When the teacher is satisfied that the students have an uncomfortable problem that they seem unable to solve she calls them back to their seats.

When they are settled, the teacher writes on the board, *Our Goals.* Under the teacher's direction, students discuss the goals and agree on one: "To make models and reports for science." The teacher then writes, *Our Problem.* A discussion follows on the problem. Each time a student states a problem, the teacher writes it on the board. If a student mentions a problem that has already been identified, the teacher shows him the duplication and makes a mark beside the previous sentence to indicate that it was mentioned more than once. After the statements have been written, the teacher helps the students select the key statements. One or more key problem statements may be identified from this process. These key statements are rewritten under the heading *Our Problem.* The teacher then writes on the board, *Possible Solutions.* The group then lists solutions that the teacher writes on the board.

After a number of solutions have been written, the teacher writes on the board, *Probable Consequences.* The teacher helps students consider the probable consequences of each solution, and describes those consequences in abbreviated form on the board. After the group has considered the consequences of each solution, the teacher asks for an identification of the best solution. If agreement cannot be reached, the teacher may wish to direct the students back to the earlier considerations of *Problems, Solutions,* and *Consequences.* Eventually a consensus agreement will be reached. (The first few times a teacher uses group discussion, the only way to reach agreement may be by voting. But with voting, the minority is usually not committed to the decision.) The next time science class is held, the students will try the solution identified today. Before the group meets again the teacher will write all of the solutions on a chart.

First Grade.   Students are having difficulty with materials in the art corner, which contains the easel and poster paints. Students are spilling paint on other students and on the floor; they are not cleaning up after themselves. Many students have complained to the teacher. After a particularly disruptive period in the art corner, the teacher calls all of the students to a discussion circle in the front of the classroom. The teacher says that there seems to be a problem in the art corner. A number of students begin to accuse each other of various offenses. The teacher explains to the students in a firm voice that in a discussion only one person speaks at a time.

The teacher asks the students about the purpose of the art center. After a number of purposes are suggested, the teacher summarizes the comments and writes them on the board. Then the students are asked whether they seem to be accomplishing these objectives. They all agree that they are not, and the teacher asks why. After a brief discussion the teacher asks what they should do to make the art corner a success. The teacher writes on the board, *Rules for the Art Corner,* and encourages the students to suggest some rules. When a student states a rule, the teacher writes it in simple enough form so that the students will be able to read and understand it. After each rule is written the teacher asks what might happen if that rule is enacted. When a student suggests a rule that essentially duplicates one already written, the teacher helps the student understand that it is a duplicate. The teacher should not worry that a particular rule, considered to be critical, is not mentioned. If it is really critical, its lack will be noticed when the students try out the rules. The discussion ends with the teacher saying that he will write the rules on a chart and they will be put into effect the next time the art corner is used.

The initial phase ends when solutions are suggested. The solution for the fifth-grade science project consists of the steps the students will follow in preparing their dioramas and reports. The solution for the first-grade art corner consists of a set of rules.

Delegate Responsibility The first time a teacher uses the Initial Phase of group discussion the teacher should expect students to be skeptical and unprepared to take responsibility for their actions. If the students are not yet sufficiently responsible to suggest a serious set of solutions, the teacher should let them try the ones they do suggest, and let them face the consequences. The worst that can happen is that they will not progress in their science unit for a few days, or that paint will be spilled again. The important thing is that the teacher move on to the Continuing Phase. The motto the teacher should try to abide by is: The only way one learns to behave responsibly is by having the opportunity to behave irresponsibly and then facing the natural consequences.

Continuing Phase Strategy

The Continuing Phase is intended to give the group opportunities to test out the effectiveness of their suggested solution and to demonstrate its value. The more thoroughly convinced students are that the solution they suggested enables them to reach their goals, the more firmly committed they will be to it. When they are firmly convinced of its value, the solution will function as a group standard, and the students will influence each other to adhere to it.

The Continuing Phase is intended to keep the decision-making process moving until a satisfactory solution has been identified. When students are able to recognize the value of one solution, it becomes thoroughly frozen as a group standard.

Summary The Continuing Phase has three steps. They are:

1. *Planning.* The group reviews the solution proposed earlier and discusses how they will carry it out.
2. *Execution.* The group performs the activity, including the solution.
3. *Evaluation.* The group discusses how well they carried out the solution. Often they will decide to revise it. Eventually, a satisfactory solution will be identified that everyone will agree on. That final solution becomes the group standard.

The Continuing Phase of group discussion occurs every time the activity is carried out. Once the best solution has been identified and codified by being placed on a chart, the teacher may wish to shorten the time devoted to the planning and evaluating steps. The Continuing Phase will be illustrated with the fifth-grade science project and the first-grade art corner.

Fifth Grade.   At the beginning of the next science period, the teacher presents the chart with the suggested solution. The teacher asks each group to explain how they intend to carry out the solution. Then the class begins working. The teacher circulates between groups, offering help and giving guidance. Ten minutes before the science period ends, the teacher halts the activity, assembles the students for discussion, and begins a group evaluation of the activity. Each group is asked to report its progress in carrying out the solution. After all of the groups have reported and the students have had an opportunity to comment on the reports, the teacher leads the class in discussing any revisions that might be needed in the solution. These changes are written on the chart. The same procedure will be followed each time the science activity is carried out.

First Grade.   At the beginning of the period when the first grade uses the art corner, the teacher presents the chart, *Rules for the Art Corner*. The teacher leads the students in a discussion of the rules, what they mean and how they will be carried out. This need not take more than a few minutes for it only involves recalling previous decisions. The activity then begins. The teacher should try to avoid intervening in the art corner, unless it becomes so disruptive that it must be closed. Just before the end of the period, the teacher leads a discussion of how well the students carried out their rules. The rules may need to be altered somewhat. The same procedure will be followed each time the art corner is used, keeping the discussion brief, but meaningful. If there are a number of independent activities going on, the teacher may wish to have the group prepare a suitable set of rules for each. These rules might be posted near the activity area or in a designated section of the room. Eventually the rules will become group standards and the teacher will need to intervene only when a student is not responding to the influence exerted on him by his classmates.

Leading Discussions

The teacher's success with group discussions is directly related to her competency in handling two critical elements: creating a genuine student problem, and maintaining a facilitative manner.

A Genuine Student Problem Students will become actively involved in a group discussion, and firmly committed to its decisions, only if their shell of complacency is broken. They must see the problem as their problem, as something that impedes progress toward their goals.

The teacher can do a number of things to help students feel it is their problem:

Let the Situation Make the Students Uncomfortable. The teacher should make sure that a problem situation arises and that it inconveniences the students. She should not intervene in the problem unless the students are in a position to suffer physical harm. In the first-grade art corner, for example, the teacher should not walk up to the corner as soon as a fracas occurs or paint is spilled. When the teacher intervenes, it then becomes her responsibility to solve the problem.

Offer No Solutions. The teacher should not offer solutions. When a student in the fifth-grade science project asks what he is supposed to do, the teacher should be noncommittal but friendly and say something like, "I don't know, it's your project. Perhaps we need to talk about it as a group."

Allow Testing of Their Solutions. If the first graders decide in their initial-phase discussion that no rules are necessary for the art corner, the teacher should abide by that solution, even though she is convinced otherwise. The matter can always be raised again in a continuing-phase discussion.

A Facilitative Manner The teacher will be most successful in leading group discussions that lead to the establishment of group standards when she displays six characteristics.

Democratic Discussion Leader. The teacher should be a democratic discussion leader. She should not be authoritarian and use the discussion as a forum for presenting her own ideas. On the other hand, she should not encourage anarchy by conducting the discussion in an unrestrained and unstructured way, letting each student express himself whenever and however he wishes. The teacher must be a firm leader and must insist that democratic procedures be followed at all times.

Be Unemotional and Factual. The teacher should try to be as unemotional and factual as possible. Group discussions should not be conducted when the teacher is upset or angry. At times of high emotion she will find it almost impossible not to preach to the children. Most discussions can be postponed until tempers cool.

Be Vague. The teacher should avoid giving absolute-sounding conclusions, bluntly telling students why they behaved as they did. There will be times when she will want to give her conclusions. After all, she is also part of the classroom. But those conclusions should always be presented in a vague and indefinite way and introduced by saying things such as, "I wonder whether . . . ?" or "Could it be that . . . ?" This vagueness allows students to accept or reject the teacher's conclusions and provides an incentive for them to suggest their own.

Lively Discussion. The teacher should keep the discussion lively so that students can display wide participation and active interest. But the discussion should not move along so rapidly that conclusions are reached before most children have had the opportunity to understand what the problem is. The discussion can be kept lively by such actions as asking a student whether he agrees or disagrees with a suggestion, and then asking him to explain his reasoning. The teacher might suggest something and then ask for an opinion: "I wonder how it would work if we only allowed three people to be in the library corner at one time. Maria, what do you think about that?"

Describe Behaviors. The teacher should help students compose statements that clearly describe behaviors. A rule that states, "Be good in the art corner," does not provide much guidance. The teacher should insist on statements that describe behaviors, such as, "Clean paint brushes" and "One person at a time."

Be Sympathetic and Understanding. The teacher should show sympathy for the student's feelings. This means that the teacher must at all times accept as fact the student's statement of his feelings. The teacher should not state that a student's feelings are silly or evil. The student's feelings must be treated as a given, like the law of gravity.

ROLE PLAY

Role play offers students a means of looking at problems from different perspectives, from the eyes of different people. They are able to experience the effect of their actions from the perspective of another person. They are able to "step into another's shoes" and feel what that person feels. The first-grade student who does not clean the paint brushes when he is finished may do so, in part, because he does not appreciate how much it upsets other people to have to clean dirty brushes before they can start painting. Role play gives him an opportunity to experience others' feelings.

Role play is primarily useful in solving problems involving a relationship between two or more persons. It allows the participants an opportunity to try out different actions in a search for the most mutually beneficial one.

Strategy

Role play is carried out in seven steps:

1. *Prepare the Class.* A real problem should be identified. It could be a classroom incident, like the first-grade art corner, or something that happened outside the classroom, in the library, on the school bus, on the playground. The problem should be one that ends with a decision a student must make, whether to clean the paint brushes or not, whether to speak sharply to another student on the bus or not. The teacher might read a description of the problem, ending with the decision to be made. The problem should be discussed briefly to focus interest and understanding.

2. *Select Participants.* A group discusses the characters in the incident. Who they were and how they might have felt. Students are chosen to play different roles. Initially it is generally a good idea to choose those students who by their actions and remarks reveal an identification with certain roles. The actors are given a short time to plan what they are going to do. They do not prepare dialogue, only a line of action.

3. *Prepare the Audience.* While the actors are planning the action, prepare the rest of the students to be active observers. An important quality of role play is its power to evoke discussion. The value of the discussion depends on the meaning the audience receives from watching. Tell the audience that laughter spoils the play. Tell them that they will have a chance to reenact the situation and show what they might do. And, very importantly, make clear that the way an actor portrays a role is no reflection on him as a person. He is simply acting out a characterization as he sees it. He should not be condemned by the teacher or by anyone else because of his interpretation of the role.

4. *Enact the Play.* The actors play their parts. The play may be very short or very long.

5. *Discuss the Play.* The discussion should focus on identifying different ways of behaving in a specific problem situation. The teacher leads the discussion, playing the role of the moderator. When a different way of behaving has been identified, it is tried in a reenactment.

6. *Reenact the Play.* The same actors may try playing their roles differently, or new actors may be chosen. Reenactment gives the students an opportunity to try a variety of different approaches, and to discover what will happen naturally with each one. The play may be reenacted a number of times, with each enactment followed by a discussion.

7. *Generalize the Experience.* The last step is the most critical because it helps students generalize from the play to their lives. Discussion follows the last enactment. The teacher can focus the discussion on the children's own lives by asking, "Do you know anyone to whom this kind of thing has happened?" The teacher should also deal with how different persons in the situation probably felt, and why they acted as they did.

Conducting Role Plays

The teacher's success with role play is directly related to her competency in handling two critical elements, spontaneity and a facilitative manner.

Spontaneity

Spontaneity is achieved by having actors work out only the line of action. They should not be given sufficient time to prepare the detailed dialogue found in regular stage plays. The teacher should never suggest dialogue; she should only outline the problem.

Spontaneity is also achieved by selecting only those situations that pose real dilemmas for students. The more real the problem is to the students, the more eagerly they will enter into the role play and the more effective it will be.

Facilitative Manner

The teacher must achieve the same balance between permissiveness and directiveness that is essential in the strategy of group discussion. The purpose of role play is for students to experience a situation and then to express their feelings about it. To accomplish this the teacher must be permissive and encourage children to find solutions based on an openly honest recognition of their feelings and actions. Their feelings can be recognized only if they surface. Students will allow their feelings to surface only if the teacher is supportive. The teacher can facilitate recognition by sometimes being vaguely reflective, saying, for example, "Do you feel angry? I think I would if I were in that situation." While the teacher must be permissive about the expression of feelings, he must not be permissive about maintaining orderly democratic procedures. Students must talk in turn, and be quiet enough to hear one another. They must also respect one another. The teacher should encourage students by personal example and explanation to express their feelings without attributing characteristics or traits to another person. For example, it is not permissible to say, "Johnny is messy." Students should learn to analyze their feelings about Johnny's messiness by saying things like, "I hate to have to clean a dirty paint brush before I start painting. I wish Johnny would clean up after himself." The first statement casts Johnny forever in the same behavior pattern. The second separates him from his behavior, thus allowing room for change.

The essential teacher behaviors are identical to those necessary for conducting effective group discussion—democratic discussion leader, unemotional and factual, vague, lively, clear, and sympathetic and understanding.

MORALE BUILDING

The purpose of morale building is to increase group cohesion by stressing the attractiveness of membership in the classroom group. The more attractive the group is for students, the more they will be influenced by its standards. While satisfaction will be a natural by-product of group projects, group discussions and role plays, there are other things teachers can do to develop group cohesion.

Strategy

1. Make favorable appraisals of the group when this is warranted and avoid unfavorable appraisals. When they do something especially well as a group, praise them.
2. Heighten student awareness of the various attractions the class offers. This might be accomplished by presenting a preview of the activities at the beginning of the day and ending the day by reviewing all the interesting activities they accomplished.

3. Stress satisfactions that will be derived from working well with other students in the class. For example, when a group has been particularly cooperative in completing a group project, provide them ample opportunity to share it with others and to explain how personally satisfying it was.

4. Emphasize their prestige as members of this group. This is the "old school spirit" routine. They are now the first graders in Room 18. That is more desirable than being in any other grade or classroom. Classroom spirit can be developed by adopting a class insignia, playing games as a class against other classrooms, and sitting in designated sections in the cafeteria.

5. Obtain favorable appraisals of the group from sources outside the classroom, such as other students, teachers, the principal and parents. When students have done something especially well, ask the principal to compliment them. Provide opportunities for them to share what they have done with other classrooms by having a traveling road show, such as a puppet play that gives performances in other classrooms. Invite parents to culminations of group projects, such as social studies units where students present a play and explain things they have studied and constructed.

DESIST TECHNIQUES

The purpose of desist techniques is for the teacher to use personal influence in a way that is least wasteful and yet most effective in controlling students' misbehavior. Desist techniques are actions the teacher must take "right now" in order to maintain a minimum level of order. They must be used with all students on some occasions, and with some students on all occasions.

Overdependence on desist techniques causes many of the problems teachers have with classroom management. The consequence of using desist techniques as the only or even the major strategy for group leadership is illustrated by the authors' experience with their dog. They have patiently disciplined the dog not to walk on the white carpet in the living room. He obediently stays off the rug, but only when the authors are at home. He has obviously learned that he need obey only in the presence of the authority.

When the dog wishes to retaliate against the authors for something they have done, such as not taking him on a trip, he makes a mess on the white rug. He could do this on other rugs in the house, on a tiled entryway or on wood floors; he always chooses the white carpet. It is as if he knew that the most effective way of retaliating against them for an unfairness done to him is by doing this in a forbidden area. He is absolutely correct.

Teachers need to be realistic about the fact that when desist techniques are the only group-leader strategy they use, their students can be expected to behave much like the authors' dog. The students comply only in the presence of the teacher's authority. And, they punish the teacher by acts of retaliation. The acts of retaliation may be against the teacher and the school (particularly against those things considered especially important by the teacher and school), or, students may retaliate against themselves by going on an intellectual sit-down strike. "You can make me sit down, but you can't make me learn." The severity of these acts of retaliation will depend on the harshness of the desist techniques and how unfair the students think them to be.

While desist techniques must sometimes be used, teachers should be aware that the more desist techniques are used, the less effective they become. In some cases they can even become counterproductive. Teachers who depend heavily on desist techniques for classroom management usually find that they must keep using a forceful level of personal influence in order to achieve the same results they once achieved with a less forceful level of personal influence. At one time they were able to get students to quiet down by asking in a soft and friendly voice, "Please sit down and pay attention." Now they find that students will respond only to a moderately loud and angry voice laced with threats, "If you don't sit down immediately you'll get an extra assignment to do."

Desist techniques should be used only when group influence is not effective in controlling students' misbehavior. Desist techniques must be used with those deviating students who are either unattracted to group membership or who have been rejected by the group. For example, if most of the students have accepted the action of walking in an orderly way from the classroom to the playground, but one or two students insist on running and pushing, the teacher must use desist techniques with the offenders. She might give them points for walking or inflict on them the punishment of sitting out the recess period. In addition, desist techniques must be used with whole classrooms when group standards have not been established for an activity. For example, if students have not yet accepted as a group standard the action of walking to recess, the entire class might receive tokens for walking or might be punished by spending part of their recess practicing walking. These desist techniques should be viewed as stop-gap measures used during the time the teacher endeavors to bring the deviants into the group and to establish group standards for all activities.

Strategy

There are two major types of desist techniques, reward and punishment. With reward methods, a student is rewarded when he behaves in a desired and defined way and ignored when he misbehaves. With punishment methods, a student is ignored when he behaves properly and punished when he misbehaves. As a general rule, reward methods achieve more effective results and are less wasteful of the teacher's personal influence. But reward methods are more difficult for teachers to use because they must follow the cardinal rule of ignoring misbehavior.

Desist techniques that use rewards are based on the notion that behavior that is rewarded will persist while behavior that is unrewarded will be extinghished. If something pleasant happens every time a student walks in the hallway, and nothing happens when he runs, he will soon start walking. Rewards may be in the form of primary reinforcers (directly met physiological or psychological needs) or secondary reinforcers (tokens that are redeemable for things that will directly meet physiological or psychological needs). Primary reinforcers may be such things as candy, first choice of play equipment, small gifts, choice of extracurricular activities or seeing a movie. Secondary reinforcers are tokens in the form of points or tickets that enable a person to purchase a primary reinforcer—six tickets enable a person to see the movie on Friday, three tickets are needed to get a gum drop.

Reward Methods

Planning a Reward Program.   Four things must be considered in the planning of the use of rewards. The more thoughtful attention the teacher gives to planning, the more effective the reward methods will be and the less difficulty the teacher will have in using them.

   1. *Clear Definition of Desired Behavior.* The behavior desired should be clear to the student and observable to the teacher. The teacher should avoid having the student play a "guessing game" where the teacher is perceived to be arbitrary. An unspecified definition like, "Be good and stay out of trouble," forces the student into a guessing game about what exactly is good behavior and what is the

teacher's mood. The same action that is considered all right on one of the teacher's good days may not be considered all right on a bad day. This lack of clarity encourages students to gamble, and like all gamblers, to accept losses philosophically: "Win a few, lose a few."

Reward methods will be most effective if the teacher selects one item at a time to correct. The teacher might start with something simple, such as walking to the pencil sharpener without hitting anyone. The behavior is specific enough so that the teacher can demonstrate it to the student. The teacher could walk to the front with his arms at his sides, and say, "This is how I want you to walk to the pencil sharpener. Notice that my arms are at my sides and I have not bumped into anyone. Now, let me show you how I don't want you to walk to the pencil sharpener." The teacher could then have the student practice walking in the right way and the wrong way. The behavior is clearly defined so that both the student and the teacher will likely agree on when it has been achieved. The only argument might be about whether someone else started it. But if the behavior states no hitting, it should not matter who started it, only that this student hit.

The teacher should identify only those behaviors that the teacher can observe. Walking to the pencil sharpener is a suitable behavior only if the teacher can observe the student doing it. The teacher should not be overly concerned that much of the student's misbehavior is not observable. Modifying some of the student's misbehavior has a positive ripple effect. When the student has learned not to hit people while walking to the pencil sharpener, he will usually stop hitting them at other times as well.

2. *Identify a Suitable Reward.* The item or items selected as a reward must be something the student desires. Some possible rewards are mentioned below.

REWARDS

Toys, such as balloons, model airplanes, stuffed animals.
Awards, such as ribbons, badges, stickers, a "happygram" sent to parents.
Points, such as gold stars, colorful stickers, rubber stamps, play money.
Money, given by parents over and above regular allowance.
Parent Activity, such as a weekend camping trip with father.
Special Activities, such as getting to use the typewriter, hit the punching bag, sit at the teacher's desk and wear the teacher's hat or sunglasses, read comics, do something of one's own choice, use the viewmaster, or listen to recordings. The activities should be something not normally done.

Food, such as fruit, popcorn, raisins or peanuts.

Special Privileges, such as early dismissal at recess or lunch, taking class
    pets home over the weekend, handing out athletic equipment or
    books, or being the first in line.

The teacher might determine a suitable reward by asking a student
what she would like. The teacher also might mention a number of
possible rewards, such as those above, and ask the student to identify the one she most desires.

3. *System for Dispensing Rewards.* The teacher must decide
whether to use primary reinforcers or secondary reinforcers. When
primary reinforcers are used, the student receives the reward immediately after the desired behavior is observed. For example, if the student walks to the pencil sharpener without hitting anyone, the teacher immediately walks over to her and does something, such as placing
an award on her shirt or stamping her hand. When secondary reinforcers are used, the student immediately receives a token that is
later traded for a reward. A certain reward might require a specified
number of tokens. For example, in order to be able to take a camping trip with his father the student might have to collect ten tokens
in one week. Secondary reinforcers are much easire to use in the
classroom.

The teacher must decide how the student will be paid and how
the payments will be recorded. The teacher might keep a record
sheet on which a mark is made each time the student exhibits the
desired behavior. The teacher should indicate to the student when a
mark has been made by giving a sign, such as a wink or nod of the
head. The student can see how she is doing by looking at the teacher's record. On the other hand, the student might keep a record
sheet on which the teacher makes a mark, or the student makes a
mark when the teacher gives a sign. The latter has the advantage
of keeping the student constantly apprised of her progress, which
is motivating. It has the disadvantage of allowing the student to cheat.

The payment procedure must provide for two critical characteristics of effective reward techniques, consistency and promptness. The student should be rewarded everytime the desired behavior
is observed. The technique loses its effectiveness if the reward
is given intermittently, for that encourages gambling. The more
promptly the reward follows the desired action, whether it is a
primary or secondary reinforcer, the more effective the technique.
Consistency and promptness are more easily achieved with secondary
reinforcers than with primary ones.

4. *Periodic Planning and Evaluation Conferences with Student.*
A weekly or biweekly conference with the student (or class, depending on the object of the technique) should be held to discuss how the
program is going. The desirability of the reward and payment procedures should be discussed, and possibly changed. For example, a
boy trying to earn a camping trip with his father may be getting discouraged because he always comes up one or two tokens short at
the end of the week. The teacher may decide to reduce the number
of tokens required so that the boy can earn his reward. The teacher
could decide to raise the number of tokens required because the
student is progressing well, or even to drop the use of the technique
altogether. The sooner this is accomplished the better.

Conducting a Reward Program.   Teachers will be most successful in
using reward methods when they have a well planned program and
when they exhibit three critical behaviors—fairness, lack of emotional involvement, and sympathy. The teacher should strive to
"stick to the agreement." Any arbitrary behavior on the teacher's
part encourages gambling on the student's part. For example, if
the student walks to the pencil sharpener without hitting anyone or
saying anything, which is the behavior agreed upon, but does so in
an insolent way, the reward should not be withheld because the
teacher did not like the student's manner.

The teacher must also combine a lack of emotional involvement
with sympathy. That is really like saying, "love the student, but hate
his behavior." For example, if the student goes through a day without earning one token, the teacher should express sympathy for the
student's plight. "It's tough, isn't it. Well, let's see how it goes tomorrow." The teacher should avoid becoming angry. This might
encourage the student to get back at the teacher by making him
angry. Sympathy and firmness are the most effective ways of dealing
with students.

Punishment Methods   Desist techniques using punishment are based on the notion that
when something unpleasant happens every time a certain behavior is
exhibited, that behavior will be extinguished. Pain is such a universal
experience for all of us that its use as punishment is equally universal. But pain should not be thought of as the only effective punishment. In fact, its use in school is usually prohibited by law, as it
should be. The major problem teachers have with punishment
methods is being sufficiently subtle in their use. Teachers usually
employ too little variety in their punishments and are overly forceful.

Planning a Punishment Program. Teachers may find it helpful to visualize punishment as existing at different places on a set of stairs. On the bottom step is the minimally forceful thing that might be done. The top step has the maximally forceful thing. The minimum force that might be used is to look across the room at a student and frown. The maximum force is to isolate the student from the class by having him stay in an isolation booth, out in the hallway, or sending him to the office. Somewhere in the middle is a quiet appeal to the student. Too many teachers start near the top of the stairs and thus leave themselves little room to escalate. If the first thing the teacher does is loudly call out a student's name and tell him to stop playing, about all the teacher has left to do is move to the top step and isolate the student. Consequently, the teacher spends a great deal of time yelling and isolating, and so overuses her personal influence that it wastes away.

Teachers will find it helpful to construct their own individual punishment stairs, from minimum to maximum force. In the space provided in Figure 8.1, plan your punishment steps. Identify ten levels, starting with a glance and ending with isolation. The first three steps and last step are given. Plan the ones in between. Write in the space provided or on another piece of paper. You can compare your responses with those of other teachers by looking at Figures 8.2, 8.3 and 8.4.

> *The Idea: Escalation.* The idea is to start at the bottom step and move up
> step by step as necessary. If the teacher glances at a student and he
> stops misbehaving but then immediately starts again, the teacher
> moves over beside him. If he continues to misbehave, the teacher places

MY PUNISHMENT STAIRS

Step One   —*Establish eye contact with the student and frown or shake your head.*

Step Two   —*Without stopping a lesson, or even indicating your intent, move over beside the student.*

Step Three—*Without stopping the lesson, gently place a hand on the student.*

Step Four

Step Five

Step Six

Step Seven

Step Eight

Step Nine

Step Ten   —*Isolation*

Figure 8.1

a hand on his shoulder. The teacher's hope is for the misbehavior to stop with the minimal use of force. The teacher must expect that sometimes she will have to go all the way up the stairs to the top.

Isolation. The ultimate punishment, isolation, should not be viewed as a physically uncomfortable experience—it is simply a place out of sight from other students. Create a spot that is separate and attractively decorated and comfortable. It may be a desk outside the room or a table in the principal's office. The isolation area should have things to do, such as coloring books, puzzles, and quiet games. When a student is sent to isolation, casually observe him, but pay no obvious attention. Do not worry if at first he spends most of the day there. Isolation has a way of making class routine look more attractive. The purpose of isolation is to reduce the alternatives open to the disruptive student and bring the realization that he has only two choices: (1) to be in class and behave; or (2) to be outside and sit. While he is outside you are not going to hurt or reject him, which would let him rationalize his misconduct on the basis of his dislike for you.

Compare Your Responses. In order to help you plan a suitable set of punishment steps, sample responses from a group of teachers to the exercise in Figure 8.1 are shown in three categories: (1) Escalation May Be Too Rapid; (2) Escalation Probably Appropriate; and (3) Escalation May Be Too Slow. Escalation is too rapid when the teacher has gone as far as he can go in five steps. Escalation is too slow when the biggest jump occurs between Step Nine and Step Ten. Escalation is appropriate when the steps are equal in terms of the increase of force. Notice how rapidly escalation occurs between Steps Three and Five in Figure 8.2.

In examining Figure 8.1, notice that the use of force escalates so rapidly, that by Step Four or Five the lesson has been disrupted. The teacher has stopped the lesson that other students are receiving in order to deal with the misbehavior of one student. Disrupting a lesson should be avoided as long as possible.

Notice the more evenly spaced escalation in the punishment stairs shown in Figure 8.3.

In the punishment steps shown in Figure 8.4, escalation is too slow, and so there is a big jump between Steps Nine and Ten. For example, with Teacher Eight, the Ninth Step is to tell the student about his misbehavior and the Tenth Step is isolation—that is a big jump. These punishment steps could be improved by making the Eighth and Ninth Steps a bit firmer.

Conducting a Punishment Program. Teachers will be most successful in using punishment methods when they have identified an

ESCALATION MAY BE TOO RAPID

Teacher One

1. *eye contact*
2. *shake head negatively*
3. *hand on student*
4. *call student's name—possibly suggest conference*
5. *shake the shivers out of him or her*
6. *threaten trip to office or parental conference*
7. *make trip to office and discuss problem*
8.
9.
10. *isolation*

Teacher Two

1. *eye contact*
2. *move to student*
3. *hand on student*
4. *take student out of room and talk with him about his behavior*
5. *take away his classroom job (privileges)*
6. *no recess privileges for the day*
7. *see the counselor about his behavior*
8. *have the student put his head down and sit in his desk for an extended period—no activity*
9. *scold*
10. *isolation*

Teacher Three

1. *voice*
2. *eye contact*
3. *move to student*
4. *hand on student*
5. *lose recess*
6. *note to parent*
7. *note from parent*
8. *after school*
9. *isolation*
10. *principals office*

Figure 8.2

appropriate set of punishment steps and when they exhibit six critical behaviors.

1. *Firmness.* Teachers must sound and act like they mean what they say. Firmness is not achieved by the level of force used, but by the teacher's manner in exercising that force. Even a simple but firm glance will usually be more effective than a whining plea, "Come on, let's cut this out now. Okay?"

2. *Loving.* The student must not feel personally rejected. Teachers must manage to communicate to the student that, "I like you but I cannot condone your behavior."

ESCALATION PROBABLY APPROPRIATE

Teacher Four

1. *eye contact*
2. *hand on the student*
3. *firmer hand on the student*
4. *move the student closer to the front of the row*
5. *talk privately with the student, explain the classroom rules*
6. *move other "catalystic" students*
7. *bargain with student placing the responsibility of his behavior on him*
8. *quietly remind student of your agreement*
9. *move student out of row to front or back of room*
10. *complete isolation*

Teacher Five

1. *eye contact. Look at him. Stare!*
2. *move to the student. Stand near him.*
3. *place hand on the student—gently, lovingly*
4. *call student to your desk—have a private talk about behavior*
5. *sharp tone—speak firmly to student*
6. *warning—"If you continue, we will have to take other measures"*
7. *move the student to another seat in the room temporarily*
8. *deprive student of recess or other privileges*
9. *isolation within the room but in sight of others (corner by teacher's desk)*
10. *isolation where they see nobody at all*

Teacher Six

1. *eye contact*
2. *shake head*
3. *walk near student*
4. *"sh—"*
5. *hand on shoulder*
6. *speak to student (do you need help?)*
7. *change activity*
8. *give adjustment time*
9. *caution that next step is isolation*
10. *isolation*

Figure 8.3

3. *Consistent.* Teachers must either tolerate a certain behavior all the time or none of the time. Teachers encourage gambling when they are not consistent about the behavior they tolerate, and this results in more misbehavior. Teachers should also endeavor to respond in the same way to all students. Teachers should try to overcome their unconscious bias against low-status boys. (See the discussion of teacher bias against low-status boys in the portion dealing with Group Structure in chapter 7.)

4. *Clarity.* Clarity is achieved by specifying the actions you wish the student to exhibit. Telling a student to pay attention is clearer than just calling her name or telling her to be good. And telling her to look up at the chalkboard and keep her hands to herself is clearer than

ESCALATION MAY BE TOO SLOW

<u>Teacher Seven</u>

1. *eye contact*
2. *move to student—get closer to student, don't talk*
3. *hand on student*
4. *"That's a no-no"*
5. *body language—shake head*
6. *talk to them by themselves—what good did that do?*
7. *do you want some help in controlling yourself or do you think you are getting grown up enough to do it by yourself?*
8. *stand and hold up hand with peace sign*
9. *stand and be quiet and wait for them to get quiet, take time off their recess until they get the idea, then just look at your watch*
10. *isolation—pleasant place—no social life—raisins—coloring book—time out booth—solitary confinement*

<u>Teacher Eight</u>

1. *acknowledge behavior with body movement*
2. *eye contact with student*
3. *move closer to student (within 10 feet)*
4. *move next to student*
5. *make "1-word" verbal response*
6. *just touch student (allows awareness of presence)*
7. *place a hand on the student*
8. *firm grip*
9. *tell student about his misbehavior*
10. *isolation (time-out room)*

Figure 8.4

telling her to pay attention. James Thurber was reported to have said that, "A word to the wise is not sufficient if it doesn't make any sense."

5. *Rationality.* Always try to explain to the student a logical reason why his behavior is unacceptable. For example, "You may find the addition of fractions very difficult if you don't carefully watch the instructions that I am giving." That statement relates the student's behavior to his learning, and thus informs him that his misbehavior is only hurting himself. The student's misbehavior might be hurting other students, and thus the teacher might say, "I cannot help Barbara and Luis if I have to watch you all the time. Help them by doing your assignment quietly." Even if the misbehaving student couldn't care less about whether he hurts Barbara and Luis, he at least knows that the teacher is being fair with him, and is simply doing what must be done.

6. *Calmness.* Try to be as unemotional as possible. When a student succeeds in making a teacher angry, she has exerted power over the teacher. The teacher who manages to stay calm in the face of student misbehavior will have far more personal influence with that student, and with all students, than one who loses his temper frequently. Calmness does not mean tolerating misbehavior. It just means that teachers do not respond as if the student's misbehavior is a personal attack on them.

SUMMARY

The group-leader strategies are summarized in the form of observation guides that can be used in evaluating the teacher's use of the strategies. The observation guides can be used by one teacher for self-evaluation or by two teachers working together as a team and evaluating each other.

I. GROUP PROJECT

	Rating		
Yes	So-So	No	

_____ Activity   _____ Date

Note: Each group project should be evaluated separately. For example, the evaluation should be done once for the play one group does and again for the mural done by another group.

    A. *Characteristics*
      1. *Cooperation.* The project is organized so that it can be successfully completed *only* through the *cooperative* efforts of two or more students.

      Suggestions: _____

      _____

      2. *Intrinsically Motivating.* The project is organized so that it provides students an opportunity to be active (physically and intellectually), to socialize, and to feel secure.

      Suggestions: _____

      _____

      3. *Meaningful.* Meaningfulness is achieved by (check one or more):
        a) relating the project to school subjects. (Social studies, science unit, etc.
        b) relating the project to total school effort.
        c) sharing the project with other groups such as students in this class, other classes, and parents.

      Suggestions: _____

      _____

    B. *Critical Teacher Behavior*
    Delegating Responsibility. The teacher has managed to delegate responsibility for successful completion of the project by helping students feel responsible for the project's outcomes.

    Suggestions: _____

    _____

Rating

Yes   So-So   No

II GROUP DISCUSSION

Note: Evaluation should be accomplished in two sessions, one for the Initial-Phase Discussion and one for the Continuing-Phase Discussion.

A. *Characteristics*
1. *Initial-Phase Discussion*

Situation   Date

a) *Problem Experienced.* Students are allowed to experience a situation where they are unable to achieve a goal they desire and the teacher does not intervene (except where absolutely necessary).

b) *Problem Defined.* Students are (check each):
   1) called into an orderly discussion group after they experience the problem.
   2) helped to identify the goal of the problem situation they experienced.
   3) helped to identify the reasons they were not achieving the goal.

c) *Alternatives Identified.* In the discussion (check each):
   1) the teacher directs the discussion to the consideration of solutions.
   2) the teacher elicits suggestions for solutions from students.
   3) the teacher writes each suggested solution down in full or in abbreviated form.
   4) the teacher indicates when a duplicate solution has been suggested.

d) *Consequences of Alternatives.* In the discussion (check each):
   1) the teacher directs the discussion to a consideration of the probable consequence.
   2) the teacher elicits suggested alternatives from students.
   3) the teacher allows for differences of opinion about what students consider to be the likely consequences of a specific solution.

e) *Solution Proposed.* The discussion concludes by (check each):
   1) the teacher directing the discussion to a consideration of which solution this group wishes to select.
   2) the teacher lets students select the solution by a procedure of consensus (all agree).
   3) the teacher records the agreed-upon solution on a chart or piece of paper.

Suggestions: _____

_____

Rating

Yes   So-So   No

2. Continuing-Phase Discussion

_____   _____

Situation   Date

a) *Planning.* At the beginning of a period when a solution will be applied, either for the first or "umpteenth" time (check each):

1) students are called into an *orderly* discussion group.

2) the solution proposed earlier is read by the teacher or students.

3) the teacher elicits from the children explanation of how they intend to carry out the solution.

4) the teacher indicates that the solution will be discussed at the end of the period.

b) *Execution.* During the period the teacher intervenes in the problem only when absolutely necessary

c) *Evaluation.* At the end of the period (check each):

1) students are called into an orderly discussion group.

2) the solution is read.

3) the teacher elicits from students examples of how *well* or *poorly* the solution was carried out.

4) the teacher directs the discussion to a consideration of changing the solution.

5) the discussion ends with a solution identified.

Suggestion: _____

_____   _____

B. *Critical Teacher Behaviors*

1. *Helping Students Perceive a Situation as a Problem*

a) the teacher allows students to experience the problem situation and to be inconvenienced by it.

b) the teacher does not intervene in the problem situation by disciplining students unless they might suffer physical harm.

c) the teacher does not offer solutions for the problem while students are experiencing it.

d) when students become intolerably disorderly, the teacher calls them into a discussion group rather than intervene by disciplining them.

2. *Manner While Conducting Discussion*

a) the teacher insists that orderly democratic procedures be followed, and is neither too authoritarian nor too permissive.

b) the teacher leads the discussion in an unemotional and factual way.

c) when the teacher makes conclusions, they are presented in a vague and indefinite way.

d) the teacher keeps the discussion sufficiently lively that students display wide participation and active interest.

e) the teacher displays an understanding and sympathy for students' feelings and attitudes.

Suggestions:_____

_____

III. ROLE PLAY

_____   _____

Situation   Date

A. *Characteristics*

Role plays are carried out in seven steps (check each):

1. *Prepare the Class*

    a) the teacher identifies a problem that is real for this group of students—something that has happened or could happen.

    b) the problem does not present a solution. Students must decide on that.

2. *Select Participants*

    a) the teacher leads a discussion of the actions and feelings of the people in the problem situation.

    b) the teacher chooses participants who are likely to be expressive.

    c) students are given only enough time to prepare for the play so that they are able to decide on the story line but not on the specific dialogue.

3. *Prepare the Audience*

    a) the teacher discusses "good" audience behavior.

    b) the teacher emphasizes that the actors are only "playing out" their roles.

4. *Enact the Play*

    The actors play their parts.

5. *Discuss the Play*

    The teacher focuses the discussion on how the actors actually behaved, and how they might have behaved differently.

6. *Re-Enact the Play*

    The same problem situation is enacted again, either with the same actors or new actors. Each reenactment is followed by discussion.

7. *Generalize the Experience*

    The teacher focuses the discussion on the implications for their particular situation.

Suggestions: _____

_____

Rating
Yes   So-So   No

   B. *Critical Teacher Behaviors*
       1. *Maintaining Spontaneity*
          The action portrayed is spontaneous rather than planned.
       2. *Manner While Conducting Play* (Check each):
          a) In discussions, the teacher insists that democratic procedures
             are followed, and is neither too permissive nor too authori-
             tarian with respect to group behavior.
          b) The teacher is very permissive and encouraging with respect
             to students' honesty in expressing their feelings.
          c) The teacher leads discussions in an unemotional way.
          d) When the teacher suggests actions or feelings, they are stated
             in a vague and indefinite way.

       Suggestions: _____

       _____

   IV. MORALE BUILDING

   Note: Keep a record of each time a characteristic is observed.

   Characteristics
   1. *Favorable Appraisals*
       Dates Observed_____

       Suggestions_____

   2. *Attractions of Group Membership.* The teacher heightens stu-
       dents' awareness of the various attractions this class group offers.

       Dates Observed _____

       Suggestions _____

   3. *Satisfactions from Cooperative Behaviors.* The teacher stresses
       the satisfactions that are derived from working cooperatively with
       other students in the class.

       Dates Observed _____

       Suggestions _____

   4. *Prestige of Group Membership.* The teacher emphasizes the
       prestige of belonging to this group as opposed to membership in
       another group.

       Dates _____

       Suggestions _____

5. *Favorable Appraisals.* The teacher obtains favorable appraisals from persons outside the group such as other students, teachers, the principal and parents.

   Dates _____

   Suggestions _____

V. DESIST TECHNIQUES

   A. *Use of Reward Methods*

   Note: Record each occurrence in the space provided.

DATE   NATURE OF REWARD   SITUATION

PRIMARY REINFORCERS Things that directly meet student's needs.	
SECONDARY REINFORCERS Tokens representing primary reinforcers.	

Rating
Yes   So-So   No

B. *Use of Punishment Methods*
Note: Record each occurrence in the space provided.

DATE	NATURE OF PUNISHMENT (i.e., eye contact calling a student's name, isolation)	PUNISHMENT THAT IMMEDIATELY PRECEDED IT, IF ANY (This is intended to indicate escalation.)

C. *Critical Teacher Behaviors*
    1. *Reward Methods* (check each):
        a) *Reward Not Mixed with Punishment* Reinforcers are either given or withheld. They are never taken away.
        b) *Suitable Reward* The reinforcers seem to be something a student really wants.
        c) *Desired Behavior Specified* The desired behavior is clearly enough specified for a child that he knows when he is exhibiting it and when he is not.
        d) *Consistency* Every time a student exhibits the desired behavior he is rewarded.
        e) *Promptness* The reward is issued immediately after the student exhibits the desired behavior.

        Suggestions: _____

        _____

    2. *Punishment Methods* (check each):
        a) *Firmness.* The teacher sounds and acts like he really means what he says.
        b) *Loving.* The teacher displays an affection for the student and a dislike of his behavior
        c) *Consistency.* The teacher responds every time the student misbehaves and he responds in like manner to all students.
        d) *Clarity.* The teacher is specific about what the student did that constituted misbehavior.

	Rating	
Yes	So-So	No

e) *Rationality.* The teacher explains why a certain behavior cannot be tolerated.

f) *Unemotional* The teacher does not respond in anger.

Suggestions: _____

_____

For Further Reading

For a particularly thorough and practical guide to educational games, see:

Gordon, A. K. *Games for Growth: Educational Games in the Classroom.* Chicago: Science Research Associates, Inc., 1970.

For a more extensive discussion of role play, see:

Shaftel, G., and Shaftel, F. *Role Playing: The Problem Story.* An Intergroup Education Pamphlet, National Conference of Christians and Jews, 1952.

Assessment

To determine whether or not educational goals are being attained, they are assessed. The assessment instruments used in the group-leader role are intended to measure the conditions that create a healthy classroom atmosphére. The two types of conditions are the teacher's personal influence and the influence of the group. The three things that affect group influence are group cohesion, group standards, and group structure. Instruments and interpretation procedures suitable for assessing each group-leader condition are explained in this chapter.

THE TEACHER'S PERSONAL INFLUENCE

The four factors that determine the personal influence teachers have with their students were previously identified. They are:

Student Affection. The stronger the sentimental tie between teacher and student, the greater the teacher's influence with the student.

Student Perception. Teachers' personal influence is affected by the way students perceive their knowledge, teaching competence, and status as an adult.

Misuse of Influence. Teacher's personal influence declines if it is used too frequently.

Degree of Individualization. Individualization affects the teacher's personal influence because it determines the ways by which students can maximize their rewards and minimize their punishments.

Instruments and interpretation procedures are suggested for assessing student affection and student perception. To assess the misuse of influence, teachers can carry out group-leader strategies identified and then evaluate them. The degree of individualization is altered by changes in the grouping patterns.

Instruments

Instruments are suggested for assessing student affection and student perception.

Student Affection In assessing student affection, teachers attempt to identify what their students like or dislike about them. Teachers then try to strengthen the tie between student and teacher by improving the things students dislike and maintaining those they like.

A suitable instrument that has a multiple-choice format is shown in Figure 9.1. Listed are qualities that students might like or dislike about a teacher. Students are asked to rate their feelings. Each student receives a form like that shown in Figure 9.1.

Students sometimes need help in expressing their feelings accurately on a rating form. Figure 9.2 shows practice forms that can be used at the lower and upper grades in helping students learn to express their feelings on a rating form. It is important when using the practice forms that the teacher stress to the student the importance of saying how that student feels. The student should not worry about others. Also, it should be stressed that the answers are strictly confidential. No names are written on the papers.

A less complex, multiple-choice instrument for assessing affection is shown in Figure 9.3. Students are asked to indicate the presence or absence of certain characteristics.

The two questions asked in Figure 9.3 can be presented in a free-response format which provides less restriction on student's answers. An instrument having a free-response format is shown in Figure 9.4. The instrument is suitable only for the upper grades.

An Instrument suitable for the lower grades is shown in Figure 9.5. It has a multiple-choice format and uses an identifying sign for

Directions   *Tell how you feel about the teacher by indicating your responses. Do not write your name on the paper.*

My Teacher:	Not at all	Not very often	Some-times	Quite often	Almost all the time
Helps me when I need it.					
Is pretty (handsome)					
Is fair with everyone					
Is polite					
Is patient					
Has a nice voice					
Talks too loudly					
Talks too much					
Has class pets					
Is too strict					
Has bad breath					
Looks nice					

Figure 9.1

each item rated and faces to represent rating levels. The teacher identifies each item by the sign, has the students point to the sign, and then reads the item beside that sign aloud. Students indicate their rating by placing a mark on one face.

The teacher must establish an atmosphere of trust in order to assure that students are reporting their *true* feelings rather than just something they consider *safe.* The teacher must convince the students that the only reason for the assessment is to help the

Lower Grade Levels

1. *Watching TV*			
2. *Eating spinach*			

Upper Grade Levels

This is how often I like:	*Not at all*	*Not very often*	*Some-times*	*Quite often*	*Almost all the time*
Watching TV					
Eating Spinach					

Figure 9.2

teacher to become a better teacher. Also, when students answer the questions they are helping to make the classroom better. The teacher should never tease or criticize students about their responses.

Student Perception In assessing students' perception of the teacher's knowledge and competence, teachers attempt to identify the areas where students respect them. Teachers' personal influence will be greatest in those areas where students have the highest respect for their knowledge and competence. Teachers can increase their personal influence by demonstrating their abilities in the areas where students have the least respect for them. For example, a teacher who is not respected for her sports ability can increase her personal influence with students by playing a credible game of four-square or kickball. The more areas students respect, the more personally influential the teacher will be.

Directions: *Tell how you feel about the teacher by checking the statements which apply. Do not write your name on the paper.*

1. Some things I like about my teacher are:

_____ *helps students when they ask questions.*

_____ *is fair to students.*

_____ *cooperates with students on their problems.*

_____ *treats everyone equally.*

_____ *is pretty (handsome).*

2. Some things I do not like about my teacher are:

_____ *talks too loudly.*

_____ *talks too much.*

_____ *dress.*

_____ *is unfair to students.*

_____ *doesn't help students when they need it.*

_____ *expects too much of students.*

Figure 9.3

Directions: *Tell how you feel about your teacher. Do not write your name.*

1. Some things I especially like about my teacher are:

_____

2. Some things I especially dislike about my teacher are:

_____

Figure 9.4

An instrument suitable for assessing the teacher's knowledge and competence is shown in Figure 9.6. It has a free-response format.

A multiple-choice format could be used to focus students' responses on particular knowledges and competencies of the teacher. A suitable instrument is shown in Figure 9.7. Notice that it asks for

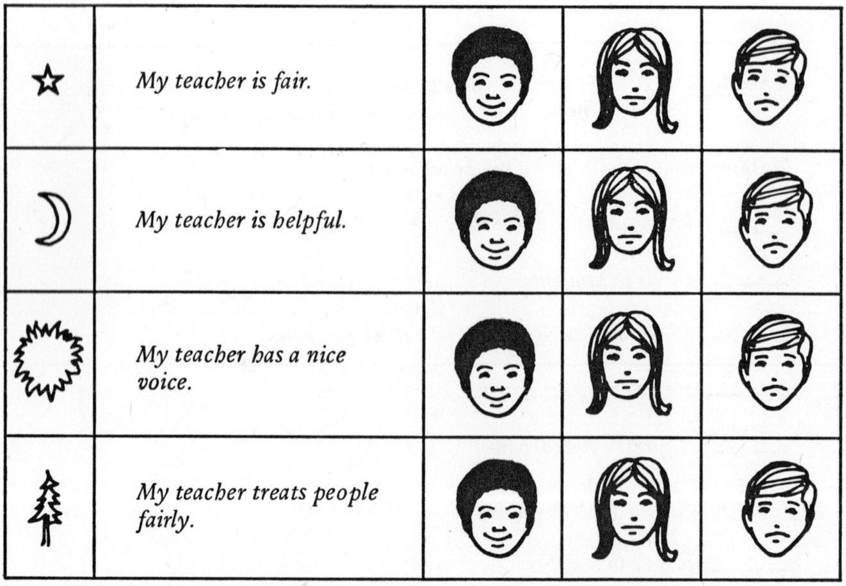

Figure 9.5

Directions: *Complete these sentences about your teacher. Do not write your
name.*

1. Some things my teacher knows a lot about are:

_____

2. Some things my teacher does not know much about are:

_____

Figure 9.6

ratings in a number of areas, including perception of misbehavior—
the ability might be called "having eyes in the back of one's head."

The instrument shown in Figure 9.7 can be designed in a way
suitable for the lower grades by using a format like that shown earlier
in Figure 9.5. In addition, the teacher could make the instrument
more interesting by having a picture for each ability.

Interpretation

In order for the assessment instrument to be of much use to the
teacher, students' responses must be interpreted. Two processes for

My teacher knows a lot about:	I agree almost always	I agree more than I disagree	I agree as often as I disagree	I disagree more than I agree	I disagree almost always
Directions: *Indicate how you feel about your teacher by making a check in one of the boxes beside each statement. Do not write your name on the paper.*					
1. *How to teach math.*					
2. *How to teach reading.*					
3. *How to teach P.E.*					
4. *How to teach art.*					
5. *How people are behaving in the room.*					

Figure 9.7

interpreting assessment instruments are explained here. Each process has a different purpose, and both can usually be accomplished with the same instrument.

The purpose of numerical interpretation is to derive a number, a score. The score allows for comparison over a period of time. If a score of 2.5 is identified as the level of student affection for September, and a score of 3.3 is identified for October, and a score of 3.9 for November, the teacher knows that the level of student affection is improving. This indicates that the teacher's personal influence is increasing. There are three steps in making a numerical interpretation.

Numerical Interpretation

Assign a weighted score to each response a student makes. With a multiple-choice item each response is assigned a score, with the weights indicating the degree of positiveness and negativeness. The item shown in Figure 9.8 has five possible responses. A weighted score of 1 is assigned to the most negative rating (Not at all) and a weighted score of 5 is assigned to the most positive rating (Almost all the time). The response and weighting are shown in Figure 9.8.

With instruments having three rating steps, like that shown in Figure 9.5, weights of 1, 3, and 5 should be assigned to the three steps.

The first step of numerical interpretation is accomplished differently when a free-response format is used. With a free-response item, the teacher designs a key which is used in assigning a *weighted* score to *each* response a student makes. The key is shown in Figure 9.9. The same weighting procedures would be used with a multiple-choice checklist like the one in Figure 9.3. Each thing checked is counted as a different response.

The first step of numerical interpretation is completed when a weighted score is assigned to *each* response a student makes. If an instrument is used like that shown in Figure 9.1, then each student will have twelve different weighted scores, one for each item. The scores of one student's paper would be like that shown in Figure 9.10. With the procedure shown in Figure 9.9 there are a total of two weighted scores, 15 and 4.

Determine a total score for each student. A student's total score is the *average* of the weighted scores for each response. For example,

Student's Response					
	Not at all	Not very often	Some-times	Quite often	Almost all the time
My teacher helps me when I need it.			X		
Weighting Assigned for This Response			3		

Figure 9.8

Items	Weighting Key
1. Some things my teacher knows a lot about are: (Each thing mentioned is counted as a different response.)	A weighted response is computed by counting the number of things the student mentions, and multiplying that by 5. Thus, if a student mentions three things the teacher knows a lot about, a weighted score of 15 is assigned to the item.
2. Some things my teacher does not know a lot about are: (Each thing mentioned is counted as different response.)	A weighted response is computed by counting the number of things the student mentions four things the teacher does not know a lot about weighted score of 4 is assigned to the item.

Figure 9.9

Student Paper #1

Item 1	3	Item 5	1	Item 9	1
Item 2	5	Item 6	4	Item 10	4
Item 3	2	Item 7	3	Item 11	5
Item 4	2	Item 8	1	Item 12	5

Figure 9.10

with the weighted scores shown in Figure 9.10, the student score is computed by:

1. *Adding* the weighted scores for each of the twelve response items. (The sum of the twelve scores is 36.)
2. *Dividing* the sum of the scores by the number of response items. (36 divided by 12 is 3.) *The total score for the student in Figure 9.10 is 3.*

With the weighted scores shown in Figure 9.9, the student score is computed by:

1. *Adding* the weighted scores for the two items. (The sum of 15 and 4 is 19.)

2. *Dividing* the sum of the two scores by the number of responses. (There were *three* responses in the first item and *four* responses in the second item, or *seven* responses altogether. Thus, the sum of 19 divided by 7 is 2.7.) The total score for the student in Figure 9.9 is 2.7.

Determine the class score.   The class score is the average of the individual student scores. The class score is computed by:

1. *Adding* the individual student scores.
2. *Dividing* the sum of individual scores by the number of students. The result is the class score.

The class score for each month might be recorded on a form like that shown in Figure 9.11. The class scores for student affection shown in Figure 9.11 indicate that the teacher is successfully increasing personal influence. That increase in personal influence is evidenced in the classroom by a decreasing problem with discipline. In November, students seem to respond quicker and more positively than they did in September.

Diagnostic Interpretation   The purpose of diagnostic interpretation is to identify specific areas where problems seem to be occurring, or where progress should be made. For example, if a teacher using the instrument shown in Figure 9.1 found that most students rated him rather negatively in "Talks too loudly," then he knows that he can probably increase student affection by lowering the volume of his voice. If the same teacher found that students rated him negatively in "Has Class pets," then he knows that he must give more attention to responding in similar ways to all students. If a teacher using the instrument shown in Figure 9.7 had a generally negative rating for "My Teacher Knows a Lot About How to Teach P.E.," then the teacher knows that she should spend more time playing with the students. She may decide to take additional inservice coursework in order to develop more competency in P.E. On the other hand, she may decide to write off P.E. as a lost cause and concentrate on other areas where she has more chance of demonstrating an improvement in competence. She may, for example, concentrate on increasing her rating in art, where she has more natural ability.

GROUP COHESION

Group cohesion refers to the feeling of "we-ness" among members of a classroom group, meaning that they are likely to think and

Student Affection						
Sept.	Oct.	Nov.	Dec.	Jan.	Feb.	Mar.
2.5	3.3	3.9				

Figure 9.11

speak in terms of "we" rather than "I." The feeling of "we-ness" can be assessed in two ways. One way is to assess how students feel about being in their classroom, and the degree to which they would rather be in this class than in any other. A second way is to identify the range of mutual friendship choices, and the existence of cliques and cleavages. The wider the range of mutual friendship choices and less evidence of cliques and cleavages, the more cohesive the classroom group. The assessment of friendship choices, cliques and cleavages will be explained later, in the part dealing with Group Structure. The instruments and interpretation explained at this time refer to how good students feel about being in the classroom.

Instruments

An instrument designed to assess group cohesion is shown in Figure 9.12. Notice that the questions are of two types: (1) they refer to the satisfaction of being in *this* class; and (2) they ask for comparisons between *this* class and *other* classes. The instrument uses a multiple-choice format.

The same questions can be used in a free-response format. Figure 9.13 shows a free-response format for the first two questions.

At the lower grade levels the questions given in Figure 9.12 can be organized in a format similar to that shown in Figure 9.5. Notice that assessment instruments used in the lower grades usually have only three rating steps, in place of the five steps used with instruments intended for older students. That is about as much distinction as younger students are able to make.

Interpretation

Two types of interpretation are explained next, numerical and diagnostic. The purpose of numerical interpretation is to derive a number.

Directions: *Tell how you feel about this classroom by indicating your response to each question. Do not write your name on the paper.*

	Feelings				
Questions	*Not at all*	*Not very often*	*Some-times*	*Quite often*	*Almost all the time*
1. Do you like being in this classroom?					
2. Do people in this classroom stand up for each other outside the class-room?					
3. Would you rather be in this classroom than in another?					
4. Do people in this class show pride in what they do in the class?					
5. Do you tell friends in other classes what you do in this class?					
6. Do you know people in other classes who wish they were in this class?					

Figure 9.12

1. Do you like being in this classroom? Why? _____

2. Do people in this classroom stand up for each other? Why?

_____

Figure 9.13

The purpose of diagnostic interpretation is to identify specific problems.

The steps in making a numerical interpretation are identical to those explained earlier in this chapter.

Numerical Interpretation

1. Assign a weighted score to each response a student makes.
2. Determine the total score for each student.
3. Determine the class score.

You may want to review that earlier explanation. You may also want to examine again the record form shown in Figure 9.11. The same kind of form could be used in recording progress in developing group cohesion.

You should not attempt a diagnostic interpretation with instruments designed to assess how students feel about being in this class rather than in some other class. Treat the instrument as a whole and do not attempt to determine the meaning of scores on separate items, as would be done with instruments designed to assess personal influence.

Diagnostic Interpretation

GROUP STANDARDS

Group standards are the implicit agreements existing between members of a group about the behaviors that all members of the group ought to exhibit. When a teacher assesses group standards she tries to determine the degree to which certain behaviors are accepted by most members of the classroom group. A certain behavior is a group standard, and members will influence each other to exhibit it, only when there is a high degree of agreement about the *properness* of it.

Group standards can then be thought of in terms of two components: (1) the *behavior,* and (2) the *degree of acceptance* of that behavior. The teacher wants to determine the *degree of acceptance* students have for a certain *behavior.* If the degree of acceptance is very high then students can be expected to carry out the behavior without teacher supervision. For example, if most class members accept the behavior of *cleaning up the paint brushes after each use,* the teacher can assume that group influence will function to keep the art corner clean. But the teacher also needs to identify those particular students who do not accept the behavior of cleaning the paint brushes, because if personal influence is not exerted on them through the use of desist techniques then they could turn the art corner into a disaster area. The two components of *behavior* and *acceptance* are identified both through the design of assessment instruments and the interpretation of students' responses.

Instruments

The degree of acceptance of certain behaviors can be determined with an instrument like that shown in Figure 9.14. It is intended to determine students' degree of acceptance of three behaviors.

Notice that students are asked to write their names on the assessment instrument shown in Figure 9.14. This enables the teacher to identify students who do not accept the same behavior that most other members do. But asking students to put their names on the paper may result in invalid responses. They may give the answer they think the teacher wants rather than the one which represents their actual feelings. One way to check the validity of their responses is to give the same instrument a week later, the second time without names. If the same numerical interpretation is made each time, the results are valid. If the numerical interpretations differ, the teacher will want to disregard the set of instruments with names.

In the lower grade levels, a format like that shown in Figure 9.5 might be used. Also, at the lower grade levels it is extremely critical to teach students how to rate their feelings before trying to assess their acceptance of certain behaviors. Instruments designed to teach students to rate their feelings were shown in Figure 9.2.

	I agree almost always	I agree more than I disagree	I agree as often as I disagree	I disagree more than I agree	I disagree almost always
Name _____					
Directions: *How do you feel about these things? Put an X under the response that best describes your feelings about each statement*					
A. Asking the teacher for help is a good thing to do.					
B. After a person has finished painting it is good to clean the brushes.					
C. It is good to help other students with their work, except during tests.					

Figure 9.14

Interpretation

The tallying of students' responses is accomplished most easily by using one of the student instruments. Tallied responses from a classroom are shown in Figure 9.15.

The easiest way of making a numerical interpretation is to identify the *modal number,* the one that is the largest. The three sequences of tallies from the form shown in Figure 9.15 are given in Figure 9.16. The *modal number* in each sequence is circled.

Cleaning Paint Brushes is the most highly accepted behavior

Numerical Interpretation

Name _____

Direction: *How do you feel about these things? Put an X under the response that best describes your feelings about each statement.*

	I agree almost always	I agree more than I disagree	I agree as often as I disagree	I disagree more than I agree	I disagree almost always
A. Asking the teacher for help is a good thing to do.	4	18	10	1	0
B. After a person has finished painting it is good to clean the brushes.	15	14	2	1	0
C. It is good to help other students with their work, except during tests.	8	10	12	1	2

Figure 9.15

Behavior		Tallies			
Asking	4	(18)	10	1	0
Cleaning	(15)	14	3	1	0
Helping	8	10	(12)	1	2

Figure 9.16

and *Helping Other Children with Their Work* is the most poorly accepted, although not rejected. The teacher will want to work at getting students to want to help each other.

These data have meaning only when compared with data collected at an earlier or later time in the same classroom. While *Helping Children* is not a highly accepted kind of behavior now, the teacher will know that progress is being made if that behavior is more highly accepted now than it was a month ago.

A more exact numerical interpretation can be accomplished by identifying the *mean number,* the average. A weight is assigned to each level of choice. The number of tallies at each level is multiplied by the weight, and the weighted tallies are then averaged to find the *mean.* In Figure 9.17 the procedure is described with the first behavior assessed, *Asking the Teacher for Help.*

The number 3.7 refers to the mean placement along the weighted five-point scale. If the next time the teacher gives this assessment instrument the mean is 4.5 then she knows that substantial progress is being made in establishing a certain behavior as a group standard.

A monthly record can be kept of group standards by recording the mean scores for each behavior on a form like that shown in Figure 9.18.

The monthly record provides the teacher with evidence of the success of his use of strategies. With the classroom shown in Figure 9.18, the teacher has been able to maintain the behaviors of *Asking* and *Cleaning,* and has been very successful in gaining a much greater acceptance of *Helping.*

Diagnostic interpretation goes on at two levels when assessing group standards, the group and the individual.

Diagnostic Interpretation

	Asking the Teacher For Help				
Tallies at Each Level	4	18	10	1	0
Weights Assigned	5	4	3	2	1
Weights Times Tallies	20	72	30	2	0
Sum of Weights Times Tallies					124
Mean (Sum Divided by Number of Children—124 ÷ 33 = 3.7)					3.7

Figure 9.17

Behavior	Dates						
	Sept.	Oct.	Nov.	Dec.	Jan.	Feb.	Mar.
Asking	3.7	3.9					
Cleaning	4.4	4.5					
Helping	3.6	4.3					

Figure 9.18

Group Level. In terms of the group, tallies used in identifying the modal level of acceptance sometimes indicate different ranges of acceptance for different behaviors. For example, the data shown in Figure 9.16 indicates that the range acceptance for *Asking* and *Cleaning* is much narrower than the range for *Helping.* With the first two behaviors most of the tallies fall into two levels. With *Asking,* 28 out of 33 fall into the second and third highest levels. With *Cleaning,* 30 out of 33 fall into the highest and second highest levels. But with *Helping,* the tallies are spread over three levels. Students seem to be in more agreement about how they accept the behaviors of *Asking* and *Cleaning* than about how they accept the behavior *Helping.* The relative lack of agreement among students with respect to the behavior of *Helping* probably indicates that more arguments will arise about *Helping* than about the other two behaviors. If a behavior has a low level of acceptance, the teacher can expect that desist techniques may have to be used for classroom management.

Incidently, notice that mean scores can mask the actual range of agreement. Compare the mean scores shown in Figure 9.18 (September only) with the modal scores shown in Figure 9.16. If one looked only at mean scores then the real differences in agreement between *Asking* and *Helping* would not be recognized.

Individual Level. A diagnostic interpretation of individual scores can be accomplished by comparing group scores and individual scores. The one student who is in the second lowest level for *Cleaning,* when 30 out of 33 of the rest of the students fall into the top two levels, deviates markedly from the group standard. That student can be expected to be a continual irritant to other students and the teacher because he will probably be the one who does not clean the paint brushes after using them. If the teacher does not take some definite action with this deviating student, she can expect that there will be numerous unpleasant incidents in the art corner, and eventually that type of behavior will be less accepted by many students. One deviating student, if not properly handled by the teacher, can make activities like the art corner such a disaster that they must be discontinued. One or two students should not be allowed to have such a depressing effect on the educational program.

The student who deviates markedly from the group standard may do so for two reasons. First, the student might not feel like a part of the group, and evidences this lack of acceptance by rejecting those behaviors that others think are important. If he cannot join, he will fight. If the student's feeling of lack of acceptance is the problem, it will probably also show up on a sociometric measure, where he will be found to be an isolate. (Sociometric measures are explained later.) The teacher should do everything she can to raise this person's status in the group, and to make him feel like an important member of it. The more the student comes to feel accepted by the group, the less he will reject their standards and act in contrary ways to them and to the teacher.

The second reason for a student deviating markedly from the group standard may not be rejection, but social blindness. The student might have such poorly developed social antennae that he simply does not perceive the subtle behaviors by which members of a group communicate with each other about their standards. This student is like the person who dresses inappropriately for a party, seems totally unaware of it, and then is hurt when people reject him. An instrument that can be used to assess students' perception of norms is shown in Figure 9.19.

Each student's response is compared with the modal scores determined earlier (Figure 9.16). The more a student deviates from the mode, the poorer his perception of norms. The reference score could also be the class mean. The accuracy of a student's perception of norms can be determined by using the form shown in Figure 9.20. 0 indicates that the students' choice was identical to the mode. A +1 is one above, +2 is two above. A sample computation is shown.

The results indicate that Robert and Maria perceive group standards accurately. Hank, on the other hand, is very inaccurate. The teacher should do everything she can to develop Hank's social consciousness in order to help him get more socially in touch with others. Hank will benefit from *role play,* where he can be helped to see himself through the eyes of others. Participation in *group*

	Almost All	Many	About Half	Some	Only a Few
Name_____					
Directions: Put an X to tell how you think your classmates feel about these things. There are no right or wrong answers					
Asking the teacher for help is a good thing to do.					
After a person has finished painting it is good to clean the paint brushes.					
It is good to help other students with their work, except during tests					

Figure 9.19

Name_____		Behaviors	
	Asking	Cleaning	Helping
Robert	0	0	0
Maria	−1	0	0
Hank	−2	−2	−1

Figure 9.20

projects and *group discussion* should also help him to develop social maturity.

GROUP STRUCTURE

Groups are characterized by a system of social stratification where individual members have a certain status and are involved in definite patterns of interaction. The higher a person's status in the group is, the more attractive group membership is, and thus the greater influence the group has over that individual. Students having low status are underestimated by both the teacher and other students, and they are poorly motivated, frequently ill, do poorly academically, and are likely to be hostile to both the teacher and other students. Groups as large as classrooms have a tendency to split into subgroups. If the subgroups become more than loosely organized friendship clusters, and cliques and cleavages develop, the healthy atmosphere of the classroom group is adversely affected.

The purpose of assessment and interpretation of group structure is to identify the status of individual members and the existence of subgroups.

Instruments

Group structure is assessed by *sociometry*. Sociometry is designed to measure *(metric)* the social structure *(socio)* of a group. Sociometric techniques indicate the status and interaction patterns for each group member by measuring the extent of acceptance between individuals in groups.

The assessment instrument used in sociometry is called a sociometric test. In a sociometric test students are asked to indicate their choice of partners for different activities. A simple sociometric test is shown in Figure 9.21. It covers two activities and asks for first and second choices.

Name_____

Directions: *List below the people in our class that you would like to be with in the two different situations. Your answers will be in private. Only you and your teacher will know how you answer.*

1. Write the names of two people you would most like to sit with in the *lunchroom*:

   *First Choice:*_____

   *Second Choice:*_____

2. Write the names of two people you would most like to do a *science project* with:

   *First Choice:*_____

   *Second Choice:*_____

Figure 9.21

A major strength of sociometry is that it approaches people in the midst of actual life situations, not before or after them. The choices students are asked to make are *real.* The validity of the sociometric test is directly related to its realness. If students, for example, are asked who they would like to sit with in the lunchroom and work with on a science project, this should be followed by their actual assignment to science projects and lunchroom seats. Students should be asked who they would like to sit with in the lunchroom *only* if the seating there is actually assigned.

Another sociometric test is shown in Figure 9.22. It identifies three activities and asks for first, second, and third choices. Notice that both sociometric tests include a variety of academic and non-academic activities. The sociometric test shown in Figure 9.22

Name_____

Directions: *Read the sentences below and tell who you would like to be with in three different situations. This will be private, only you and the teacher will know how you answer.*

1. *Social Studies*   What member of our class would you like to be on a social studies committee with?

    *First Choice:*_____

    *Second Choice:*_____

    *Third Choice:*_____

2. *Field Trip*   If our class was going on a field trip, who would be your choice to sit with on the bus?

    *First Choice:*_____

    *Second Choice:*_____

    *Third Choice:*_____

3. *Party*   If you had a party at your house, who would you like to invite?

    *First Choice:*_____

    *Second Choice:*_____

    *Third Choice:*_____

Figure 9.22

had a social studies committee, a field trip, and a party. A variety of activities is critical because the teacher wants to determine general student status and subgroup organization. As you will see later, student choices vary in different activities. One person may be chosen frequently for an athletic activity but never chosen for an academic activity. What the teacher wants to know is the person's frequency and pattern of choices in a representative sampling of activities.

If students do not know each other's names well, a class list could be distributed. If students have name cards on their desks, as is common in the primary grades, these can serve to remind students of names.

Interpretation

The results of sociometric tests are tallied on a chart like that shown in Figure 9.23. The test used was the one shown in Figure 9.21. First and second choices for lunch are indicated by the number placed to the *left* of the slash. Thus, the designation 2/ indicates that the person was chosen *second for lunch.* First and second choices for science are indicated by the number placed to the *right* of the slash. Thus, the designation /1 indicates that the person was chosen *first for science.* Further, the designation 2/1 in the same box indicates that the person was chosen second for lunch and first for science. The slash could be eliminated if colored pencils were used; a green number indicating choices for lunch a red number choices for science.

When no number appears in a box it indicates that the person was not chosen first or second for either activity. The numbered names in the horizontal rows indicate the *Choosers.* The numbers in the vertical columns refer to those *Chosen* by the persons shown in the horizontal rows. The numbers in the horizontal rows are the same as those in the vertical columns. (Number 1 is Betty and Number 15 is Norm.) The names are arranged by the alphabetical order of students' last names.

Examine the *Totals* given on the bottom of the chart shown in Figure 9.23. The total for *Lunch* is determined by adding the number of times the person was chosen either first or second. Thus, the number 1 in the row labeled *Lunch* indicates the person was chosen either first or second by at least one person. The number 2 indicates that the person was chosen either first or second by at least two

Chooser	1	2	3	4	5	6	7	8	9	10	11	12	13	14	15	16
						Chosen										
1. Betty		2/1	2/								/1					
2. Maria						2/					1/2		/1			
3. Harriet						1/		/1								2/2
4. Joan						1/					2/2		/1			
5. Robert			2/								/2					1/1
6. Ted			2/								1/1		/2			
7. Jaime					1/			2/					/1			/2
8. Charles			1/			2/					/1		/2			
9. Peter											2/2					1/1
10. Nick						2/		/1				/2				1/
11. John				2/		/1							/2			1/
12. Larry						2/	/2							1/	/1	
13. Tonia	1/1								2/						/2	
14. Harry				/2							2/		/1	1/		
15. Norm		2/				1/						/2	/1			
16. Karen			1/					/1			2/2					
TOTALS																
Lunch	1	2	5	1	1	7	0	1	1	0	6	0	0	1	1	5
Science	1	1	0	1	0	1	1	3	0	0	8	2	8	0	2	4
Social Status	2	3	5	2	1	8	1	4	1	0	14	2	8	1	3	9

Figure 9.23

persons. With this chart, no weighting is assigned to first and second choices. (But the teacher may wish to assign differential weights, perhaps a weight of 1 to second choices and a weight of 2 to first choices.) The total for *Social Status* is determined by adding the numbers given for *Science* and *Lunch*. Thus, John (11) has a total social status of 14 and Nick (10) has a total social status of 0. Nick is an *isolate* and John is a *star*.

Numerical and diagnostic interpretation is carried out with the data summarized in a chart like that shown in Figure 9.23.

The purpose of a numerical interpretation is to derive numbers that indicate a certain situation. The numbers derived in a numerical interpretation of sociometric data indicate social status and subgroups. For example, the chart shown in Figure 9.23 assigns Nick a social status score of 0, indicating that he is an isolate. As a means of helping you understand both the meaning and value of numerical interpretation, data from two classrooms will be examined and compared. A portion of the pattern of sociometric choices for both classrooms is shown in Figures 9.24 and 9.25. Only a portion of the data is shown and examined because a complete visualization of the sociometric patterns requires the use of colored lines.

Numerical Interpretation

Examine the sociogram shown in Figure 9.24. It shows the first and second choices in science for the classroom that was tested with the sociometric test shown in Figure 9.21 and summarized with the chart shown in Figure 9.23. This is called a *circle sociogram,* and is the easiest sociogram to construct. Names are arranged in a circle and choice lines drawn between them.

The sociogram shown in Figure 9.25 is arranged in a way that visually displays subgroups. It is more difficult to construct than the circle sociogram shown in Figure 9.24. The *subgroup sociogram* is constructed by placing together those having *mutual* choices. John and Robert are mutual choices because they chose each other. Those who do not choose each other are placed far apart. A subgroup sociogram is constructed by starting with those most frequently chosen, and then placing close to them the names of those they have chosen. For example, Eugene is frequently chosen and so his name is written first. The names of the persons he chose are placed near Eugene's name. In order to simplify the sociogram, only first choices for the activities are shown in Figure 9.25.

The classroom shown in Figure 9.25 has both *cliques* and a *cleavage.* The four subgroups are *cliques* because there are no mutual choices between them. For example, John who is in the group to the upper right, chose Diane, who is in the group to the upper left, but she did not reciprocate that choice. Jane, who is in the group to the upper left chose Eugene, but he did not reciprocate that choice. A *cleavage* exists between the two upper subgroups and the two lower subgroups because there are no choices between them, either reciprocated or not. A *clique refers to no mutual choices between members* in different subgroups. A *cleavage refers to no choices between members* in different subgroups. Cleavage involves a higher degree of alienation between subgroups than does a clique. Groups

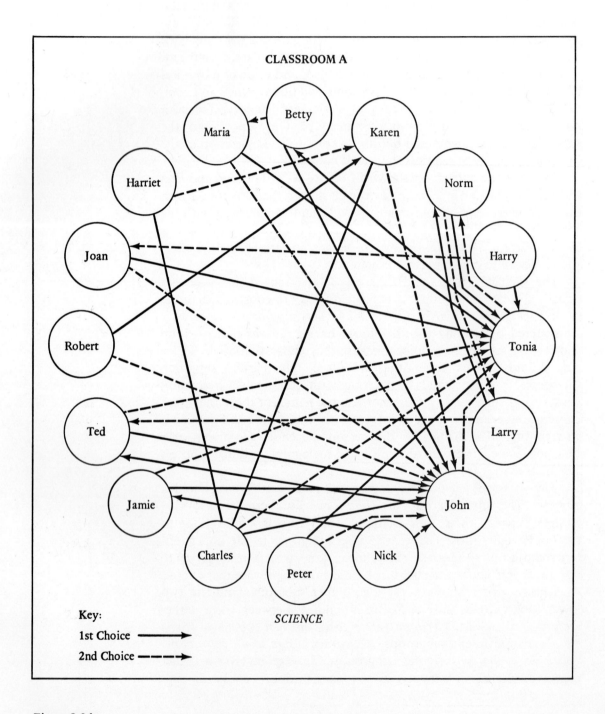

CLASSROOM A

SCIENCE

Key:
1st Choice ——————▶
2nd Choice – – – –▶

Figure 9.24

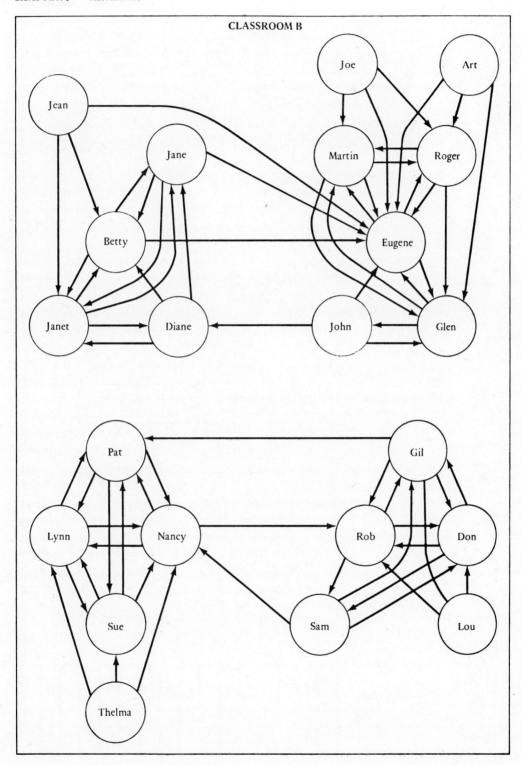

CLASSROOM B

Figure 9.25

having cleavages are less healthy than those having only cliques, and groups having cliques are less healthy than subgroups having only loosely formed friendship clusters. On a sociogram, the latter type of classroom looks like one big subgroup; no cliqued or cleaved subgroups can be identified.

Three types of numerical interpretation will be explained: (1) raw score, (2) median, and (3) percentage.

Raw Score. The bottom row in Figure 9.23 provides a raw score interpretation. The bottom row is shown in Figure 9.27. The classroom has one *isolate*, Number 10. The major *star* in the room is Number 11. The class has four stars altogether: Numbers 6, 11, 13, and 16.

The teacher's goal is to reduce the number of isolates in the classroom. If the teacher with the class shown in Figure 9.26 is successful, the next time the sociometric test is administered there will be no isolates. If the health of the classroom is declining, there is likely to be more than one isolate the next time the sociometric is administered. Classroom A, shown in Figure 9.24, has a healthier classroom atmosphere than Classroom B, shown in Figure 9.25 because Classroom A has *one isolate out of sixteen students,* and Classroom B has *five isolates out of twenty-two students.*

Median Score. A median score provides an indication of the degree of unity in the classroom group. The more unified the classroom group the more widely choices are distributed, and thus the less the range between those receiving many choices and those receiving only a few. The median score is determined by arranging social status scores from high to low. For example, if the social status scores shown in the bottom row in Figure 9.26 are arranged from high to low, they would look like Figure 9.27. The midpoint, or median, is also shown. The median is equally distant from each end; in this case, it is the point eight from the top and eight from the bottom.

Student Number Codes	1	2	3	4	5	6	7	8	9	10	11	12	13	14	15	16
Social Status	2	3	5	2	1	8	1	4	1	0	14	2	8	1	3	9

Figure 9.26

Social Status   0   1   1   1   1   2   2   2 ↑ 3   3   4   5   8   8   9   14
median

Figure 9.27

If equivalent data were available for Classroom A (Figure 9.24) and Classroom B (Figure 9.25) then the median scores of these two classrooms could be compared. Classroom A would probably be found to have a higher median score than Classroom B. The higher the median score, the more healthy the classroom atmosphere. The goal of the teacher is to raise the median score.

Percentage Scores. Percentage scores can be determined for a number of classroom characteristics that indicate the health of a classroom. The most important scores and their meaning are:

1. *Percentage of isolates.* The lower the percentage of isolates, the healthier the classroom atmosphere.
2. *Percentage of mutuals.* The higher the percentage of mutual choices, the healthier the classroom atmosphere.
3. *Percentage of unreciprocated choices.* The lower the percentage of unreciprocated choices, the healthier the classroom atmosphere.
4. *Percentage of inter-group choices* (sex, ethnic, racial). The higher the percentage of intergroup choices, the healthier the classroom atmosphere.

The steps of computing two of these percentages are shown for Classrooms A and B. The computation is shown in Figure 9.28.

The numerical interpretation of the two characteristics shows the differences between Classrooms A and B to be great. The summarized numerical interpretation is shown in Figure 9.29.

The goal of the teacher in both classrooms should be to lower the percentage of isolates and increase the percentage of intergroup choices. The teacher in Classroom B will have improved the group climate in that room if the next time the sociometric test is given the percentage of isolates is less than 22 percent and the percentage of intergroup sex choices is higher than 9 percent.

The purpose of diagnostic interpretation is to identify specific areas where problems seem to be occurring, or where progress   *Diagnostic Interpretation*

Computing the Percentage of Isolates

Step	Figures
1. Identify the number of children.	Classroom A—16 Classroom B—22
2. Identify the number of isolates.	Classroom A—1 Classroom B—5
3. Divide the number of isolates by the number of children.	Classroom A—1 ÷ 16 = .06 Classroom B—5 ÷ 22 = 22.
4. Multiply the dividend by 100. *This is the percentage of isolates in the classroom.*	Classroom A—6% Classroom B—22%

Computing the Percentage of Intergroup Sex Choices

Step	Figures
1. Identify the number of children.	Classroom A—16 Classroom B—22
2. Identify the number of choices each child can give.	Classroom A—2 Classroom B—3
3. Multiply the number of choices by the number of children. This gives the total number of choices.	Classroom A—16 X 2 = 32 Classroom B—22 X 3 = 66
4. Identify the number of intergroup sex choices. Count the number of times a boy chooses a girl and a girl chooses a boy.	Classroom A—16 Classroom B—6
5. Divide the number of intergroup sex choices by the total number of choices.	Classroom A—16 ÷ 32 = .50 Classroom B—6 ÷ 66 = .09
6. Multiply the dividend by 100. *This is the percentage of inter-group sex choices in the class room.*	Classroom A—50% Classroom B—9%

Figure 9.28

should or could be made. Diagnostic interpretation should be directed at two levels, the individual and the group.

Individual Level. It would be helpful, for example, to have some *possible* explanations of why Nick (Figures 9.23 and 9.24) is an isolate. Is he new to the class? Is he from a different racial, ethnic, or social background than the rest of the students? Does he have

Index	Classroom	Percentage
Isolates	A	6%
	B	22%
Intergroup	A	50%
Sex Choices	B	9%

Figure 9.29

some particularly obnoxious characteristics? Is he socially immature? The explanation can lead to a hypothesis about remediation. If Nick is new to the class, then the teacher might hypothesize, "If I find ways for other students in the class to become better acquainted with Nick, then they will be more likely to choose him for activities." The teacher might then organize a *group project* where Nick is assigned with students of higher status. The teacher might conduct a *group discussion* about how the class should treat people that are new. The class might *role play* being a new student. The teacher might give Nick an assignment where he must interact frequently with other students, such as the job of distributing the athletic equipment at recess time.

On the other hand, if the possible explanation for Nick's isolation is his immature and ego-defensive behavior, the teacher may want to try *counseling strategies* and *role play*. Perhaps if Nick had an opportunity to view his behavior as others view it, he would realize that it alienates him from other students. The class might be helped to show more understanding and restraint if they participated in *group discussions* and *role plays* where problems like Nick's were examined.

Group Level. A teacher with a group like Classroom B (Figure 9.25) will want to try and explain the basis for the cliques and cleavages. An examination of Figure 9.25 leads one to suggest a possible explanation for the cliques; the boys and girls are in different cliques and so sex seems to be the reason for the alienation. That explanation leads logically to the hypothesis, "If I find ways to involve the boys and girls in cooperative activities, they will be more likely to choose each other." The teacher might organize *group projects* and assign boys and girls to work together on the same project.

Figure 9.25 contains insufficient information to suggest a possible explanation for the cleavage between the top two subgroups and the bottom two subgroups. The teacher will want to examine other information that might provide some insight. The teacher should give particular attention to such stratification criteria as sex, age, personality, size, looks, material possessions, athletic ability, race, ethnicity, and social class. If the teacher concludes that the cleavage seems to be on the basis of social class—the top two groups are bussed from a low income area—then the teacher can devise appropriate remedial measures. *Group projects* might be initiated where students from both social classes are assigned to the same project. The class might *role play* problems involving social class. They might conduct *group discussions* about how they can deal with problems created by social class differences.

Teachers faced with cleavages or cliques too often make the mistake of trying to ignore the basic problem. It is almost as if they believed that if the problem is not mentioned, it will go away. But it usually does not. A straightforward discussion of such problems may not result in solutions for the society, but it will result in a more healthy classroom atmosphere and the increased satisfactions that come with participation in healthy classrooms. With those satisfactions will come increased motivation, academic improvement, more self-direction, and fewer discipline problems.

10

Situational Examples

SITUATION 1

As a result of an unexpectedly large student enrollment, Mrs. G. was hired a month after school started in the fall. Nine or ten students selected from the existing fifth grades in the school formed her new class. The class was housed in a temporary building next to the school. Most portable buildings are drab, noisy, and lack aesthetic appeal, and hers was no exception.

Teacher: The first morning I felt the students' antagonism and apprehension. Apparently the rumor had been about for two weeks that a new class would be formed, but all at once it was a reality and I was confronted with children who felt displaced and rejected. I tried to begin by getting acquainted. We played some new games, but the general mood varied from uneasiness to apathy.

Comment: Preparation for change is important at any age. The small child needs it as well as the adult. To suddenly be flung into a new situation is disconcerting. Not surprisingly, many students feel rejected, "Why was I chosen to go?" Feelings of rejection are particularly strong when good friends are split up.

Teacher: After we arranged the seats and put some things away, it was recess time. Later I found out from the other teachers that during recess they either played with their old classmates or complained to their former teachers that they wished to go back to their "old" room.

Comment: This is to be expected and the teacher should not feel discouraged. A teacher coming in after school has been in session awhile is at a disadvantage. By then, a classroom has become a group and students feel secure in a certain routine. Mrs. G. will need to instill a new routine (which is relatively easy) and build group morale (not as easy).

Teacher: That first week we had some art projects to decorate our rather drab room. The children worked well together and created some colorful artistic murals and mobiles. They were obviously pleased with their efforts and several stayed after school to hang them. I noticed that later in the first week many of them played together during recess.

Comment: Cohesion isn't built overnight, but this class seems to be well on the way to identifying with Mrs. G. Building morale in a class, whether newly formed or well-established, is important. "We belong to Room 12," is a spirit that brings identification and cooperation.

Possible Solutions

1. Invite the principal into the room to verbally reward the children. This could be just a few words of praise about the art work they are exhibiting.
2. Enlist children in a joint task, a clean-up day, a talent show, or the writing and production of a play.
3. Invite parents to come and see the play or talent show. Committees could be formed to greet and seat the parents, have them sign a guest book, and prepare and serve simple refreshments.
4. Arrange sports events with other classrooms. The preparation for and competition of a kickball game or a track meet can bring a group together. Reward both the losers and winners with ribbons and simple refreshments.

SITUATION 2

Miss K.'s class has a high level of activity. Several children seem to border on being hyperactive and it is difficult to hold their attention for more than a few minutes.

Teacher: The children in my class seem unable to work independently at either academic or extracurricular tasks. They talk and squabble incessantly. I have a police whistle that I blow to get their attention. This quiets them down temporarily.

Comment: Combating noise with more noise is emotional, rude, and ineffective.

Teacher: I have a sentence that I make children write either as a group or as individual punishment. They write, "I'm glad Miss K. is teaching me to be good." They must write it twenty-five times and this quiets them down.

Comment: This may quiet the culprits temporarily but it in no way changes the behavior of the group or individuals. In fact, the sentence would more accurately describe the situation if it read, "Miss K. is teaching me to dislike school."

Teacher: Some of the children in the class write these sentences ahead and when I hand out the punishment, they have them already written. This bothers me, and I'm not sure what to do about it. Maybe I should give a different sentence each time.

Comment: Rather than different sentences, this teacher needs to think of alternatives to her punishment strategy.

Teacher: No matter where I place about eight children in the class, there is trouble. I've tried putting them in all seating arrangements imaginable but no matter what I do there is constant bickering. The noise level in the classroom is always high.

Comment: There are two different aspects to scrutinize here. First, there is apparently general discord among the students in the class. Second, the teacher may be overly concerned about noise level.

Possible Solutions

1. When gaining class attention it is usually just as effective to use quiet means as noisy ones. Usually lights are on in the classroom during school hours. Simply turning out these lights can bring a hush to the class. Other quiet signals are raising hands and humming a quiet tune. Different techniques work at the various grade levels, but all respond to gentle persuasion.

2. Chronic misbehavior by many in the class points to more maladjustment than the mere writing of sentences can cure. It might help to find out the social composition of the class through a sociogram.

3. Find out how the students feel about the teacher. Use one of the forms illustrated in the chapter on assessment.

4. Have a class discussion to elicit ideas from the students about how the class might view punishment for deviant behavior.

5. Get some group projects going that might eliminate bickering.

6. Set up learning centers to which children can go when they are capable of working independently.

SITUATION 3

Mrs. R.'s fourth-grade class seems to be well-behaved only when the teacher is present and directing the class. When Mrs. R. leaves the room, even momentarily, or talks to a visitor, the class immediately explodes.

Comment: This is an example of an autocratic classroom. Anarchy reigns in the absence of the authority figure, the teacher. A democratic classroom is more likely to function well without a teacher present.

Teacher: Yesterday Mrs. B., a mother of one of the students, came into the class to tell me about a new home situation that might effect the child's behavior at school. The children were writing their spelling words. After about one minute the noise level in the room rose sharply.

Comment: The parent should have made an appointment to speak with the teacher at a more convenient time. A matter of this nature requires a setting where both parties can share thoughts without outside interference. Nevertheless, there are situations where a hasty conference seemingly cannot be avoided.

Teacher: I turned to the class twice to ask for quiet. The second time I called out the names of three or four troublemakers. This settled them for a few seconds but soon it was back to the same din. I felt embarrassed and found it hard to concentrate on what Mrs. B. was trying to explain.

Comment: After becoming used to being repressed, children (and adults) find freedom hard to handle because they have not built up a normative pattern of inner restraints. The result is often bedlam.

Teacher: Finally, in exasperation, I turned to Alice and asked her to write down the names of people misbehaving or talking on the chalkboard. Things seemed to quiet immediately and I was able to finish the conversation.

Comment: Poor Alice! She has been placed in a police role. Why was she chosen? Is she an isolate among her classmates because she wins the favor of the teacher? Or, does she maintain control of the class because she is a leader and has gained the respect of her peers?

Teacher: When Mrs. B. left, I turned to the class and told them how rude they had been. I said they lacked consideration for others and that they could give up their recess to sit and think about it.

Comment: This class probably needs recess to vent some of that energy it has just been trying to show. Sitting quietly may well build additional resentment that will be exhibited next time a similar occasion occurs.

Possible Solutions

1. Have a class *discussion* (not a lecture!). The teacher might express to the class how she felt during this interruption in class routine. She could elicit from the class possible ways of dealing with the situation. She might list the class's decisions on the chalkboard and later write them on a chart.
2. Role play the situation. Mrs. R. might select students to play the role of the visitor and the teacher. This could be done several times with an evaluation of each alternative. Role playing helps children understand the feelings of others and builds an appreciation of the importance of self-control.
3. Make certain that children are aware of acceptable things to do when they complete their assigned tasks.

SITUATION 4

The learning centers in Mr. H.'s classroom seem to be havens for club meetings, giggling parties, water fights, and jousting matches.

Teacher: It's not that the children don't get along. Rarely do they fight or have disagreements. It is just that they feel that it is "do your own thing time" when the teacher isn't giving them attention.

Comment: Learning centers can become bastions for such activities if well-meaning teachers have not planned carefully.

Teacher: Yesterday as I was teaching a group of three children, the principal walked in to tell me that the neighboring teachers were complaining about the noise from my room. I realized it was a legitimate complaint as I observed and listened. Frankly, sometimes I become so engrossed in what I am teaching that I shut out the outside sounds and concentrate on the lesson at hand.

Comment: This can be an asset as well as a liability, but quite obviously, someone must be aware of what is going on in the total classroom.

Teacher: After I got the children's attention, I decided it was time for a council meeting. I called the chairman up and I presented the problem to her. She then asked for discussion from the class and I observed the meeting.

Comment: This is an excellent way to bring an awareness to the class that there is a problem which involves them and that they have a responsibility to help solve it.

Teacher: A suggestion was made that we have rules posted at the learning centers. At the present time there are six centers, so the class divided into groups of about five students each. Each committee worked on rules for a particular center. After fifteen minutes the students returned to their desks and the meeting resumed. Each group presented the rules they suggested for a center. There was little disagreement as students seemed to readily accept the rules from the various committees.

Comment: Beautifully done! This teacher seems to be innovative and perceptive.

Possible Solutions

1. Make sure all learning centers are within eye range of the teacher as he is working with the individuals or small groups.

2. Try to shorten the time the children are ,left to work independently at the centers.

3. Have children keep individual records of what they accomplished during their independent work time.

4. Try to have fewer children involved in learning centers at a time. Some children might do independent reading or writing at their desks for a portion of the period.

SITUATION 5

To a casual observer, Miss J.'s third-grade classroom seems to function smoothly, but there is difficulty at every recess. Children come into the room upset, shouting accusations. Some are in tears. The common difficulty is conflict between boys and girls for play equipment and for water at the drinking fountain, and interference in playground games. The results of these everyday shouting and chasing matches are torn shirts, hot tempers, and, on the part of the teacher, frazzled nerves.

Comment: This is typical of the power struggle that occurs when there is cleavage in a group. The cleavage in this case is between the boys and girls.

Teacher: Hardly a recess goes by without a confrontation between the boys and girls arising. I dread opening the door and seeing their lines outside. I have a girls' line and boys' line, but you never would know it by looking at them. This boy-girl thing is getting out of hand.

Comment: Why have a girls' line and boys' line? This only serves to widen that already deep chasm. If lines are abolutely necessary (ideally they should be eliminated altogether) there might be a Line A and a Line B with boys and girls in each.

Teacher: After the children come in and calm down, I try to hold a discussion to find out the cause of the difficulty. By the time each side's story is told, the root incident is so obscured by the various versions that I give up. We've already wasted fifteen minutes of our math time and all to no avail.

Comment: Are there class officers? If so, someone else should chair these discussions besides the teacher. It removes the teacher from the situation and places the responsibility for a solution on students.

Teacher: Yesterday I spoke with the physical education teachers about the problem. They, of course, don't encounter this because the boys go to Mr. G. and the girls to Mrs. K. for physical education twice a week. Each teacher spoke with praise about the group and said that there was always a cooperative spirit.

Comment: First, separate lines and now we discover separate P.E. instruction. We begin to wonder to what extent this sex separation exists in other areas. The cleavage between boys and girls is an expected consequence of this separation.

Possible Solutions

1. Find out the structure of the classroom by using a sociometric test. It will provide information about the interaction patterns for each cleaved subgroup. Obviously, there is a boy-girl cleavage, but does it apply to both the playground and the classroom?

2. Involve the class in a number of group projects where boys and girls are assigned to the same group. These might include a play for social studies, an art project, or a writing assignment that includes interviews and cooperative skills.

3. Have small group discussions at times when things are on a less emotional level—not just after recess. Arrange a lunch time dialogue with ten students at a time. In a relaxed atmosphere, it is easier for everyone to obtain objectivity and propose solutions.

Counselor Role

11

Conditions

We are born helpless. As soon as we are fully conscious we discover loneliness. We need others physically, emotionally, intellectually; we need them if we are to know anything, even ourselves.

C. S. Lewis, The Four Loves

Death is not the greatest loss in life. The greatest loss is what dies inside us while we live. The unbearable tragedy is to live without dignity or sensitivity.

Norman Cousins, Saturday Review, June 14, 1975

Someday, after mastering the winds, the waves, the tides and gravity, we shall harness the energies of love, and then for the second time in history man will discover fire.

Teilhard de Chardin

Teachers begin to harness the energies of love when they act on the realization that students' misbehavior is purposive and directed toward the attainment of needs. Students' behavior has a purpose, even if the students fail to recognize it. Misbehaving students have the same needs as other students, but they have incorrect ideas about themselves and less socially acceptable ways of achieving their needs. Unless a student can learn to attain needs in constructive ways, undesirable and destructive ways will be used. The need for affection, for example, is better achieved by misbehaving and being punished than by being so good that the teacher ignores you. Even negative attention is better than no attention at all.

Misbehaving students can be redirected and helped to develop better ideas about themselves by any teacher who is able to win their confidence and understand their ideas and behavior patterns. The teacher can win a student's confidence by endeavoring to establish emotional contact at what Martin Buber called the "I-Thou" level—being sensitive to the student's feelings, treating them as valid feelings, and respecting the student's dignity and treating the student as a unique individual.[1] The teacher can understand a student's behavior patterns and ideas about self by searching for common denominators of the student's actions. Two basic types of actions, self-concept and coping devices are described in this chapter. Self-concept refers to the students' ideas about themselves. Coping devices refer to the students' learned ways of dealing with stresses that arise from situations they encounter daily.

It is critical for the teacher to view adjustment as a continuum rather than as a pole wherein a student is considered to be either *adjusted* or *maladjusted*. To define either pole of adjustment or maladjustment is a fruitless task. The temptation is to define one as the absence of the other. It is closer to reality to think in terms of more adjustment and less adjustment. Karl Menninger views mental illness and mental health as a continuum: "The goal of therapeutic intervention is the expediting of the upward trend of the illness-recovery process. To accomplish this the positive factors must be

---

1. M. Buber, *Between Man and Man* (New York: The Macmillan Company, 1965). Buber distinguished between the "I-Thou" and the "I-It" relationships. The difference between the two kinds of relationships is not the nature of the object, whether human or non-human, but the nature of the relationship. An "I-Thou" relationship is open, direct, mutual and present. It occurs only when individuals actively experience the other side of the relationship, and, thus, achieve a state of "inclusion."

The "I-It" relationship, by contrast, is the typical subject-object situation wherein one uses other persons or things without allowing them to exist for themselves in their own uniqueness. The teacher is in an "I-It" relationship with a student when the student's misbehavior is viewed solely as something that must be curbed because it reflects unfavorably on the teacher when viewed by other students, the principal, other teachers, and parents. An "I-Thou" relationship occurs only when the teacher experiences personally the misbehaving student's feelings of discouragement, and the student, in turn, experiences the teacher's feelings of frustration in dealing with the student's misbehavior.

identified as well as the negative or pathogenic factors, the former to be supported and the latter combated."[2] A teacher can expedite students' upward trend of adjustment by helping them develop more adequate self-concepts and more constructive ways of coping with stress.

Teachers must be realistic about their limited ability to help students with serious personality maladjustments. First, the problem does not usually originate in the school, but in the home and neighborhood, and sometimes from a brain injury or genetically determined temperamental traits. Therefore, the amelioration of these conditions is largely beyond the teacher's control. There is little a teacher can do to change the home conditions of the "latchkey" child whose parents work, thereby leaving the child alone for long periods of time. The teacher alone can do little to change the home situation of a student whose anti-social behavior is the result of living with a brutal father and an overly permissive mother. Second, making a valid diagnosis and providing suitable treatment for serious personality disorders requires training and experience that is beyond what is expected of teachers. The most the teacher may be able to accomplish is to refer the student to other agencies that offer diagnosis and treatment. But teachers can try to help other students in the classroom get along with and accept the maladjusted student.

SELF-CONCEPT

Self-concept refers to the way one sees oneself. It is the totality of a person's understanding, attitudes and feelings. The view remains constant regardless of whatever environmental situation the person may be in at a given moment.

The concept people have of themselves can be inferred from the way they describe themselves. Physical features can be described, such as "I am five feet, three inches tall and I have brown eyes." Personality characteristics can be described such as, "I talk and laugh a lot." Feelings can be described, such as "I'm dumb."

Concepts of self are often complicated by false ideas. The tall, lanky, adolescent girl thinks she is severely malformed and handicapped and for this reason she feels men do not like her. The boy with slow reading-ability development thinks he is a poor reader.

---

2. Karl Menninger et al., *The Vital Balance* (New York: The Viking Press, 1963), p. 402.

One of the most depressing descriptions of false ideas about self is provided by black psychologist Kenneth Clark:

> When Negro children as young as three years old are shown white- and Negro-appearing dolls and asked to color pictures of children to look like themselves, many of them tend to reject the dark-skinned dolls as "dirty" or "bad" or to color the pictures of themselves a light color or a bizarre shade like purple. But the fantasy is not complete, for when asked to identify which doll is like themselves, some Negro children, particularly in the North, will refuse, burst into tears, and run away. By the age of seven most Negro children have accepted the reality that they are, after all, dark-skinned. But the stigma remains; they have been forced to recognize themselves as inferior. Few if any Negroes ever fully lose that sense of shame and self-hatred.[3]

People attempt to preserve a consistent image of themselves as they interact with their environment and interpret their experiences in that environment. They attempt to maintain that self image even in the face of later evidence that refutes its validity. If a boy has a concept of himself as a poor speller, he will remain a poor speller until convinced otherwise. He may possess the intellectual capacity to become an excellent speller, but will remain a poor speller. Clark describes a sense of inferiority among black children that causes them to work well below their actual capacities. Moreover, the depressing effect their negative self-concept has on their general performance in school, and especially in test situations, will usually keep the teacher from ever realizing their actual potential. These students will continue to perform below their actual capacities until they develop a more positive self-concept. They will work below their capacities even though the teacher is competent and uses outstanding methods of individualization and motivation.

Development of Self-Concepts

Self-concepts are developed from experience. As Overstreet noted:

> His estimates of himself reflect the treatment he receives from the key figures in his environment; it is not something he makes out of nothing, but something he makes of other people's responses to him. As others see him, so he gradually tends to see himself.[4]

---

3. Kenneth B. Clark, *Dark Ghetto* (New York: Harper & Row, 1965), pp. 64, 65.
4. B. W. Overstreet, "The Role of the Home in Mental Health," in *Mental Health in Modern Education*, N. B. Henry, ed., Yearbook of the National Society for Social Studies Education, Part II, vol. 54, 1955, p. 91.

A person's estimates of self are developed in two ways. First, judgments are formed based on inferences derived from interaction with the environment. The girl who fails at school tasks develops a concept of self as "dumb in school." The boy who notices that he can throw and catch a football better than others in his class develops a concept of self as "a good football player."

Second, judgments of others are internalized. If the teacher tells a girl she isn't good in arithmetic, and she accepts that as being accurate, she will develop a concept of self as "I am not good in math." If a parent tells a child that people who live on this side of the highway are superior to those who live on the opposite side, and the child accepts this as valid, the child forms a concept of self as "better than those people."

When a person's experiences coincide with the judgments of others, the development of the self-concept is almost assured. The boy who does poorly on reading worksheets, and is repeatedly told by the teacher that he is poor in reading, will surely develop a concept of self as "poor in reading."

Schools and Teachers

The school's role in developing adequate self-concepts is becoming increasingly critical as parental influence declines. The changing role of parents is illustrated by the "parent gap," which refers to parents ceding influence over their children to schools, television and children's peer groups.[5] The cause of the "parent gap" is not intentional parental neglect, but social and economic factors over which many parents have no control, and therefore they feel overwhelmed and inadequate. In these times it is almost impossible to raise a child without substantial outside help.

One symptom of the declining influence of parents, and an act that probably represents the ultimate crisis of self-concept, is suicide, now the second leading cause of death among young Americans between the ages of fifteen and twenty-four. If the teacher is not successful in changing the inadequate self-concepts of the increasing numbers of children coming from homes where there is a "parent gap," the teacher's other instructional efforts will most likely be wasted, no matter how well intentioned they may be or how competently they are executed.

---

5. See "Parent Gap," *Newsweek* (September 22, 1975).

Albert Schweitzer noted that a person's acceptance of self is the primary requisite for an adequate self-concept and a reasonably well-integrated personality.

> It is only by confidence in our ability to reach truth by our own individual thinking that we are capable of accepting thought from outside.[6]

In fact, acceptance of self is so closely related to acceptance of others that one cannot determine which is cause and which is effect (Burger 1952). Thus it is advisable for teachers to work on both of them simultaneously.

Summary

Self-concept refers to one's perception of one's self—one's physical and personality characteristics and one's feelings of worth and adequacy. People try, albeit unconsciously, to behave in ways that are consistent with the image they possess of themselves; in a very real sense, as a person thinks he is, so he is. If one *thinks* he is dumb, he will *behave* in a dumb way, even though he may actually have average or above average ability. The fact that self-concepts are frequently inaccurate makes remediation especially important.

Concepts of self are developed out of experiences, from inferences derived through interacting with the environment—if I can hit a baseball better than other people my age then I am a good baseball player—and by internalizing the judgments of significant others—if my mother says I am stupid, then I must be stupid. If the teacher is not successful in changing a student's feelings of inadequacy then the student will likely learn little in school, regardless of how enlightened and well intended the teacher's methods may be.

The school's role in developing adequate self-concepts is becoming more critical as parental influence declines. It is becoming ever more true that schools that attempt to teach only the "3 R's," and neglect the development of self-concepts, will become progressively less effective at teaching even the "3 R's."

---

6. A. Schweitzer, *Out of My Life and Thought* (New York: Henry Holt, 1933), p. 173.

COPING DEVICES

Coping means encountering something in our environment that is new or not yet mastered—a novel situation, an obstacle or a conflict. Samuel Butler, a novelist in the early part of this century, offers a clear and poetic description of the process.

> All our lives long, every day and every hour, we are engaged in the process of accommodating our changed and unchanged selves to changed and unchanged surroundings; living, in fact is nothing else than this process of accommodation; when we fail in it a little we are stupid, when we fail flagrantly we are mad, when we suspend it temporarily we sleep, when we give up the attempt altogether we die. In quiet, uneventful lives, the changes internal and external are so small that there is little or no strain in the process of fusion and accommodation; in other lives there is great strain, but there is also great fusing and accommodating power; in others great strain with little accommodating power. A life will be successful or not according as the power of accommodation is equal to or unequal to the strain of fusing and adjusting internal and external changes.[7]

The dynamic process of coping is directed at attaining needs. In the words of Karl Menninger, the individual,

> . . . pursues his ends, seeking to express his intentions and fulfill his needs as he perceives them and as he finds opportunity. He tries to survive, with minimal pain and maximal pleasure. . . All this requires an infinitude of doing, of trying and failing, of trying and succeeding, of trying and partially succeeding and having to compromise. It involves going ahead, stepping aside, stepping back, perhaps even running away. It involves fights and embraces, bargains and donations, gestures and conversations, working and playing, reproaches, rewards and retrenchments.[8]

Coping devices are the behavioral sequences a person uses in dealing with stresses caused by challenges. A student is challenged to differing degrees by situations such as accidently dropping a full tray of food in the cafeteria, being assigned to work on a mural with other students, being informed of tomorrow's spelling test, and being nominated for the position of class president. These situations are likely to be so sudden and challenging that they initiate a minor disturbance of the person's steady state, which then results in the

7. S. Butler, *The Way of All Flesh* (New York: Dutton, 1903).
8. Menninger et al., *The Vital Balance*, p. 126.

person feeling increased stress. Coping devices serve to relieve or regulate the feelings of increased stress and restore the balance of the steady state.

Some Common Coping Devices

Some of the more common coping devices healthy and reasonably well-adjusted individuals use in dealing with minor emergencies are discussed here.[9]

Physical Activity   The individual, when aroused may move in a way intended to reduce the challenge. The movement may be toward or away from the situation. If the individual's curiosity is aroused by a strange object, he may move to pick it up and examine it. If someone presents a challenging argument, the individual may speak up. On the other hand, if the situation seems dangerous or personally threatening the individual may retreat.

Different people have different physical reactions to identical situations, but all responses are intended to reduce stress. For example, one student who drops a tray of food in the cafeteria will immediately begin picking up the spilled contents. Another will turn to the person next to him and loudly blame that person for the accident and insist that he clean it up. A third student will run out of the cafeteria. A fourth student will try to ignore the spilled tray, acting as if someone else dropped it.

The different ways students have learned to cope physically with a challenge will have differing degrees of effectiveness in reducing their level of stress. The student who immediately begins picking up the spilled contents of the tray will probably achieve a steady state more quickly and more permanently than the one who blames others for the accident. The student who blames his neighbor creates a challenge with which the neighbor must deal that will likely result in yet another challenge for the student who initially spilled the tray.

Reassurance   The individual, when challenged, may seek reassurance. For the infant this can be accomplished by moving into the mother's arms. As the person grows older the soft touches and soothing sounds he

---

9. For an excellent discussion of coping devices seen Menninger et al., *The Vital Balance*, pp. 133–145.

sought as an infant take on other and more subtle forms. Reassurance for the child and adult may be in the form of spoken comments: "I know you're afraid. I won't leave you." "I know it hurts." or "You must feel badly, but it happens to everybody at one time or another." Reassurance may be in the form of personal gestures, such as a gentle pat on the back. Regardless of age, challenged individuals seek reassurance of their lovableness and of the protecting attitude of those who prize them even in times of error and danger.

Different individuals can be expected to seek differing degrees of reassurance. With the tray dropping incident, one student will feel sufficiently reassured when the teacher gives a pleasant smile, a shrug of the shoulders, and says, "Happened to me last week." Another will be so shaken by the same incident that the teacher will have to hold the student in her arms.

Individuals may meet a challenge by trying to assert intellectual *Self-Discipline* control over their immediate and natural emotions. There is a game where one player uses verbal abuse in an effort to incite another to anger and physical reprisal, while the challenged individual attempts to maintain self-control. Students play a variation of this game with each other. They say insulting things to each other, "Fatty, fatty, two-by-four, Can't get through the kitchen door." In our social system, a high value is placed on the insulted person responding nonviolently to the verbal abuse, and even saying something clever, and equally abusive, like, "Rather be fat than a skinny bean pole like you." Children may also be physically abusive to each other. On his way to sharpen a pencil, a boy intentionally knocks another student's paper off the desk. The most valued response in our society is for the offended student to suppress the immediate impulse to jump up and start hitting and, instead, wait and get even in some particularly clever way, such as "accidentally" dropping a messy crayon on the boy's completed paper. Bradlee in his book on John F. Kennedy, identified the rule of self-discipline of the Boston Irish political jungle: "Don't get mad. Just get even."[10]

In the process of growing up one must learn that some impulses have to be suppressed, some temptations resisted, and some frustrations endured. Students who have difficulty using the coping device of self-discipline are usually the most troublesome for the teacher because they often respond violently to challenges. They

---

10. B. C. Bradlee, *Conversations with Kennedy* (New York: Norton and Company, Inc., 1975).

start yelling, pushing and hitting when people crowd in front of them in line or bump them. Their violent reactions create challenges for those around them, and an accelerating cycle of abusive behavior is initiated and maintained.

Escape Valve Laughing, crying and swearing provide instant tension relief. Laughing discharges some tension in the form of humor, either at one's own expense, or at someone else's. The student who responds to being called "Fatty, fatty, two-by-four," with the comment that it is preferable to "being a skinny old bean pole," is using humor. The student who drops a tray in the cafeteria and starts laughing about it is reducing stress. Rather than admonish the person who dropped the tray in the cafeteria, and then started laughing, for not taking the accident seriously, the teacher should also recognize the humor of the incident, and thus help the person reduce the tension level. Grotjahn noted that "Laughter . . . as it provided a permissible release of unconscious aggressions, is one of the best safeguards of mental health."[11]

Crying lowers the general level of emotional feeling and allows the painful and dominant energy of the shock to be worked off gradually. With the child and the adult, the reduction of energy induced by the shock frequently declares itself in a distinct sigh of relief. Unfortunately, in our society crying is usually considered to be an unacceptable coping device for boys and men. Boys and men who have not learned to use the other more acceptable valves of laughing and swearing will find that the energy is worked off in ways destructive to physical health, such as hyperacidity and hypertension, which can eventually lead to ulcers and heart attacks.

Swearing, like laughing and crying, brings about a sense of relief from tension. But swearing is a device that is easily and often abused. When it becomes a habit, it loses its value as an escape valve. Swearing is commonly used by boys and men, simply because crying in our society is not considered masculine. Most teachers are understandably reluctant to allow students to use certain four-letter words; they should be encouraged to use more generally acceptable substitutes. For example, counting to ten may have the same tension relieving effect.

Talking Talking and being listened to, are basic universal forms of human interaction. Not surprisingly, they are the medium of most psychiatric

---

11. M. Grotjahn, "Innocent Merriment," *Commonweal* 67 (1958):605.

therapy. Talking about a problem with an interested listener offers two benefits. First, it implies the establishment of a meaningful contact with another human being. "I truly exist because you are listening attentively." Second, significant ideas may emerge just by hearing one's own thoughts being spoken aloud. There is always the possibility that a friendly and supportive listener may suggest something helpful, but this is an unexpected dividend.

An example of the effect of being listened to is demonstrated by the experiment at the Western Electric plant in Hawthorne.[12] The experiment demonstrated the beneficial effects of giving employees opportunities to speak freely to noncritical listeners. The researchers were attempting to identify the physical surroundings that workers on an assembly line found most pleasant, and that resulted in the highest level of worker productivity. After talking with the workers about what they liked, the researchers tried different physical surroundings. At different times they changed the light level, provided music, and painted the walls. Each change, including the reintroduction of the original surroundings, resulted in an increased level of productivity. The term "Hawthorne Effect" is used frequently in education to explain why so many experiments with new methods usually have positive results. The effect of involving teachers in trying out a "new method" for teaching reading has much the same effect as involving workers on an assembly line in experimenting with new physical surroundings.

Teachers can help students cope with many frustrations by being attentive and noncritical listeners. The teacher can say, "Want to tell me about it?" when a student comes in from the playground after some particularly painful incident, such as a bigger student taking away a ball, or being pushed out of line and missing a turn. Teachers must realize that even though they probably cannot rectify the person's problem, it does help the student to talk about it. The only additional action the teacher may want to take is using another coping device, *reassurance.* The teacher might say, "I imagine it must be very frustrating to have one of the boys take the ball away. I know I would be upset. I certainly understand why you are so mad."

Fantasy Formation

The importance of dreams and daydreams has long been recognized by psychoanalysts, and studies have demonstrated their vital necessity as coping devices (Dement 1960). Fantasies may involve carrying

---

12. See F. J. Roethlisberger and W. J. Dickson, *Management and the Worker* (Cambridge, Mass.: Harvard University Press, 1939).

out aggressive attacks—perhaps on the boy who causes so much anguish on the playground—or they may involve compensation, gratification, and indulgence. They can give pleasure and they can relieve stress.

Teachers can encourage students' use of fantasy by having them draw pictures of irritating situations, and of the solutions they would like to see occur. Teachers will find that "talking it out" sometimes results in the student describing an imaginary solution to a crisis situation. The main thing the teacher must remember is to be uncritical and supportive. The fantasy is not the intended solution, it is only a means of relieving stress. The normal use of fantasy becomes abnormal when the person confuses the fantasy with reality.

Coping Styles

Murphy suggests the concept of coping styles to refer to the pattern of coping devices that a particular person uses.[13] A person may use a wide range of coping devices, or only a few. A person may use any one coping device in the same way, or may alter its use in different situations.

For example, Steve's behavior is characterized by a tendency to use physical activity, but not self-discipline. Moreover, he usually restricts his use of physical activity to finding scapegoats. He is the one who drops the tray in the cafeteria and then loudly blames the accident on the person next to him. If he does poorly on a spelling test he is likely to state in a loud and belligerent voice that the teacher did not say the words loud enough or did not give him enough time to write them. In neither situation does he seem able to use self-discipline, which would be evidenced by a sort of "grin-and-bear-it" response. In neither situation is his physical activity directed toward eliminating the real cause of the problem, either by immediately picking up the spilled tray or by devoting more time to studying the spelling words.

Jim's behavior, on the other hand, is characterized by a tendency to direct his physical activity toward the cause of the problem, be it a spilled tray or poor spelling performance. But before doing so, he frequently uses the escape valve device of laughter. When the tray of food spills he behaves as if it is a comical event. He continues giggling while he is cleaning up the mess.

13. L. Murphy, *The widening World of Childhood* (New York: Basic Books, Inc., 1962).

Jim and Steve have comparable mental abilities, are about the same age, and come from almost identical socioeconomic and family backgrounds. Somewhere along the line, in the process of growing up, they developed different coping styles.

Coping and Physical Health

Few teachers realize that a student's inability to cope successfully with stress frequently results in physical symptoms as well as mental health symptoms. The student who appears morose may be suffering from unrelieved stress rather than from illness, malnutrition, or inherited deficiency. The idea that physical health is influenced by psychological factors is not new. Ulcers, hypertension, hyperthyroidism, rheumatoid arthritis and asthma have long been attributed to psychosomatic causes. But recent medical evidence suggests that any distinction between psychosomatic and nonpsychosomatic disease is arbitrary. Many medical researchers argue that physical disease is not the result of any single, specific agent, such as a germ or virus, but is the consequence of many factors, including demands placed on the individual, and the individual's ability or inability to cope with resulting stress.

The relationship between the ability to cope successfully with stress and physical health is seen in the "Broken Heart" studies of the increase in the death rate among recent widowers. Scientists at the Institute of Community Studies in London studied 4,486 widowers and found that widowhood appears to bring in its wake a sudden increment in mortality (Young, Benjamin, and Wallis 1963). Compared with other men the same age, the widowers studied had a mortality rate that was 40 percent higher in the first six months.

Holmes and Rahe developed "The Social Readjustment Rating Scale" to aid in their study of the relationship between stress and physical health.[14] Reasoning that different kinds of accommodations strike us with different force, Holmes and Rahe listed as many stress-causing events as they could, had numerous persons rate the comparative seriousness of the events, and then assigned a score to each event according to how much impact people felt that it had. A top score of 100 was assigned for the death of a spouse, 47 for getting fired, and a low score of 11 for minor violations of the law.

In a later study, the "Social Readjustment Rating Scale" was

---

14. T. H. Holmes and R. H. Rahe, *Journal of Psychosomatic Research* 11 (1967): 213–218.

administered to 3,000 sailors about to depart for six months of sea duty (Gunderson, Rahe, and Arthur 1968). During sea duty it was possible to maintain exact medical records on each man. After the men returned, the medical records were examined. The researchers discovered that the men who scored in the upper 10 percent on the scale—those who had to accommodate to the most stress-causing events in the year preceding the cruise—had an illness rate 150 to 200 percent above those who scored in the bottom 10 percent on the scale. Moreover, the higher the score the more severe the illness was likely to be. The researchers concluded that there is a clear connection between the body's defenses and the demands for coping that are placed on the individual. They reasoned that various noxious elements, both external and internal, are always present and always seeking to explode into disease. They explode when the body's defense systems are unable to cope with the demands that come pulsing through the nervous and endocrine systems.

Schools and Teachers

As the impact of the traditional institution on the family continues to decline, community institutions such as the school become more important. Where schools once augmented the home, and were primarily concerned with academic matters (reading, writing and arithmetic), they must now be concerned with the whole person, and particularly with an area traditionally reserved for the home—students' mental health.

The serious state of students' mental health is seen in the rising incidence of symptoms of unrelieved stress, such as the spectacular rise of teenage drug use, alcoholism, suicide, juvenile delinquency, runaways and illegitimate births. While these symptoms have been previously considered to be found with greater frequency among students from poor and nonwhite families the symptoms are seen with increasing frequency among middle- and upper-class groups.

Schools must be vitally concerned with students' ability to cope successfully, because mental health directly affects learning. Ausubel notes that "it has been generally found that anxiety facilitates rote and less difficult kinds of meaningful reception learning, but has an inhibitory effect on more complex types of learning tasks that are either higher, unfamiliar or more dependent on improvising skill than on persistence."[15] The student with feelings of unrelieved

---

15. D. P. Ausubel, *Educational Psychology: A Cognitive View* (New York: Holt, Rinehart and Winston, Inc., 1968), p. 405.

stress will be able to memorize rote material, but will be largely unable to learn strategies for improvising satisfactory solutions to novel, conceptual-level problems. Schools must be vitally concerned with developing the student's ability to cope successfully.

It is encouraging that teachers can improve students' ability to cope successfully with stress. Escalona and Heider identify the four most important factors in changing a young person's use of coping devices:

1. Improved health
2. Drive
3. Persistent effort toward mastery
4. Consciousness of coping style and recognition of its effectiveness [16]

Schools can improve student's physical health by providing health-care services and nutritional meals. Teachers can affect students' drive by providing motivating school activities that maximize their opportunities to achieve the basic needs of movement (both physical and intellectual), socialization and affection. Teachers can affect students' persistent effort toward mastery by utilizing more individualized instructional strategies, and thus assure them of success and recognition of their success.

Teachers can make students conscious of their coping style and help them to recognize its effectiveness by using counselor role strategies. Essentially, these strategies are used to determine what a student's coping style is, how successful it is, and communicating this information to the student in a way that has maximum impact.

It is important to state here that teachers must realize that coping is something they must learn to do well. Teachers suffering from unrelieved stress will not only be ineffectual in helping students cope, they will usually manage to become a major source of stress for the student. For example, there was probably a supervising teacher in the cafeteria when the trays were accidently dropped. The spilled tray presents a sudden and challenging situation to both the student responsible for dropping it and the teacher responsible for maintaining order. The teacher who reacts violently, either physically or verbally, only increases the level of challenge with which the already frustrated student must deal. The teacher might better use the coping device of self-discipline and simply repress the impulse to be angry. The teacher might use the coping device of talking and

---

16. S. Escalona and G. Heider, *Prediction and Outcome* (New York: Basic Books, 1959).

say to herself, "That kid is all thumbs, but he didn't mean to do it, so I should try to be understanding." The teacher might use the coping device of reassurance and bring the topic up later in the teachers' room so she can feel better about the fact that the same thing seems to happen all the time on lunch duty.

Summary

Coping devices refer to the learned ways of dealing with the stresses that arise from situations people encounter daily. Coping devices are used in relieving or regulating stress.

Six coping devices used by healthy and reasonably well adjusted individuals are identified:

1. Physical Activity. Individuals, when aroused, may move physically in a way intended to reduce the challenge.
2. Reassurance. Individuals, when challenged, seek reassurance of their lovableness and of the protecting attitude of those who prize them even in times of error and danger.
3. Self-Discipline. Individuals meet the challenge by trying to exert intellectual control over their immediate and natural emotions.
4. Escape Valve. Laughing, crying and swearing provide instant tension relief.
5. Talking. Talking, and being listened to, usually reduce stress, and sometimes even produce possible solutions.
6. Fantasy Formation. Fantasies give pleasure, and in some curious way, relieve stress.

Students' inability to cope successfully affects not only their mental health, it may also affect their physical health. As the beneficial effects of the family decline, the importance of the school in helping students learn to cope successfully becomes increasingly critical. In a very real sense, for all too many students, school is their last hope for happiness and adjustment.

References

Burger, E. 1952. Relation between expressed acceptance of self and expressed acceptance of others. *Journal of Abnormal Social Psychology* 47(1952): 778-782.

Dement, W. 1960. The effect of dream deprivation. *Science* 131:1705–1707.

Gunderson, E. K.; Rahe, R. H.; and Arthur, R. J. 1968. Social and environmental factors in illness behavior. Paper presented to the Annual Meeting of the Western Psychological Assn., San Diego, Calif.

Young, M.; Benjamin, B.; and Wallis, C. 1963. *Lancet* (August 31):454–456.

12

Strategies

The goal of the teacher as a counselor is to help students develop more adequate self-concepts and to learn coping devices that will be successful in reducing stress. The teacher can make progress toward the goal by altering the three environmental factors that a student encounters at school: the behavior of other students; instructional tasks; and, the behavior of the teacher.

BEHAVIOR OF OTHER STUDENTS

A teacher can beneficially alter a student's peer environment by using the group-leader strategies of role play and group discussion. For example, one teacher used group discussion as a means of altering the way students in her second-grade classroom treated a new boy. The boy's family had arrived from out of state prior to the opening of school in the fall. The boy's first few weeks in the class were marked by strife and grief. Although normally a very cheerful and peaceful person, he was involved in numerous fights at school, and was frequently chased home by groups of jeering, rock-throwing classmates. The teacher recognized the situation, and used group discussion to relieve the harmful peer pressure being exerted on the boy. One day the teacher sent him to the office on a prearranged errand designed to keep him out of the room for about fifteen minutes. As soon as the boy left the room, the teacher initiated a discussion about the boy's problem. The class discussed how he must feel as a newcomer, as the only newcomer in the class. They suggested some things they might do to make his life more pleasant. Almost immediately the incidents of fighting and rock-throwing stopped, and the boy began making friends and showing academic progress.

Teachers should recognize that misbehaving students are not only a problem for the teacher, they are usually a problem for the other students as well. A student with some maladjustment problems can easily get into a cycle of abusive behavior with other students that only serves to increase the student's degree of maladjustment and, consequently, the amount of misbehavior with which the teacher must deal. The strategies of group discussion and role play are very effective in dealing with this type of problem because they help students in the classroom understand how the maladjusted person feels and the probable reasons for his disturbing behavior. In addition, the strategies lead the students to discussing practical solutions for the problem, and encourage them to try out the solutions they suggest.

Often, the source of stress comes from outside the classroom, with the result being unpleasant relationships within the class. Group discussion and role play are effective in helping students understand and deal successfully with outside sources of stress. For example, a group discussion held in a sixth-grade classroom evenly composed of white and black students illustrates how a teacher might deal with racial strife arising from outside forces, but reflected in relationships within the classroom. The day before the discussion the class had participated with students from other schools in an outdoor education activity. A fight had taken place between two white boys, one from this class and one from a class in a predominantly white school. The fight started when a white boy from the other school called a black boy in this class a "dirty black nigger." A white boy from this class didn't appreciate his classmate being called that, and said so. The first boy accused the boy in this class of being a "nigger lover," and the fight began. The next day the teacher initiated a group discussion of the incident by having the two central figures in this class describe the events of the previous day. The discussion soon led to a surprisingly frank review about whites and blacks. Students expressed the feeling that whites and blacks were just people, some were good and some were bad. The group identified some solutions on how to deal peacefully with a situation similar to the one just described. The discussion improved the atmosphere of the group and it helped both white and black students learn alternative ways of coping with stressful situations.

A student's peer environment will be beneficially altered by any improvements in the classroom atmosphere. The healthier the classroom atmosphere, the more tolerant students will be of the unpleasant antics of their maladjusted classmates. In a healthy classroom group, students function in a cooperative and helping relationship with each other rather than in a competitive and adversary relationship.

INSTRUCTIONAL TASKS

Teachers can improve students' self-concepts and their ability to cope successfully with stress by using instructional-manager strategies. When a continuous-progress curriculum is used with an individualized-grouping pattern the student can be given instructional tasks that he is able to master successfully. Thus, he is not subject to the ridicule of his classmates. The objectives are so specific that the student can experience a genuine feeling of academic success after only five to ten minutes at his task. As success follows success, the student begins to alter his concept of "I'm too dumb to learn." The reduction of challenge allows him to learn other more successful coping strategies than avoidance of school-related tasks and aggressive responses to other students. By contrast, the student's degree of maladjustment can get worse if he is given instructional tasks that are too difficult for him to accomplish successfully, and if he is given these tasks in group settings where his inabilities are continually displayed to his classmates.

The use of an individualized-grouping pattern provides a degree of intimacy between teacher and student that is missing in most other group-related activities in the classroom. The one-to-one relationship enables many students to meet their need for adult affection.

Independent activities, especially learning centers and group projects, reduce a student's level of stress because the emphasis is on doing things that are interesting, and doing them without direct supervision. Students who have experienced failure in school-related tasks can benefit greatly by doing intrinsically motivating activities where there is little chance of failure.

TEACHER BEHAVIOR

The three intangible factors governing the behavior of effective teachers were identified two thousand years ago by Saint Paul: "Faith, Hope and Love. Of these," he declared, "Love is the greatest." Teachers who make these three factors their basic philosophy will usually be effective in helping their students develop more adequate self-concepts and learn to use coping devices that will more successfully reduce stress.

The remainder of this chapter is devoted to an explanation of counselor strategies that can be used to alter students' behavior. The four counselor strategies are:

1. Making Contact
2. Listening
3. Encouraging
4. Enlightening

MAKING CONTACT

The importance of the teacher attempting to "make contact" with students from their first encounter is underscored by Menninger. He emphasizes the importance of making contact in psychiatry:

> Making contact with a psychiatric patient is of the utmost importance. In physical illness, given a pain somewhere in the body, no one is too much offended by the doctor's manner of approach. . . . With a psychiatric illness it is different. Loss of contact with others is the very thing the patient suffers from, and the doctor who muffs the approach can easily thereby destroy all possibility of being helpful, or at least postpone it a long time.[1]

The teacher who follows the old adage "Be tough at first, then loosen the reins," is just as liable to muff the approach and destroy all possibility of being helpful as is the doctor who is clumsy, gauche and rude during the first appointment. From the first class meeting, teachers should try to let students know that they care about them as individuals.

---

1. K. Menninger, M. Maymann, and P. Pruyser, *The Vital Balance* (New York: The Viking Press, 1963), p. 348.

Strategy

The communication of caring can be accomplished, in the words of Jersild:

> . . . by being an understanding adult who lets the child know that the teacher realizes the struggle the child is undergoing. He can do this by means of a glance or by noticeably keeping his mouth shut. He can do it by a kind of understanding patience which allows the child to express his annoyances . . . or to voice his grievances.[2]

A teacher can communicate caring to a student by recognizing the student's struggle and expressing sympathy for his feelings. For example, if a student says, "I am stupid," the teacher should accept this feeling as genuine, but should express sympathy for how much the person must suffer from the feeling. The teacher should not get into an argument about whether or not the student ought to feel that way. The communication of caring might be expressed in this way:

Roberto: I am stupid.

Teacher: You really feel that way don't you? You really think you're not smart.

Roberto: Yeah!

Teacher: That must make you hurt inside a lot.

Roberto: Yeah!

Teacher: You must be afraid in class that I will call on you, and you won't be able to give the right answer. You must be afraid that if you don't give the right answer the other children will laugh.

Roberto: Yeah! That happened yesterday in math. I didn't know the answer, and the kids laughed.

Teacher: And you felt they were laughing at you?

Roberto: Yeah.

---

2. A. T. Jersild, *Child Psychology,* 4th ed. (Englewood Cliffs, N.J.: Prentice-Hall, 1954), p. 235.

Teacher: Well, Roberto, you have a different opinion of yourself than I do. I think you are a very nice person, and not at all dumb.

While this brief conversation alone will not change Roberto's self-concept, it could plant a small seed of doubt. The earlier judgments Roberto formed from interacting with the environment are not supported by the present judgment of his teacher. And, very importantly, his teacher understands how he feels, and cares that he feels badly. This intimate conversation serves to establish contact with Roberto.

Evidence of the powerfully beneficial effects of communicating caring is seen in the phenomenon known in medicine as the "placebo effect."[3] Placebo means "I will please," the implication being that the remedy is given to please the patient rather than cure him. But the pleasure often has the effect of a cure.

The teacher will be more effective in establishing contact if a higher priority is initially placed on communicating caring than on immediately teaching subject matter. This priority is expressed by Jo Ellen Hartline, a fourth-grade teacher in Phoenix, Arizona. She states that:

Even as a beginning teacher, I felt deep within me the need to establish rapport between a child and myself before I tried to teach subject matter.

She tells the following personal story to her students as a way of communicating her caring to them.

One night when my daughter was learning to read, she and her dad were sitting on the couch. His arm was around her, and she was reading away. Passing through the room, I stopped and said, "Just listen to her. Isn't that great! Aren't you proud of her?" He slowly turned his head and looked at me and said, "Why, I was proud of her when she couldn't read one word."[4]

Mrs. Hartline uses the story to communicate to her students that while they may have academic problems, the problems can be handled. She likes and loves them for being themselves; they will work together on the academic problems.

---

3. A similar phenomenon is the "Hawthorne Effect," which was discussed in the previous chapter in a discussion concerning talking as a coping device.

4. Related in a special issue on motivating students, *Today's Education,* National Education Association (September-October 1975):25.

LISTENING

Menninger notes that in psychiatry:

> Listening is one of the most important tools the psychiatrist possesses. Listening has both diagnostic and therapeutic functions.[5]

The psychiatrist's listening, like the teacher's, is of a "professional" type rather than the lay type of our everyday lives. Professional listening is characterized by noting not only what the person says, but what he does not say, or says by means of gestures, postures and facial expressions. It is listening with both the mind and the heart.

Strategy

The professional listener listens in a way that encourages students to recognize and express their feelings. This encouraging kind of listening was described clearly by magazine writer Brenda Ueland:

> Who are the people . . . to whom you go for advice? Not to the hard practical ones who can tell you exactly what to do, but to the listeners; that is, the kindest, least censorious, least bossy people that you know. It is because by pouring out your problems to them, you then know what to do about it yourself . . . .
>
> Now, how to listen? It is harder than you think. I don't believe in critical listening, for that only puts a person in a strait jacket of hesitancy. He begins to choose his words solemnly or primly. His little inner fountain cannot spring. Critical listeners dry you up. But creative listeners are those who want you to be recklessly yourself, even at your very worst, even vituperative, bad-tempered. They are mentally saying as you express these things: "Whee! Hurrah! Good for you!" For true listeners know that if you are bad-tempered it does not mean that you are always so. They don't love you just when you are nice; they love *all* of you. Besides critical listening, there is another kind that is no good: passive, censorious listening . . .
>
> In order to learn to listen, here are some suggestions: Try to learn tranquility, . . . begin to hear not only what people are saying, but what they are *trying* to say . . . watch you self-assertiveness. And give it up.[6]

---

5. Menninger, Maymann, and Pruyser, *The Vital Balance*, p. 349.

6. Brenda Ueland, "Tell Me More," *Ladies Home Journal* (November 1941), © 1941, Downe Publishing, Inc. Reprinted with permission of *Ladies' Home Journal*.

Professional listeners are "creative listeners." They recognize that a student's feelings are real. They are genuinely joyful when the student is actually able to recognize and express his feelings. Above all, the professional listener does not behave in a critical and censorious way that might cause students to bury their true feelings within themselves.

Nondirective Method
While professional listeners should not behave in ways that the student will interpret as being critical and censorious, they should be able to keep the conversation going and keep it focused on the student's problem. Carl Rogers developed a "nondirective" method by which a counselor or teacher can be a creative listener.[7] This method forms the core of Roger's "Client-Centered Therapy." The two basic techniques in the method are: (1) repeat the person's last statement of the key idea (the person's expression of the problem); and, (2) if that fails, ask for clarification. The application of the two techniques of repetition and clarification are shown in Figure 12.1.

Technique		*Dialogue*
	Kari:	(Crying) No one likes me.
Repeat..........	Teacher:	(Waits three to five seconds, or until it becomes obvious Kari will not continue.) You think that no one likes you.
	Kari:	Yes. I don't have any friends.
Repeat..........	Teacher:	(Waits three to five seconds, or until it becomes obvious Kari will not continue.) You say that you have no friends.
	Kari:	Uh, huh!
Clarification	Teacher:	(Waits three to five seconds, or until it becomes obvious Kari will not continue.) Why do you think you have no friends?
	Kari:	Because no one will play with me.

Figure 12.1

---

7. Carl Rogers, *Client-Centered Therapy* (Boston: Houghton Mifflin, 1951).

The teacher could also have said some other things as ways of repetition or clarification. When Kari said, "Uh, huh!" the teacher could use the technique of repetition by saying the statement that Kari made some time back, "A little while ago you said that you have no friends." In Figure 12.1 when Kari said, "Uh, huh!" the teacher used a why question to get clarification. Another way the teacher could ask for clarification would be to ask for an example, "Tell me about a time when someone showed she didn't like you."

ENCOURAGEMENT

Research indicates that there is a web of intriguing interrelationships between teacher distribution of approval and disapproval, and other variables such as students' beliefs of what teachers think of them, what they think of themselves, their academic achievement, and their general happiness with school.[8] The clear implication of this research is that teachers can affect, both positively and negatively, students' self-concepts, academic achievement and general motivation by the way they distribute teacher approval and disapproval.

Strategy

A study by Staines involving two junior high school classrooms, illustrates how the strategy of encouragement can be carried out, and demonstrates its effectiveness.[9] At the beginning of the study the self-concepts and general achievement of the students in both classes were assessed. The teacher in Classroom A was not informed of the results of the assessment, or even that an experiment was being conducted. The teacher in Classroom B studied the self-ratings of each student in the class and noted the profile of high and low scores. The teacher then attempted to raise the low self-ratings and maintain the high self-ratings by tailoring teacher comments and actions to each person's profile. For example, if a boy had an unrealistically negative evaluation of his ability in mathematics, the teacher tried to avoid showing disapproval of his work in mathematics, and made approving

---

8. See L. E. Longstreth, *Psychological Development of the Child* (New York: The Ronald Press Company, 1968), pp. 461–466.

9. J. W. Staines, "The Self-Picture as a Factor in the Classroom," *British Journal of Education* 28 (1958):97–111.

comments whenever possible. The teacher would say things like, "Your arithmetic paper was better today than yesterday. That's great!" If a girl was very conscious of being short, she was asked to take the role of a mother or an aunt in a play rather than the role of a little girl. The teacher in the experimental classroom made no other changes in the instruction.

At the end of twelve weeks all of the students' self-concepts and general achievement were again assessed and compared. Students showed more improvement in those areas in the classroom where the teacher made a conscious and deliberate effort to match approving comments and actions to each person's self-concept profile than they did in the classroom where the teacher ignored their self-concepts.

The chain of causation between teacher approval and disapproval, on the one hand, and students' self-concepts and academic achievement on the other, means that students' self-concepts and academic achievement can be improved by the teacher praising, reinforcing good behavior, and passing along nice comments. When a person is praised, the latent powers of adjustment seem to be released in ways that beneficially affect learning and self-confidence.

Important Factors   Teacher effectiveness in using encouragement depends on two factors: (1) the authenticity of the encouragement; and, (2) the deliberateness with which it is given.

Authenticity. The teacher should follow the old adage, "Actions speak louder than words." Encouragement depends more on underlying teacher attitude than on specific concrete actions. It is not what one says and does, but how one says and does it. If a teacher frowns when stating, "That's very good!" it is likely that the frown will be noticed rather than the positive comment, and the frown will be interpreted as disapproval.

In order for encouragement to be authentic it must be realistic. A child should not be told that he did outstanding work on his arithmetic paper when he obviously did not. But the teacher could state, quite honestly, that the paper is better than yesterday's. That improvement can be honestly noted and praised.

Deliberateness. Encouragement will be most effective when it is used in the same deliberate way the teacher used it in the Staines experiment. The teacher studies each person's profile of self-concepts.

(Suitable assessment instruments are given in the next chapter.)
Areas where encouragement might be given to each person are noted:

> Joe—be positive about arithmetic
> Mary—be positive about height

The teacher then plans specific opportunities where encouragement
might be given:

> Joe—be positive when he shows any improvement in arithmetic
> Mary—plan a role play with an adult part for Mary

The teacher should identify specific instances where encouragement
can be given, and not leave the process to chance. When teachers do
nothing more than admonish themselves to "be more encouraging,"
they usually find that nothing happens.

   With some students the teacher will have a difficult time finding
specific instances where encouragement can honestly be given. But
we must remember that there is something in every child that can be
approved. With some children it is just harder to find. Teachers
should recognize that the students for whom it is the most difficult
to identify instances where encouragement can be given are probably
the ones who need it the most, and will benefit the most from it.

   Teachers should plan specific instances for giving encouragement,
and monitor their own behavior to make sure that they are actually
carrying out their plan. One way to monitor teacher behavior is to
record its occurrence. Make a record of the specific instances where
approval should be given, and then record each time it is actually
done. A portion of a possible record sheet is shown in Figure 12.2.
The record sheet serves as a reminder of the specific actions that
were planned, as well as a constant incentive for the teacher to be
more approving.

Names	Areas to Approve	Specific Approving Actions for Each Area	Tally of Use of Each Action
Joe	Arithmetic	1. When today's paper is better than yesterdays.	xxxx
		2. When asks for help with arithmetic	x

Figure 12.2

Another way to monitor encouragement is having another teacher observe and keep a record of what happens.

ENLIGHTENMENT

While the strategies of making contact, listening and encouraging
are usually sufficient to arrest a student's increasing maladjustment
and begin the upward process of adjustment, by themselves they
are seldom enough to help a person achieve an optimum level of
adjustment. Disruptive students with poor work habits know they
should do better, but they can do little to improve because they
do not know the reasons for their inadequate behavior, nor are they
aware of any viable alternatives. Enlightenment should help students
recognize the reasons for their behavior and make them more aware
of alternative ways of behaving.

Strategy

Enlightenment can be achieved in two ways: (1) helping students
understand the natural relationship between actions and consequences; and, (2) helping students become more knowledgeable
about alternative actions that have a greater likelihood of leading
to their desired consequences.

Action and
Consequences
Many students, like many adults, including teachers, lack insight.
They are unable to view themselves and their behavior through the
eyes of those with whom they interact. For example, after most
students have already lined up for lunch, and the teacher is not
looking, Mary tries to push toward the head of the line. When
she does, many of the other students begin yelling at her. She is
genuinely startled and hurt by their anger. She starts yelling back
and pushing those around her. Mary lacks insight. She is unable to
recognize that her action of crowding toward the head of the line
could be expected to lead quite naturally to the consequence of
other students getting angry. Most likely, she would respond exactly
the same way if someone did that to her. But she simply does not
recognize the similarity between how she would behave if someone
crowded in front of her and how others behave when she is the

one doing the crowding. If she were able to recognize this relationship, she might have behaved differently.

A conference between the teacher and Jerry illustrates how a teacher might enlighten a student by helping him understand the natural relationship between actions and consequences. Jerry was sent from the playground for fighting He is now talking to his teacher. The teacher starts the conference by having Jerry describe the incident. Jerry is hurt and angry because the other boys rejected him, and wouldn't let him play four-square. The teacher uses the strategy of encouragement by expressing sympathy for how badly Jerry must feel about being rejected by his friends and excluded from a game he enjoys. The teacher then starts using the strategy of enlightenment.

Teacher: Let me see if I understand what happened. You were the second person in line. You say that Mark was the first person in line, the one who is supposed to be the referee. You thought he was cheating because he didn't call a ball hit by his friend Jose as being out. You then grabbed the ball and insisted that Jose was out. The other people said that you were not the referee, and thereby not entitled to make the call. You said that Mark was cheating and so it didn't matter that you weren't the referee. This eventually led to a fight. Is that a good description of what happened?

Jerry: Yeah! Those dirty guys cheat all the time. They just try to keep each other in.

Teacher: Tell me, what do you think is the purpose in the game of four-square for having the first person in line be designated as the referee?

Jerry: So you have a referee, someone to call bad hits.

Teacher: Why not just let the person who hits the ball decide if its out?

Jerry: He'll cheat. He'll always say the ball is good, so he can stay in.

Teacher: Why not let the other players decide?

Jerry: They'll always say he's out, because they want to get in.

Teacher: Why not just let the people in line vote on it?

Jerry: That would take all day, and everybody would just fight.

Teacher: Could it be that the reason one person is designated as referee is so that there will be no fighting?

Jerry: Yeah. But what if he cheats?

Teacher: When the two sixth grades play baseball, and Mr. Jefferson is the referee, what happens if a player disagrees with a call Mr. Jefferson made?

Jerry: That's just too bad. Mr. Jefferson is the referee. Besides, he's the principal.

Teacher: Even if he wasn't the principal, do you think they could play the game at all if they didn't agree to have a referee, and to follow the calls he made?

Jerry: Nah!

Teacher: Could it be that the reason the other people got mad at you was because you didn't follow what the referee said?

Jerry: Yeah! Maybe!

Teacher: How do you think you would have felt if you were the first person in line, and the second person said that you were cheating, and grabbed the ball and wouldn't let the game go on?

Jerry: Well, they would be wrong. I don't cheat.

Teacher: Isn't it possible that Mark might feel the same way? Maybe he doesn't think he cheats either. Is that possible?

Jerry: Yeah, I guess so.

Teacher: How would you feel if Mark said you were cheating?

Jerry: I would be mad.

Teacher: Is it possible that Mark reacted just the way you would?

Jerry: I guess so.

Teacher: How do you feel when you are in line and someone else, in back of the referee, grabs the ball and says that the referee is cheating, and then won't give up the ball until everyone agrees with him?

> *Jerry:*   I get mad.
>
> *Teacher:*   Could it be that other people respond the same way to you when you are the one who grabs the ball?
>
> *Jerry:*   Yeah. I guess so.

In this conference the teacher tries to help Jerry understand that the reactions of the other people were natural consequences of his actions toward them. They behaved much the same way he would have if the situation had been reversed.

Jerry's conversation with the teacher can benefit both his self-concept and his feeling of stress. First, in terms of self-concept, the conversation helps debunk the possibility in Jerry's mind that his friends "hate him." They were just behaving naturally, as he would have done in the same situation. Second, in terms of coping, the conversation serves as a talking and reassuring coping device for Jerry. Talking about the incident makes him feel better, as does the teacher's obvious concern about how badly he feels. As a result of the conversation, Jerry no longer feels stress, and his steady state is restored. He is now better able to deal rationally with things. He can now benefit from a discussion of alternatives.

Alternative actions can be developed from the different coping devices. Jerry used the coping device of physical activity, which had a different consequence than what he expected. Let's examine the other coping devices Jerry could have used. If he had used these other devices he may have remained in the game.

Knowledgeable about Alternatives

Self-Discipline. Jerry might have tried suppressing his immediate impulse to be angry. Eventually, Jose, or someone else, would have made a hit so obviously bad that even Mark would have had to call it out. Then Jerry would have moved up to the head of the line and become referee.

Identifying Alternatives

Reassurance. Jerry could have tried being reassured by others in the line. He could have turned to the person behind him and said, "Did you see that? He does that all the time." Jerry would have felt somewhat reassured if the other person had said, "Yeah! I know."

Escape Valve. Jerry might have tried swearing, crying, or laughing. Swearing would be satisfactory as long as the person to whom he swore was not too offended. The swearing would be less offensive if it were done "under his breath." Jerry could also have cried "under his breath."

Talking. Jerry might have just yelled at Mark that he was cheating. He might have gone even further and said that when he became referee Mark had better watch out because then he too would cheat and help his friends. As most teachers on playground duty are only too painfully aware, talking—nay, yelling—is a coping device commonly used by children.

Fantasy Formation. Jerry might have reduced his feeling of stress if he had continued in the game and then later drawn a picture of how he felt about Mark's refereeing. If he had withheld the impulse to fight, and waited until later to draw a picture, he would have continued to be a more or less happy participant in the game and would not have been alienated from his friends.

Communicating Knowledge of Alternatives The teacher's intent is to convey to the student an understanding of how each alternative coping device can work, and its probable success in achieving the consequences the student desires. This understanding can be conveyed in the same conversational setting as that illustrated by the teacher's conversation with Jerry. Let's pick up on that conference again, and see how a teacher might convey an understanding to Jerry of how two coping devices, self-discipline and escape valve, might be used.

Teacher: Were you happy with what happened in the game, being kicked out and having your friends mad at you?

Jerry: No.

Teacher: Well, let's think together of some other things you might do the next time that kind of situation arises, when someone appears to be cheating in four-square, or in any game. And you can expect it will happen again, can't you?

Jerry: Yeah. Kids cheat all the time.

Teacher: Something I try to do in a situation like that is to force myself not to say anything. I think to myself that if I say anything it will just make matters worse. Besides, my turn will come. Do you suppose that might work for you?

Jerry: No. I get too mad when people cheat. I can't keep my mouth shut.

Teacher: If you had forced yourself not to say anything, what do you think would have happened?

Jerry: I would have stayed in the game.

Teacher: Is staying in the game better than what did happen?

Jerry: Yeah! I'd rather stay in the game, and not have my friends so mad at me.

Teacher: I wonder whether it might be worth the effort to force yourself to keep your mouth shut?

Jerry: Yeah! Maybe!

Teacher: Another thing I do sometimes is to swear to myself. I say something like, "Gosh darn it. That really makes me mad." I find saying that helps make me less mad, and less liable to start yelling. Do you ever try that?

Jerry: When I swear I get into trouble.

Teacher: Well, I would too if I swore out loud. But I swear to myself. Could it perhaps help you to swear to yourself?

Jerry: Yeah! I guess it would

Teacher: What might have happened if you had said something like, "Gosh darn it" to yourself?

Jerry: I would have stayed in the game, and everyone wouldn't be mad at me.

Now that Jerry seems to understand two alternative ways he might cope with challenges and their probable consequences, the teacher might try to help him plan their use in future incidents.

Teacher: Tell me, the next time you are the second person in line in a four-square game, and you think that the first person, the referee, has cheated, what might you do other than grab the ball away from the other players?

Jerry: I could say, "Darn it" to myself. I might even say, "Darn, darn, darn." That might make me feel better.

Teacher: Suppose you are playing baseball and Mr. Jefferson makes a call you don't agree with, you think he is cheating, what might you do?

Jerry: I could say, "Darn it" to myself. Then I could say to myself that someone has to be the referee.

Teacher: We'll talk again tomorrow. You tell me about how you did those things the rest of today and tomorrow. Now, what are you going to do when you think someone is cheating?

Jerry: Swear to myself, and try and talk myself out of being mad.

Teacher: Good! Let's see how well those things work.

The teacher must remember to talk to Jerry again tomorrow, both to remind him about the alternative coping devices they discussed and to praise him for using them. The teacher will want to have Jerry describe the new challenges in such detail that the consequences of his actions become obvious to him. The teacher can then point out how the use of these alternative coping devices leads to more desirable consequences.

The Teacher's Manner

The teacher's success in carrying out the strategy of enlightenment depends on the manner of conversing. The teacher should: (1) be factual and unemotional; (2) emphasize the what rather than the why; and, (3) offer suggestions and interpretations in a vague and indefinite way.

Factual and Unemotional No matter how correct and useful the teacher's interpretations and suggestions are, they are likely to be ignored if given in a way that the student feels is belligerent. A conference with the student should be held when both the teacher and student are calm. Jerry's fracas occured during the morning recess, but the conference was postponed until noon. By then Jerry was no longer mad about the game, and the teacher was no longer quite so annoyed about being called from the teacher's room in the middle of a break. In conference with Jerry, the teacher concentrated on facts, rather than conclusions. The teacher had Jerry describe what he thought happened. If Jerry had been unable to deal with facts, and could say nothing more specific and conjectural than, "Mark cheated. He does that all the time. I hate him," then the teacher might even have had Jerry draw the events on the chalkboard, or role play them: "You show me what happened. I'll be Jose, and you be Mark and yourself You tell me what to do. Show me what you and Mark and Jose did."

A lack of patience on the part of the teacher will result in emotion. The teacher must try to remain calm with Jerry, even though it may be the third time this week Jerry has been in a fight, and each time a conference has been held. The teacher can cope with her own feelings of stress by talking to herself. "I guess I'll just have to keep trying. I'm doing the best I know how. That is all anyone can expect of me. Besides, no one else seems to have any better ideas."

The teacher should try to deal with what the student did rather than why he did it. A student is bound to feel the teacher is critical and censorious whenever the teacher starts a conference with "Tell me why you did that? What conceivable reason could anyone have for doing that?" The teacher should try not to be concerned with past behavior; it is over and done with, and cannot be undone. If Jerry were to take the same action tomorrow that he took earlier today, the outcome would most likely be the same. The teacher should try to concentrate on what different actions could have occurred and what their consequences might have been. Actions that would have led to desirable consequences today will probably lead to desirable consequences tomorrow. The student should be encouraged to try those actions when similar challenges are faced in the future.

What rather than Why

When the teacher makes suggestions, they should be offered in a vague and indefinite way. The teacher can be vague and indefinite by prefacing all suggestions and interpretations with such qualifying statements as, "I wonder whether . . . ?" "Could it be that . . . ?" "Something you might want to try that has worked for other people is . . ." The vagueness encourages the student to offer his own suggestions and interpretations, and allows him the option of accepting or rejecting those offered by the teacher. When the student has the option of accepting or rejecting the teacher's comments, he is more likely to consider them seriously, and to accept them.

Vague and Indefinite

Summary

The counselor strategies are summarized in the form of an observation guide that might be used in evaluating the teacher's use of the strategies. The guide can be used by one teacher for self-evaluation or by two teachers working together and evaluating each other.

NOTE: The most common setting for observing the use of these strategies is a conference involving only the teacher and one student. Seldom will all strategies be used in one conference.

_____   _____   _____
   Student   Date   Topic

Rating
Yes   So-So   No

I. MAKING CONTACT
   A. *Initial Contact with Students.* The teacher shows that he cares about the student as an individual.

   Suggestions: _____

   B. *Express Sympathy.* The teacher expresses sympathy for the student's feelings.

   Suggestions: _____

   C. *No Arguing About Feelings.* The teacher does not argue about whether or not the student should feel a certain way. The student's statements are accepted, and further statements are encouraged.

   Suggestions: _____

II. LISTENING
   A. *Creative Listening.* The teacher listens creatively by being genuinely joyful when a student expresses feelings. The teacher is not critical or censorious.

   Suggestions: _____

   B. *Nondirective Conversation.* (check each)
      1. *Repeat.* The teacher repeats the student's last statement of the key idea or problem.

   Suggestions: _____

      2. *Clarification.* When simply repeating the idea does not keep the conversation going and focused, the teacher asks the student to:
      (1) Explain why he might feel as he does, or
      (2) Describe an example of a time he felt that way.

   Suggestions: _____

III. ENCOURAGEMENT

A. *Shows Approval.* Count the number of times the teacher said something approving or disapproving in a given period of time.

Time Period   Times Approved

Times Disapproved

B. *Encouragement Is Authentic.* (check each)
   1. The teacher's actions support the approving words.
   2. The approval is realistic. A student is not told that something is outstanding when it is obvious to the student that it is not.

   Suggestions: _____

C. *Encouragement Is Deliberate.* (check each)
   1. The teacher has identified for each child the areas where approval is needed.
   2. The teacher has identified the specific approving actions that will be taken with each student.
   3. The teacher keeps a record of the number of times each approving action is taken.

   Suggestions: _____

IV. ENLIGHTENMENT

A. *Characteristics.* (check each)
   1. *Actions and Consequences.* The teacher helps a student gain insight by guiding him to understand the naturalness of the consequences that followed his action.

   Suggestions: _____

   2. *Knowledgeable About Alternatives.* The teacher suggested different alternative actions and the likely consequences of each. The alternatives are based on the following coping devices: (check which)
   - physical activity
   - reassurance
   - self-discipline
   - escape valve
   - talking
   - fantasy formation

   Suggestions: _____

Rating

Yes   So-So   No

B. *Teacher's Manner.* (check each)

1. *Factual and Unemotional.* The teacher deals with facts and not conclusions. The teacher is unemotional.

   Suggestions: _____

2. *Emphasize the What Not the Why.* The teacher does not expect a student to explain why something was done. The student is not asked to justify the action. The emphasis is on the action taken, and the consequences of that action.

   Suggestions: _____

3. *Vagueness and Indefiniteness.* The teacher offers interpretations and suggestions by saying things like, "I wonder whether . . .?" or "Could it possibly be that . . . ?" or "Something that you might want to try is . . ."

   Suggestions: _____

13

Assessment

Assessment is used in determining whether or not educational goals are being attained. Assessment instruments are used to determine what effect the use of counselor strategies is having on students' ideas about themselves and on their learned ways of dealing with challenges. In this chapter we shall describe instruments suitable for measuring each condition, and procedures for making numerical and diagnostic interpretations.

SELF-CONCEPT

An assessment of self-concepts should provide information about how students perceive themselves, their physical and personality characteristics and, most important, their feelings of worth and adequacy. A numerical interpretation provides a point of reference so that progress in improving a student's self-concept can be determined. A diagnostic interpretation provides a profile of a student's self-ratings. The teacher can then use counselor strategies in raising the low self-ratings and maintaining the high self-ratings.

Assessment in the Lower Grades

Instruments suitable for use in the lower grades and procedures for interpreting data collected with them are described.

Instruments Self-concepts are most commonly assessed by having students rate themselves on a series of bipolar adjectives, such as happy-sad, smart-dumb. A child's response sheet for an instrument suitable for the kindergarten and first grade is shown in Figure 13.1. It is based on the "Where Are You Game" created by Engel and Raine.[1] The teacher's instructions are as follows:

> We are going to look at some pictures and decide how we are like each picture. Look at the pictures under Number 1. The child on top is very happy. The child laughs and smiles a lot. The child at the bottom is not very happy. The child seldom laughs and smiles. Decide which child you are like. Put a mark in the box that shows the child you are like. If you are sometimes like one and sometimes like the other, mark the middle box.

A suitable story is told about each of the polar adjectives.

Figure 13.1

1. M. Engel and W. Raine, "A Method for the Measurement of the Self-Concept of Children in the Third Grade," *Journal of Genetic Psychology* 102(1963):125–137.

The instrument should be more complex when used with students above the first grade level. The instrument can be made more complex in the following three ways. First, five responses can be used instead of three, thus giving a greater range of scores to interpret. Second, more bipolar adjectives can be used, thus giving a more complete picture of the student. These adjectives might be used:

happy–sad	friendly–unfriendly
smart–dumb	athletic–unathletic
well liked–not liked	cooperative–uncooperative
attractive–unattractive	kind–mean

Third, bipolar adjectives can be made more specific, thus giving more precise information about the nature of a self-concept. These adjectives should be used in place of smart-dumb:

smart in arithmetic–dumb in arithmetic
smart in reading–dumb in reading
smart in science–dumb in science

Two types of interpretation are explained, numerical and diagnostic.   *Interpretation*

Numerical Interpretation. A numerical interpretation is made in two steps. First, assign a weighted score to each possible response. For example, with the instrument shown in Figure 13.1, a weighted score of 1 might be assigned to the highest box, 3 to the second box, and 5 to the last. The assigning of weights to the first set of bipolar adjectives is shown in Figure 13.3. Second, identify the student's score for each set of bipolar adjectives. If a student marked the box closest to the word sad in the portion of the instrument shown in Figure 13.3 the student's score for the bipolar adjectives of happy–sad would be 5.

Scores should be recorded so a student's progress can be determined. An individual record form is shown in Figure 13.4. The

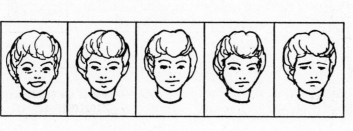

Happy   *Sad*

Figure 13.2

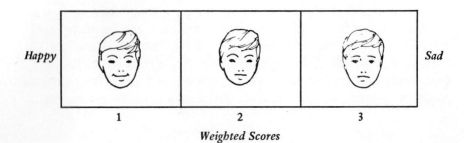

Happy ... *Sad*

1   2   3

Figure 13.3   *Weighted Scores*

		Name	Maria

SELF–CONCEPT

BIPOLAR ADJECTIVES	MONTH			
	September	October	November	December
happy—sad	5	3		
smart—dumb	5	5		
well liked—not liked	1	1		
attractive—unattractive	3	5		
OVERALL SELF-ESTEEM	3.5	3.5		

Figure 13.4

form shows the score for each set of bipolar adjectives. It also shows a score of overall self-esteem. The overall score is derived by adding the scores from the bipolar adjectives and dividing that by the number of adjectives. Thus, $(5 + 5 + 1 + 3) \div 4 = 3.5$. Maria's overall self-esteem has not changed in two months. Whatever the teacher has been doing is apparently not effective. The teacher should try other things, and then assess the results again.

Diagnostic Interpretation. The record form shown in Figure 13.4 provides a profile of one student's self-ratings. The teacher should plan a program of encouragement that will raise that student's low ratings and maintain the high ratings. Of particular concern should be Maria's concept of her academic ability. But encouragement in that area will do little good unless instruction has been sufficiently individualized so that Maria is given instructional tasks that she can master successfully with effort and without being subjected to peer disapproval.

Assessment in the Upper Grades

Instruments for use in the uppergrades and procedures for interpreting data collected from them are described.

An instrument that can be used to assess the self-concepts of upper-grade students is shown in Figure 13.5.   *Instruments*

The instrument in Figure 13.5 uses the procedure of having students rate themselves against bipolar adjectives, but it is different from the instrument shown for the lower grades in that the two poles are inferred by the rating choices rather than by being identified: happy ranges from "almost always" to "almost never." Also, students at the upper grade levels can be asked to distinguish between how they are and how they wish they were. The ratings students give for these two dimensions provide important diagnostic information beyond what is gained from the simpler type of single-dimension rating used in the lower grades. The interpretation of the information will be explained later.

Teachers should design instruments for assessing self-concepts so that they are suitable for their particular students and situations. For example, a teacher could delve further into the specific area of intelligence by using such adjectives as:

Smart—Arithmetic
Smart—Reading
Smart—Science
Smart—Things Outside of School

The teacher could include a number of adjectives about the same idea in order to provide more reliable information. For example, the three adjectives shown below refer to the same idea. The student's score for that idea is the average of weighted responses for the three adjectives:

Name_____ Date_____

Directions: *Tell how you are and how you would like to be. There are no right and wrong answers. Answer according to your feelings. Put an X to tell how you feel about each idea.*

THIS IS HOW I AM

IDEAS   FEELINGS

	Almost Always	Most of the Time	About Half of the Time	Sometimes	Almost Never
Happy	_____	_____	_____	_____	_____
Smart	_____	_____	_____	_____	_____
Attractive	_____	_____	_____	_____	_____
Friendly	_____	_____	_____	_____	_____
Popular	_____	_____	_____	_____	_____
Studious	_____	_____	_____	_____	_____

THIS IS HOW I WISH I WAS

IDEAS   FEELINGS

	Almost Always	Most of the Time	About Half of the Time	Sometimes	Almost Never
Happy	_____	_____	_____	_____	_____
Smart	_____	_____	_____	_____	_____
Attractive	_____	_____	_____	_____	_____
Friendly	_____	_____	_____	_____	_____
Popular	_____	_____	_____	_____	_____
Studious	_____	_____	_____	_____	_____

Figure 13.5

Likeable
Popular
Well Liked

Interpretation Two types of interpretation are explained, numerical and diagnostic.

Numerical Interpretation. In making a numerical interpretation of the data collected with the instrument shown in Figure 13.5 the two dimensions (How I Am, How I Wish I Was) are computed separately. The two steps identified earlier for the instrument shown in Figure 13.1 are used. First, assign a weighted score to each possible response. Assign 1 to Almost Never, 2 to Sometimes, and so forth to the fifth rating. Second, identify the student's score for each adjective. An overall score of self-esteem can also be derived for each dimension. The overall score is the average of scores for each dimension. A record sheet giving scores for one month is shown in Figure 13.6.

Diagnostic Interpretation. The record form shown in Figure 13.6 provides a profile of self-ratings for the two dimensions of I Am and I Wish. A number of conclusions can be made after examining that data:

1. Happiness and Friendliness. Larry ranks himself high both in how he thinks he is and how he wishes to be. He seems to have achieved his goals in both areas. Not much needs to be done with these areas, except to maintain the ratings.

2. Smartness and Studiousness. Larry ranks himself low both in how he thinks he is and how he wishes to be. Larry pictures himself as dumb and a poor student. That low rating will result in a low level of academic work from Larry because he is likely to behave in ways consistent with his self-concept. Those low ratings must be raised if Larry is to make academic progress. But the low ratings Larry gives himself for the dimension of I Wish indicate that he seems to attribute little importance

Name	Larry							
			MONTH					
	September		October		November		December	
ADJECTIVE	I Am	I Wish	I Am	I Wish	I Am	I Wish	I Am	I Wish
Happy	4	4						
Smart	2	3						
Attractive	1	4						
Friendly	5	5						
Popular	1	5						
Studious	3	3						
OVERALL SELF-ESTEEM	2.7	4.0						

Figure 13.6

to school work. Before raising Larry's ratings of his abilities as a student, the teacher must first help him raise his goals. He must want to be a better student. He must place a higher value on school performance. Larry's goals might be raised by using strategies that will motivate him, such as independent activities, group projects, and incentive techniques. Once Larry's goals for school work rise, the teacher can use an encouragement strategy to raise his concept of himself as a student.

3. Attractiveness and Popularity. There is a great discrepancy between how attractive and popular Larry thinks himself to be and how he wishes he were. This discrepancy is likely to result in a high level of anxiety that is evidenced in his use of coping devices in social situations that to the teacher do not seem to be serious enough to create stress. Larry might use many disrupting physical actions to get attention both from the teacher and the other children. He might also seek continual reassurance from the teacher. The teacher will want first to determine through a sociometric assessment just how popular Larry really is. If he is the isolate he seems to think himself to be, the teacher will want to raise his status in the group by using group-leader strategies involving both personal influence and group influence. If the sociometric assessment shows that Larry is more popular than he thinks he is, the teacher might use the strategies of encouragement and enlightenment.

Most diagnostic interpretations of two-dimensional self-concept assessments will fall into one of three categories discussed above.

1. Both the I Am and I Wish will be high, indicating only the necessity of maintaining the high ratings.
2. Both the I Am and I Wish will be low, indicating the necessity of raising the student's goals as well as his self-concepts.
3. The I Am will be well below the I Wish, indicating a high level of anxiety. The teacher needs to determine how realistic the discrepancy is. If it is realistic, instructional strategies are used to increase the student's ability and group-leader strategies are used to raise his status. At the same time, encouragement and enlightenment strategies are used to raise self-concept. For example, if the discrepancy were in the area of arithmetic, the teacher might initiate a continuous-progress curriculum with an individualized-grouping pattern to raise the child's level of performance in arithmetic. At the same time, the teacher would maintain records of the student's progress in arithmetic and use them in giving encouragement and enlightenment.

COPING DEVICES

Assessment of student's use of coping devices should provide information about the ways students deal with the stresses arising from situations they encounter in their daily lives. The information collected should be enough to enable the teacher to make conclusions about a student's coping style and how effective that style is in reducing the stress the student feels. The information should also provide a basis for planning counselor strategies that can be used in developing the student's ability to use other, more effective, coping devices.

Coping style is a sufficiently complex phenomenon that cannot be identified from a single instrument administered one time, as is frequently possible in identifying self-concept. With coping style, the teacher must conduct a case study of the student that utilizes such instruments as anecdotal records and self-reports, along with a systematic procedure for interpreting the information in a way that suggests appropriate teaching strategies. suitable assessment instruments and interpretation procedures are suggested.

Instruments

Two types of instruments suitable for assessing students' use of coping devices are described, anecdotal records and self-reports.

An anecdote is a written narrative of a biographical incident. An anecdotal record is a series of anecdotes collected over a period of time. A form that can be used in making anecdotal records is shown in Figure 13.7. Each time the student displays a significant behavior, the teacher writes a short description of it, and notes the date and

Anecdotal Records

ANECDOTAL RECORD

Student's Name_____

Teacher's Name_____

Record of Observations:

<u>Date</u>   <u>Time</u>   _____ Incident _____

Figure 13.7

time. The anecdotes will be recorded for as short a time as one week, or for as long as the entire school year. The student's coping style can usually be inferred by looking for common patterns of behavior that have been exhibited in a number of incidents.

Teachers who are just beginning to record anecdotes must avoid a natural tendency to confuse facts with opinions. In order for the anecdotal record to be of later use in identifying coping style, teachers must distinguish between what they actually see a student doing—the facts—and how they interpret that behavior—their opinions. Here is an anecdote that is inadequate because it mixes facts with opinions.

> 11/18/75   9:35 a.m.
>
> Robert was up to his usual antics of trying to get attention. During story-time he kept turning to the boys seated behind him, whispering and clowning whenever he thought my attention was elsewhere. He seems to be a born troublemaker. And to think this is only the first grade!

The phrases "usual antics of trying to get attention" and "born troublemaker" are statements of opinion. They provide no information about the challenge with which Robert was apparently coping. Of much greater value would be information about who the boys behind Robert were. If they turned out to be stars, and Robert was an isolate, that might suggest the challenge Robert perceived; he might have been trying to meet a need for affection. If Robert was observed in a number of situations to behave in a similar way in the presence of high-status individuals, that conclusion could be made with more assurance.

Here is how the incident with Robert might better have been recorded:

> 11/18/75   9:35 a.m.
>
> During storytime in the amphitheater, Robert turned three or four times to Jim and Mario, seated behind him, and whispered and made faces, and wiggled. Robert seemed to initiate the interchange. I motioned for him to stop each time, even called his name. About the fourth time I asked him to leave and return to his seat. He had tears in his eyes and said, "I didn't do anything!"

That anecdote contains only facts. Interpreting those facts should be withheld until quite a number have been collected, and can be examined together. Patterns of behavior indicative of coping style are more evident when a number of separate anecdotes are examined at the same time.

The recording of anecdotes can be very time consuming if the teacher does not keep the notes brief. Only significant things should be recorded. The incident with Robert could be briefly recorded in this way:

11/18/75   9:35 a.m.
Storytime. Robert started disturbing interchange with Jim and Mario. Robert would not stop when asked repeatedly, so asked to leave group. Left with teary eyes.

Though brief, this report contains the most significant events in the incident. It was storytime. Robert initiated an interchange with Jim and Mario. Robert was so intent on the interchange that he continued it even when asked repeatedly by the teacher to stop. Robert was emotionally upset, as indicated by his crying.

Because the maintaining of anecdotal records is obviously very time consuming, teachers will want to keep them on only a few students at any one time. The teacher will probably want to start with the most seriously maladjusted children, and stay with them until a coping style has been identified.

The self-report is used to get information about what concerns a student. The student's stated concerns will usually indicate situations in which the student feels stress, and, hopefully, the ways the student copes with that stress. In the upper grades students are usually able to respond directly to the question "What are some of your concerns?" Assessment can be made more directly at the intermediate and primary grades by having students identify things that cause them to be angry or happy. An instrument suitable for the intermediate grades is shown in Figure 13.8. It provides information about stressful and nonstressful situations. In the primary grades students might be asked to draw pictures of things that make them happy and mad. The teacher can help by writing a title for the pictures. Asking the student to title a picture helps the teacher understand the idea the student is attempting to illustrate.

Student Self-Reports

Information about the way students cope with stress can often be collected by having them explain what they do when something happens that makes them mad. An instrument that might be used in the intermediate grades is shown in Figure 13.9. At the primary grades students might be asked to draw pictures of things that make them mad, and then what they do about them. The teacher will probably want to ask the student to suggest a title or description that the teacher can write below each picture. The title helps the teacher understand the picture.

Name _____

Here are some things at school that make me happy:

_____

_____

_____

Here are some things at school that make me mad:

_____

_____

_____

Figure 13.8

Name _____

Here are some things that make me mad: This is what I do when I get mad:

1) _____   1) _____

2) _____   2) _____

3) _____   3) _____

Figure 13.9

CASE STUDY

Student _____   Teacher _____   Date

I. PROBLEM

A. *Coping Style*

Stressful Situations	Coping Devices
Identify three types of situations where stress might be felt:	Describe the coping devices commonly used with each type of situation:
1. *Student with Task* (math, P. E.)	1. *Identify Coping Device* (physical activity, reassurance, self–discipline, escape valve, talking, fantasy formation)
2. *Student with Other Students*	

Figure 13.10

3. *Student with Teacher*

2. *Describe Use of Coping Device*
The particular way the person carries out physical activity, and so forth.

B. *Effectiveness of Coping Style*

1. How well is the student *satisfactorly* achieving needs? Describe for each need. (Satisfactory from the *student's* point of view.)

   A. *Need for Activity* (physical and intellectual)

   B. *Need for Socialization*

   C. *Need to Feel Confident and Secure*

2. How disturbing to the teacher, other students and the school's program is the student's coping style?

   A. Disturbing enough that change is necessary immediately

   B. Not sufficiently disturbing to bother changing

C. *Other Pertinent Information*

   1. *Self-Concept*   Areas of High Self-Esteem   Areas of Low Self-Esteem

   2. *Social Standing* (sociometric data on student)

   3. *Family and Siblings*

   4. *School Achievement and Capacity*

II. SOLUTIONS

   What specific actions might be taken in terms of the following teacher strategies?

A. *Counselor Strategies*

   1. Making Contact

   2. Listening

   3. Encouraging

   4. Enlightening

B. *Group-Leader Strategies*

   1. Group Discussion

   2. Role Play

   3. Morale Building

   4. Desist Techniques

   5. Group Projects

Figure 13.10 Cont.

C. *Instructor Strategies*

   1. Continuous–Progress Curriculum

   2. Grouping

   3. Independent Activities

   4. Instructional Aides

   5. Student Contracts

   6. Incentive Techniques

Fig. 13.10 cont.

Interpretation

The purpose of interpretation is to: (1) identify the problem, which consists of situations where the student feels stress and the coping devices the student uses in dealing with that stress; and, (2) suggest solutions, which are the counselor strategies the teacher might use. Interpretation can be carried out in the steps shown in Figure 13.10. Interpretation will involve information previously collected about coping, like that shown in Figures 13.7, 13.8 and 13.9, as well as information collected in other areas, such as self-concept and sociometric status. The teacher should collect all pertinent information before beginning the steps of interpretation shown here.

14

Situational Examples

SITUATION 1

Mrs. K. has what she terms "a bright, friendly class" of sixth graders. Although the school year is barely underway, she has noticed that one child is definitely a "loner."

Comment: To recognize isolates within a classroom is a first step. So often teachers see the "different" child as a burden to cope with rather than someone to understand and to help.

Teacher: Marcy is noticeably different in my class. She comes to school poorly dressed in ill-fitting clothes and has a pale drawn look about her that is emphasized by a rather frightened expression. At recess she sits passively watching others. It appears that she is in a dream world. In the classroom she dawdles over her work, rarely finishing an assignment. She does not communicate with her classmates and only mumbles a hasty response when I try to converse. I gave a sociometric test to the class and it came out much as I predicted for Marcy—no one chose her.

Comment: Sociometric tests identify isolates and also show choices the isolates make. Students chosen by Marcy on this test would be the ones to enlist for help in drawing her into group participation.

Teacher: I feel a real need to help Marcy become part of the group. I called her home and spoke with an older sister. She said that her mother worked and she would have her call me before school the next morning. Mrs. L. called and made arrangements for a conference the following day. Her first words after arrival were, "That Marcy had better not be doing something wrong here or she'll sure get it." I found out during the conversation that Mrs. L. was working evenings, that Mr. L. had deserted the family of four children and that Mrs. L.'s oldest child, an unmarried girl of seventeen, was living at home with her baby. Mrs. L. emphasized that she wanted Marcy to do as she was supposed to do and not misbehave. I told her several times that Marcy was not misbehaving but rather was not participating. She seemed not to be bothered by this and said to let her know if Marcy "acted up."

Comment: Although this conference is enlightening in many ways, Mrs. L. is apparently not receiving the message intended. It simply does not occur to Mrs. L. that a quiet, nonparticipating child can be a problem.

Teacher: I asked Mrs. L. what kinds of things Marcy likes to do at home. Frankly, because she works evenings, I don't think she sees Marcy enough to know what Marcy does or does not like to do. There seem to be specific tasks that the child is expected to do. After that she's on her own.

Comment: Marcy apparently views her condition as hopeless. It seems she's given up and her discouragement with the world results in withdrawal and listlessness.

Possible Solutions

1. Every child needs some individual time with an understanding adult. Marcy lacks this contact. If there is a counselor in this school, Marcy should spend some time each week with this person. The teacher will usually be the deciding influence on whether or not Marcy builds self-esteem and relates to her peers. The teacher can build a personal relationship with Marcy that will encourage her to talk about some of her thoughts. Of course, this should not be in the form of "prying" on the teacher's part, which often results in just the opposite of the desired results. If the teacher creates situations in which the child can be alone in the classroom with the teacher, helping out with small tasks, a personal relationship will develop, and communication will begin to take place.

2. Marcy particularly needs encouragement. She should be put in situations where praise can genuinely be given. (Children quickly see

through false praise.) If she is not finishing her assignments, perhaps she can be placed in a continuous-progress curriculum where she feels less threatened by failure and can observe her own growth.

3. Enlist those students that Marcy chose on the sociometric test to help out. Often children will show great empathy for such a situation if the teacher frankly asks for cooperation and shows a need for their help. They might ask Marcy to join in their games at recess, or choose her to be on a committee doing a group project.

4. Marcy might be able to go into a primary grade and help the teacher with art projects or games. The younger children will accept this older helper and she will begin to have status in a group.

5. Keep a record of development of self-concepts. Watch closely to see how she views herself and if growth in self-esteem is taking place.

SITUATION 2

Glen is a hot tempered ten-year-old fifth grader in Mr. S.'s class. He blames his anger on those around him.

Teacher: Glen is continually getting into some kind of conflict. He initiates fights and arguments with those around him both in the classroom and on the playground. Because of his lack of social skills, he is completely rejected by his classmates. Other teachers complain that he teases the younger children at lunch time.

Comment: Unlike the child in the previous situation who can easily be overlooked by an insensitive teacher, Glen never for a moment lets anyone forget he exists. His overt behavior is really a cry for help.

Teacher: I called Mrs. R. several times and each time I called she had an excuse for not coming to a conference or failed to keep an appointment. Finally, she met me for a conference. She described a home situation that helped me to understand Glen's behavior. Mr. R. is unemployed and has a drinking problem. He often does not come home for two or three days, and when he is home he is very abusive to Glen and his four younger siblings. Mrs. R. appeared nervous and tired and explained that she had just started working nights as a waitress.

Comment: This gives us a good picture of Glen's home. We can begin to understand Glen's striking out. He is an angry child who views the world as a place in which one must be aggressive in order to exist. But just giving us a picture does not excuse his behavior.

Teacher: Yesterday I think Glen was having a particularly bad day. He managed to get into several arguments and fights by the first recess. I put him out in the hall with his work. He did not accomplish anything, but at least he did not bother the rest of the class.

Comment: Children who are seeking attention will go to any length to receive it. The teacher may be using too little variety in his punishment techniques, too forceful too soon. He may want to plan a wide range of techniques that will allow for more escalation.

Possible Solutions

1. The teacher should try to establish a dialogue with Glen. If Glen has an understanding and sympathetic adult with whom he can build a trust relationship, he can vent some of his emotions in more constructive ways. Encourage Glen to stay after school to help out in the classroom. Listen to him and be sympathetic with his feelings.

2. Learn how Glen views himself by using self-concept assessments. Identify areas of negative self-worth. Work to make him feel more adequate in those areas. Keep a record of the self-concept assessments so progress can be observed.

3. Work out an arrangement of incentive strategies with Glen that will extrinsically motivate him. Reward him for acceptable behavior. If he has managed to stay out of trouble for two hours, let him have a special privilege.

4. Keep an anecdotal record of Glen's behavior. These recorded incidences can be of help in evaluating overall behavior changes and determining the pattern of his behavior.

SITUATION 3

Dan is a third-grade student in Mrs. W.'s class. He has missed many days of school during the previous years. Due to such excess absences, he was in the second grade for the second time. His IQ tests show him to be of high-average intelligence. He is small and frail compared to his classmates who are all younger. He appears nervous and shy in the classroom and does not participate in the activities in the room or on the playground.

Comment: This situation requires not only an observant and sensitive teacher, but one who is willing to devote time and effort in seeking the total behavior pattern and background of this child.

Teacher: During the first week of school I noticed Dan's unwillingness to participate. He seemed afraid and sat quietly at his desk drawing small intricate pictures of rockets and spacemen. As I would call his name for the routine procedures in class, he showed a minimum of effort. He quickly withdrew again to his own world.

Comment: It seems that this child is only attending this class physically.

Teacher: The second week of school Dan was absent. I checked the records in the office and found that Dan had a history of asthma. He is an only child and previous teachers had commented that his mother had come for conferences many times.

Comment: Now would seem the logical time for the teacher to delve more fully into the situation in order to prevent this year from duplicating those of the past.

Teacher: Monday of the following week Dan was absent again. After school his mother came in and asked if she could "talk to me about Dan's problems." During the conference I learned that Dan had been home with an asthma attack and that he does not like school. He is the only child of parents who desperately wanted a child for many years before he was born. Although she was not antagonistic toward me, I felt she thought the school in general was not meeting Dan's needs.

Comment: This conference gives us a great deal of insight.

Teacher: Dan's mother said that she would take school work home for Dan to do. I asked if we could set a time to talk with the counselor and perhaps Dan's physician to determine how we might proceed to set up reasonable expectations for Dan's progress this year. Mrs. R. said there was no need to consult the doctor and that she had already talked to the counselor on previous occasions and there was nothing to discuss.

Comment: For the sake of Dan's future, firmer steps need to be taken.

There must also be a trust relationship built with this mother
before progress can be made. Proceed with caution, but do
proceed.

Teacher: With the principal's permission, I called the doctor listed on
Dan's health form. He said that although Dan had had some
respiratory problems in the past, he saw no reason why he
could not participate fully in all physical activities. In fact,
he had encouraged Dan's mother to enroll Dan in gymnastic
and swimming classes.

Possible Solutions

1. It appears that this child has been reinforced in the past for his failure
   to participate. He has been rewarded with approval by his mother for
   being delicate and noninvolved. Although this behavior has been a
   pattern for many years, it can be reversed by rewarding him for participating. Dan can find satisfaction through the efforts of an encouraging teacher.

2. Have a conference with Dan. Listen to him. Together you can set up
   simple goals that he might find of interest. Encourage him to get involved in some of the activities in the class. Get a committment on his
   part and evaluate it together.

3. If Dan has a particular interest in rockets and space, as it would appear,
   let him do some art work in this area and perhaps make a simple
   presentation to the class. Let him choose a small committee to work
   with him on some of the aspects of the study.

4. Find out how Dan views himself through a self-concept assessment.
   Let him express himself through creative writing. Perhaps through his
   writing it will become evident that there are anxieties that impair his
   learning and participation.

5. Invite Dan's mother to help in the classroom on a regular basis. Having
   her observe Dan with his peers might give her a new perspective. It
   might also build a trust relationship between her and the school. Make
   sure that her involvement, however, is completely separate from Dan's
   tasks or it could become a situation where she hovers over her son.

SITUATION 4

Alex has been dubbed "Mr. Professor" by his fifth-grade classmates.
His tests indicate he has a very high IQ, but he has trouble relating
socially to his peers. He has one sister three years of age.

Teacher: Alex has been the "know-it-all" in class from the very first day. He stands ready to correct or criticize in every situation. It is true that he is exceptionally bright but he has been rejected by the others in the class because of his superior attitude.

Comment: This child is calling out for attention and getting it in a negative way.

Teacher: Alex seems to be a compulsive perfectionist. When I give a spelling test, he writes the words so slowly and perfectly that the class has to wait.

Comment: Of course Alex is very aware of the game he is playing. It is just another one of his attention-getting actions.

Teacher: I finally said that I would give the spelling test at a reasonable rate of speed and if he couldn't keep up with the rest, he could take it after school. He sat with a smile on his face but he didn't continue the test.

Comment: This was a reward for him. Special attention would have to be given.

Teacher: After school I asked a student to give the spelling words to Alex. He began doing the same slow writing until the student came to me with complaints. I said that he must be finished with the test in five minutes. He finished in less than two minutes.

Comment: Isolated incidences, such as this, will most assuredly continue to occur. They are intended as attention-getting actions and when the teacher and fellow students comply by giving time and energy, Alex feels rewarded.

Teacher: Yesterday a student in the class was telling about a trip she had taken to a nearby state park. Alex interrupted her and said he had gone there many times and proceeded to tell about the rock formations. I didn't say anything but went over by his desk to stand. When he looked at me I was looking away but he stopped talking.

Comment: This mild desist strategy seemed to work. There was no eye contact with the teacher but just her physical presence seemed to get the message to him.

Teacher: After the students had shared their information, we had a class dicussion about courtesy toward speakers. The class gave some suggestions, one of which was "Don't interrupt." I put these suggestions on a chart in the front of the room.

Comment: It was good not to identify or accuse anyone of being discourteous, but rather to keep it objective. People like Alex are usually aware of their actions. This was apparent when he stopped talking when the teacher stood by his desk. These people cannot change because they do not understand the reason for their actions, or know of any satisfying alternatives.

Teacher: No one wants to play with him at recess. If he participates in a game and loses, he says his opponents cheated. If he wins, he brags about it and says he's the best.

Comment: This child has a great deal of potential that is at the moment improperly channeled. He needs new direction and the opportunity to comfortably change his pattern. It is uncomfortable to have this image to maintain, but it is even more uncomfortable to let it go without security. He needs to socialize but does not know how to go about it other than in negative ways.

Possible Solutions

1. The teacher will find it easy to communicate with Alex. She can be very frank about his behavior and he will recognize it as his. If she builds a good relationship with him through short, positive conversations, he will know that he has some security in change. Perhaps he can take the risk to change the image that he has put forth.

2. Alex has a great deal of knowledge to share with others. The problem seems to be in transmitting this knowledge in a socially acceptable way. Set up a situation where he and one or two others in the class with high ability can work on a special project. Let him do research on his own and present his findings to the others. Ask other teachers if they have pupils who would work well with Alex and get a special school project going.

3. If he has a skill he can share with others, such as chess or music, he might be encouraged to start a chess club or a small music group. Give him some leadership responsibilities.

4. Encourage positive reactions from the class. It is easy with such a child to let negative feelings show through. Ask for positive statements such as, "What did you like about that report?"

5. Encourage Alex to put his thoughts down on paper. He is highly verbal. Let him vent some of his feelings through creative writing. Much can be learned through this and eventually he can become more honest with his feelings. He can relate his feelings about his home, family, the school, his teachers and his peers.

6. Keep a record of his writing to see if there is any significant change as different strategies are used in the classroom.

Index